MANAGING
WORKFORCE
2000

Managing
WORKFORCE
2000

Gaining the
Diversity
Advantage

DAVID JAMIESON
JULIE O'MARA

Foreword by Warren Bennis

Jossey-Bass Publishers · San Francisco

MANAGING WORKFORCE 2000:
Gaining the Diversity Advantage
by David Jamieson and Julie O'Mara

Copyright © 1991 by: Jossey-Bass Inc., Publishers
350 Sansome Street
San Francisco, California 94104

&

Jossey-Bass Limited
Headington Hill Hall
Oxford OX3 0BW

Library of Congress Cataloging-in-Publication Data

Jamieson, David, date.
    Managing workforce 2000 : gaining the diversity advantage / David
Jamieson and Julie O'Mara ; foreword by Warren Bennis.
        p.   cm. — (The Jossey-Bass management series)
    Includes bibliographical references and index.
    ISBN 1-55542-264-0
    1. Manpower planning—United States.   2. Minorities—Employment—
United States.   3. Women—Employment—United States.   4. Pluralism
(Social sciences)—United States.   I. O'Mara, Julie, date.
II. Title.   III. Series.
HF5549.5.M3J36   1991
658.3—dc20   90-22120
                                                                  CIP

Manufactured in the United States of America

The paper in this book meets the guidelines for
permanence and durability of the Committee on
Production Guidelines for Book Longevity of the
Council on Library Resources.

A BARD PRODUCTIONS BOOK

Copy Editing: Helen Hyams
Text Design: Suzanne Pustejovsky
Jacket Design: Suzanne Pustejovsky
Composition/Production: Round Rock Graphics

FIRST EDITION

HB Printing: 10   9   8   7   6   5   4   3

Code 9117

*The Jossey-Bass
Management Series*

To

Julie's son Ryan and
Dave's sons Brian and Chris,
who will benefit from
a changed workplace
of the future

Table of Contents

Foreword

When the dust settles on the nineties and we can look back through the shining ether of time, this book by David Jamieson and Julie O'Mara will stand the test. It's a gem and will soon become a classic. Why this unbridled enthusiasm? There are three very good reasons:

1. This is the first book I've come across that confronts the critical leadership issue of management and organization of the nineties: how to manage the changing workforce. While the word *diversity* is one of the new management buzzwords and a lot has been written about it, this is the first book for managers with a systematic framework for taking action.

2. As the authors state in their preface, and as I want to underline, this book is unique in that "it starts with a broadened view of diversity, adding values, age, disabilities, and education to the more common interpretation that focuses exclusively on women and ethnic groups."

3. Perhaps most importantly, *Managing Workforce 2000: Gaining the Diversity Advantage* focuses on the managerial and organizational implications for a new workforce. It strikes at the heart of the problem: how organizations must change to accommodate to the new diversity. To say we must "embrace diversity" is all well and good but this book describes how managers actually go about the "embracing." It also describes how organizations must change policies, systems, and practices to mesh with the needs, preferences, lifestyles, and values of the contemporary workforce.

The important message of *Managing Workforce 2000: Gaining the Diversity Advantage* needs to be understood by not-for-profit as well as business organizations. To take one example close to home: In the modern university we still have a difficult time with the so-called "nontraditional" student. There was a time when students came in only four sizes: eighteen, nineteen, twenty, and twenty-one. That was true only a few years ago. Now our students are often in their thirties and forties (the average age of our graduate students is thirty-two!) and the people of color, the physically challenged, and the high percentage of women make our campuses both exciting and, in general, either apprehensive or inadequate in responding to this diversity.

On the other hand, look at the terrific job the Girl Scouts of the USA did under the stewardship of its past national executive director, Frances Hesselbein. She recognized that by the year 2000, one-third of the country will be people of color. Girls' needs are changing, and under her direction, the Girl Scouts explored ways to meet and deliver those services. As she said to me in an interview, "We have something of value to offer, and we respect the values and culture of our girls. If they open our handbooks, even if they are a minority, or handicapped, or a Navajo, we'll be there for them."

So this book is for you, *if* you want to understand what is changing about the workforce and what can be done in responding to these changes. And who doesn't?

Again, the critical issue of the nineties is how to recruit, retain, and develop workers. That's what this book is all about. I recommend it heartily to everybody concerned with this issue: human resource managers, executives, board members, and everyone concerned with a productive workplace.

February 1991

Warren Bennis
*University Professor and
Distinguished Professor of
Business Administration,
School of Business Administration,
University of Southern California,*
and
author of *On Becoming a Leader*
and *Why Leaders Can't Lead*

Preface

The changing composition of the workforce is creating new challenges for the management of work, workers, and the workplace. An unprecedented number of forces are reshaping the way we think about the management of organizations and people. Shrinking labor force growth, changing job skill requirements, significant shifts in demographics, and changing values are converging to create a new workplace in the 1990s. By attracting, integrating, and retaining an increasingly diverse, nontraditional workforce, organizations are also paying serious attention to global competitiveness and its productivity, quality, and service components.

The Purpose of This Book

We wrote this book to help managers and human resource professionals gain a marketplace advantage by addressing the needs of the diverse workforce. By gaining a diversity advantage we mean blending and capitalizing on the different skills and perspectives of people and creating an organization where everyone gives his or her best. This book will help managers and human resource professionals identify and change organizational policies, systems, and management practices that are "out of synch" with the needs and preferences of the contemporary workforce.

People want, need, and deserve a workplace free of anxiety and stress, where they each can contribute to the best of their ability and grow in their jobs. Until now, too many people have been stifled by managers who are unskilled in working with the changing workforce and by organizations that think they're still managing only younger, less educated white males. Working under conditions they deem demeaning, inequitable, or foolish, many employees simply withhold their best efforts.

The interest in the changing workforce surged with the publication of *Workforce 2000: Work and Workers for the 21st Century* by the Hudson Institute. Since then the phrase "Workforce 2000" has been used by many individuals and organizations to describe the growing changes and increasing diversity of the workforce. The Hudson Institute did a great service for U.S. organizations.

Managing Workforce 2000: Gaining the Diversity Advantage provides guidance to show managers and organizations how to move beyond rhetoric to action. It reviews the changes in the workforce and their consequences, and it introduces FLEX-MANAGEMENT, a new management mindset and framework for action. Key management strategies and 133 examples of how eighty-two organizations are proceeding make up the heart of the book. We close with implications for management development and an approach for developing a new workplace that understands the diverse workforce and gains advantage by responding to changing needs.

It is not our intent to provide a prescription, but rather to develop an approach for examining and changing organizations and to highlight ways in which some organizations are responding effectively. The opportunities to develop healthy, effective organizations with a highly diverse workforce are endless. Early steps are encouraging, but there is still a long way to go.

We hope that our book stimulates creative action, encourages greater sharing of innovations, and helps organizations and managers respond in new ways to the changing workforce.

Why This Book Is Different

This book is unique in two major ways. First, it describes a broadened view of diversity, adding values, age, disabilities, and education to the more common interpretation that focuses exclusively on women and people of color. We include age and values because people in the workforce are diverse in their values and are from many different age groups. Persons with disabilities are included because many more will be entering the workforce in the future, and we believe they represent another aspect of diversity which must be considered. Education is added because the growing gap between the highly educated and the functionally illiterate adds to management's challenges. Second, it focuses on management implications and actions, offering guidance to managers and strategies for organizations. *Managing Workforce 2000: Gaining the Diversity Advantage* blends concepts with practical examples to provide a compelling call for action and a clear model to follow.

This Book Is for You

If you manage others, train people who manage others, or influence organizational policies and systems, this book is for you. Its ideas will help you to

- Understand what changes are taking place in the workforce and their effect on the organization

- See the impact of these changes on your existing management practices and on the organization's policies and systems

- Individualize your management practices

- Influence organizational policies and systems

- Rekindle work spirit, satisfaction, and commitment

- Reduce tensions and frustration among workers and between workers and managers

- Teach others about managing with the changing workforce

Where This Book Came From

This book has deep roots for us. Our interest in this subject matter grew many years ago, during the latter part of the 1970s and into the early 1980s, as we saw the early signs of change taking place in the workforce. There was no book in our minds then and the organizational world was very different.

Some people were already experiencing "diversity" and weren't sure how to handle the issues that arose. Greater numbers of women were entering the workforce, affirmative action programs were having some impact, shifting values were becoming more evident as the burgeoning Baby Boomers entered and grew more influential in organizations, and front-line supervisors were challenged by the presence of new types of workers.

Our interest in the changing workforce began in different ways. In the 1970s, Julie traveled the country training women and men on many issues faced in the workplace. She was also teaching a course, "Women in Management," at Golden Gate University. Seeing the real issue more broadly and with the university's support, she designed and offered a course called "Managing the Changing Workforce." Unfortunately, back then no one signed up!

At about the same time, but in a different place, Dave gave his first speech on "The Changing Workforce of the Eighties." Shortly thereafter, he was involved in gathering information on future demographic and value trends that would affect public education in a southern California county.

During the early and mid-1980s, we were increasingly involved in the development of more "flexible" human resource systems such as new versions of performance appraisal and performance management programs, job posting, and assessment processes to match people with jobs. As we continued our work as designers and facilitators of planning groups, design teams, management retreats, quality programs, and team development sessions, questions about the changing workforce surfaced regularly.

We saw many organizations start or expand special training, orientation, or career programs for women and people of color.

The signs were all there! The movement had begun. Organizations began to look at the issues of access and opportunity, training, organizational policies, and management awareness as they related to the changing workforce. As the 1980s proceeded, "flexibility" began to grow through options in compensation and benefit plans, leave policies, and time and location of work.

During the past decade, we have tested our ideas through hundreds of speeches and workshops for managers from the front line to top executives, across public and private organizations, and with companies and professional groups. We have been actively involved in new designs for management and executive development programs, where human resource issues and the changing workforce are central. And we have worked with managers and human resource staff to solve the problems of their workforce and explore alternatives to existing policies, systems, and management practices.

Consequently, the information in this book comes from many sources:

- From the hundreds of employees at all levels in many organizations who have shared their stories with us over our collective "thirty-something" years as consultants

- From personal experience as Baby Boomers on the cutting edge of massive changes, and as experimenters and innovators trying to facilitate changes that would match our vision of an organization responsive to the changing workforce

- From clients who have invited us to help them solve the problems of a changing workforce through new human resource systems design, awareness and strategy sessions, climate analysis, training and development, team building, and other organizational change projects

- From the thousands who have attended our programs over the years, sharing their expertise, experiences, and ideas

- From the wave of new management literature and contemporary business periodicals that promote changes in the way we manage

- From our observations of managers who are struggling to function with inadequate concepts and inflexible policies, systems, and practices

- And from our conversations with our colleagues in human resource development around the world

What You Can Expect

We have focused on the U.S. workforce, yet each year it becomes clearer that our experience in the United States is a scenario that other nations are watching and will experience. We hope that what we are writing about today will be helpful as we move closer to a global workforce and global organizations.

Our approach is straightforward. In Chapter One we describe the challenge and opportunity for organizations, managers, and employees. We discuss the organizational culture changes needed and highlight perspectives of both managers and employees. We call for management that is beyond "one size fits all" and for a new organizational paradigm.

Chapter Two describes the changes in the workforce in terms of age, gender, culture, education, disabilities, and values. This chapter provides a framework for discussing a broader view of the workforce. Our intent is to be descriptive with statistics used only to sharpen the reality. An added element of this chapter is the identification of some of the future implications these changes have for management.

In Chapter Three we address the need for changing the management mindset. We first point out how traditional management philosophy may have developed, then go on to describe a new direction for management to take. In this chapter we introduce the FLEX-MANAGEMENT model, its strategies, and recommended actions.

Parts Two through Five are each concerned with one of the FLEX-MANAGEMENT strategies: matching people and jobs, managing and rewarding performance, informing and involving people, and supporting lifestyle and life needs. Twelve detailed chapters show how each strategy can create effective results, describe the types of actions that make such strategies real, and provide numerous examples to illustrate and reinforce the concepts that are presented.

In Part Six, we turn our attention to management development and organizational change. The focus of Chapter Sixteen is on the key management skills required to more effectively manage the changing workforce. These skills provide a basis for management development. Chapter Seventeen discusses planned organizational change, presenting a structured approach toward creating a more flexible workplace.

Finally, we provide an annotated Resources section (Part Seven), which identifies a sampling of programs, consultants, and organizations that offer resources in specific areas of workforce change. We hope that this information will help you to solve specific problems you may have.

Throughout the book, individuals are occasionally quoted without further citation. This information came from telephone interviews and personal correspondence. Names and companies are actual with the exception of the opening vignettes in Parts Two, Three, Four, and Five, which are fictitious. Also, a few examples required appropriate disguise to protect confidentiality.

As society and workforce change becomes more diverse, so does the English language. It is especially challenging—and important—to use language that is current and preferred when addressing persons with disabilities and persons of various racial and ethnic groups. The difficulty in selecting the "right" term to use is that there is disagreement between members of any one group and the preferences continually change.

In writing this book, we consulted several experts and continually evaluated our use of language. We've used the business press and preferences of the individuals and organizations mentioned (some have decided to use terminology that's consistent with legislation and general government use) as well as our own judgment in making decisions on which term to use. Where people or publications are quoted, we did not change the wording they used. Therefore, you will find many inconsistencies. Such is life and the nature of changing times.

When we use *ethnic diversity* and *multicultural* we are including race as well as ethnicity. The term *people of color* is used to describe persons or groups who are not Caucasian. We have used the words *black, white,* and *brown* to describe those racial and ethnic groups. However, it concerns us that they are not capitalized as that practice can be interpreted as considering these groups to be of less importance. We've used *black* rather than *African American* and *Hispanic* rather than *Latino,* although there's some thinking that these may become the preferred terms. We've avoided using the word *minority,* because it is becoming less accepted and, in some regions, is not accurate. Also, for many persons, it has a negative connotation. The phrase *persons with disabilities* indicates that the person is more important than the disability. That's why we've used it, rather than *handicapped* or *disabled*.

There are no conclusions in this book, only beginnings. Although we do not yet have all the information that will be needed to effectively develop organizations and manage people in the twenty-first century, what we discovered in researching this book is very encouraging. We hope to stimulate further innovation, instill greater optimism, and contribute to organizational success and workforce satisfaction in the 1990s and beyond.

February 1991

David Jamieson
Los Angeles, California

Julie O'Mara
Castro Valley, California

Acknowledgments

To manage the changing workforce, you must be flexible, individualize your approach, include and empower others in your organization, reward performance, and support the personal and professional needs of others. A manager cannot reach for the stars alone. Neither can authors.

The willingness of others to set aside their own priorities and help us not only felt great, but resulted in a much better product. It truly is impossible to acknowledge everyone, but we will try.

There are thousands who have influenced our thinking. Innovative managers transcended the pressures and confusion of day-to-day activities to think long term and meet the needs of others in the workplace. People who attended our speeches asked thoughtful questions that helped us to shape, clarify, and strengthen our concepts. Clients allowed us to test our ideas as we helped them face workplace challenges.

Other authors contributed by sharing techniques and alerting us to the range of emotions we would experience by writing a book. Their advice was invaluable. If we had followed more of it, we would have finished a year earlier. Thanks to Karl Albrecht, Geoff Bellman, Peter Block, Joan Minninger, Ron Zemke, and other authors who are acknowledged elsewhere in this section. A special thanks to Warren Bennis for showing his support by writing the foreword.

The willingness of the following persons to work with us in the early days of our thinking about the changing workforce made a significant impact. They include Alysin Brown Humes, Marti Jordan, Irv Margol, Elaine Miyamori, Michele Nuzzo, Erika Sorokin, and Dick Wolfe. Thank you for recognizing the value of our book in its infancy. We also appreciate the willingness of those who reviewed and supported our book proposal as we approached various publishers. They include Larry Greiner, Jake Landry, Earle Ormiston, Tom Peters, Stu Sobel, Bill Striedl, and Connie Wolf.

There are two events that were pivotal to developing our model and organizing our thoughts. The first—support we've received from training conferences—actually consists of many events. Since 1983, we've presented on the changing workforce at the annual conferences sponsored by *Training* magazine and later cosponsored by *Training* magazine and *Personnel Journal*. Thanks to Liz Brekke, Julie Goshens, and Lin Standke for their confidence in us. We also thank others at Lakewood Publications, especially Jack Gordon, Phil Jones, and Chris Lee, for asking us challenging questions and supporting our work by allowing us to contribute our thoughts to several articles. The second event was being part of the Management Vision series. A three-hour teleconference on our work, "The Changing Workforce: Strategies for Future Management," produced by Gary Gaal at Executive Communications, gave us exposure to a sizable corporate audience. Thank you to Dana Gaines Robinson for recommending us to Gary.

Among the richest features of this book are the examples. Some of these examples came from our work over the years, some were found in the business literature, and others were found through networking. Each example necessitated anywhere from three to ten interactions. Literally hundreds of people were involved in this process. Most are quoted or referenced in the text. Others who helped to identify examples include Bill Beach, Drake Beil, Ginny Belden, Caela Farren, Ruth Gentilman, Brian Gilmore, Jerry Gullo, Doug Hartman, Ken Ideus, Bev Kaye, Nancy Kuhn, Jim Lomac, Lynda McDermott, Donna McNamara, Pat Morris, Donna Pinkstaff, Michael O'Brien, Kathy Ryan, Ron Sepielli, Halsey Snow, Angie Twarynski, Howard Watts, Michael Winston, and Bill Yeomans. In our search to identify the perfect example to document a concept, we were often so intensely focused that we really challenged those who helped us. We appreciate their tolerance and unfailing willingness to help.

We are indebted to the many public relations and human resource persons who worked behind the scenes to organize examples and check our writing to be sure we were accurate. The majority of these persons did this task with a great deal of interest, promptness, and excitement about the focus of the book.

Interviewing and writing the examples took place over an eighteen-month period. The vast majority of this was done by Jennifer Myers. She performed this task with skill and patience. The skill was in her ability to probe for the messages we wanted to convey and to write them with interest and accuracy. The patience came into play with the energy spent in playing telephone tag. It seemed as if Jennifer placed five phone calls or fax messages for every time she connected with the person she needed.

Such is the situation when working with busy people who are doing the right things for their organizations or for their clients. She was also patient with our desire to keep making changes and shifting categories until we were satisfied.

The following persons endured reading all or parts of various manuscript drafts. Their insightful comments and tactful criticism greatly improved our work. Special thanks to Terry Broomfield, Lennie Copeland, Peggy Hutcheson, Dick Kropp, Joan Linder, Tony Patitucci, Carlene Reinhart, and Jossey-Bass readers. During the rewrite phase, we realized that we had some "holes" that needed filling—additional examples, views on workplace values, suggestions for the Resources section, and reactions to title ideas. We were overwhelmed when 147 people responded to a request for help. This response assured us that we were on the right track and motivated us to push forward. Thank you to all who responded.

Judy Bess, Janet Riehl, and Paula Statman joined the team toward the end as the manuscript deadline approached and there was still a great deal to do. They helped us meet the deadline by interviewing, helping with last-minute sections of the book, and editing. They know what works well on paper and showed great skill in helping us get it there. Francine Kendall, who takes pride in staying current on the use of language related to diversity, helped us make decisions about this controversial and sensitive topic. Don Beck provided valuable insight for our section on values.

The Apple Macintosh™ made our lives a lot easier—we can't imagine writing a book without a computer—but it would have been just another pretty face had it not been for its competent operation by Pam Swanson, who was asked to change and then sometimes change back several portions of the manuscript. She also managed the final approval process for all the examples, compiled the Resources section, and contributed numerous ideas.

A special thanks to Tom Macris who lent his quality thinking and creative eye to help us review the dust jacket art and graphic symbols.

We'd especially like to thank our friends and colleagues who have given us support—many for a long, long time. They never seemed to grow tired of asking—or prodding—us about how the book was going. We know that at times our moaning and groaning about writing the book must have proved boring. We thank them for their patience, for their willingness to remain interested and encouraging, and, even if they may have had doubts as to whether or not we'd finish the book, for keeping those thoughts to themselves. They include those already acknowledged and Lynn Baroff, Fern Beck, Bill Bradley, Dave Brinkerhoff, Jan Duke, Bob Farnquist, Joann Jorz, Margaret Law, Kitti Lawrence, Marianne Matheis, Margo Murray, Terry Paulson, Curt Plott, Bob Preziosi, Walt Ross, Joanne Sujansky, and Pat Williams.

Michele Wyman Jamieson was in the unique position of playing many roles throughout this long process and being there for special needs and critical interventions. She provided unending support, patience, and practicality. She read, reread, edited, critiqued, and suggested. And she probably attended more presentations than anyone else—always followed by constructive criticism and uplifting praise. Thanks, Michele, for the love and valuable contributions.

Not enough can be said about the role Ray Bard, our agent and book producer, has played in moving this work from concept to the printed page. His facilitative, encouraging, always positive, above-the-fray manner matched our needs perfectly. His ability to be clear-headed when we were uncertain or discouraged was often called upon. His technical competence helped us position the book, identify the best publisher, and produce a book that is inviting to read, as well as useful. We are also indebted to Helen Hyams, Pam Kern, and Suzanne Pustejovsky, Ray's capable team, and to Larry Davis for having enough confidence in us to recommend Ray.

We are fortunate to have Jossey-Bass as our publisher. We're grateful to Steve Piersanti, president of Jossey-Bass, for the concern and care he has shown us. We remember one particular dinner in New York City. Steve's intense, and at times relentless, insistence that we explain the focus of our work with great clarity helped us to find better ways to communicate our message. We also appreciate the creativity and support of others at Jossey-Bass who helped in a variety of ways. They include Rachel Anderson, Trish O'Hare, and Sarah Polster. And a special thanks to Kathryn Hall and David Roth for helping with focus and title.

We appreciate the long-term support and confidence of our parents, Sam and Esther Jamieson and Lawrence and the late Edna O'Mara.

As it is for the changing workforce, maintaining a balance between work and family is an important value for us. While both of us consider family and personal relationships a central purpose of our lives, there were times in writing this book that our behavior indicated otherwise. We appreciate everyone's tolerance and support. And now that this book is finished, we know that our friends and family share in its accomplishment. We trust that this work makes a contribution to improving the quality of all our lives.

D.J.
J.O.

The Authors

Both authors are consultants who are recognized by clients and colleagues as experts in the areas of human resource management and organizational change. They are frequently invited to speak about issues related to these topics and are known and respected by many thousands of people. Each has served a term as the elected volunteer national president of the American Society for Training and Development (ASTD), the world's leading and largest professional association dedicated to the development of the workforce and the workplace. Their clients include Aerospace Corporation; Bank of America; Citibank California; the County of Santa Clara, California; the Los Angeles Times; McDonnell Douglas; Pacific Gas and Electric; Security Pacific Corporation; Southern California Edison; Syntex; Transamerica; and Wang Laboratories.

Training magazine, one of the two outstanding publications of the human resource development profession, has published feature profiles on Julie (February 1985) and Dave (February 1986), recognizing them as key contributors to the human resource profession.

David Jamieson is president of the Jamieson Consulting Group, a national consulting organization. Dave has been in management consulting since 1970, with a generalist orientation and an emphasis in organization design and development and human resource management. He has consulted widely with organizations of varying sizes, across different industries, and at multiple levels. He is currently pursuing interests in revitalizing the management of people and organizations, creating effective work settings for the changing workforce, developing strategic thinking, improving quality and service, and designing and facilitating strategies for change.

In 1986, Dave became codirector of the Master of Science in Organization Development (MSOD) program at Pepperdine University; he has also served on the adjunct faculty at the University of Southern California and at the University of California, Los Angeles. He serves as lead faculty in human resource management for the Command College of the California Police Officers' Standards and Training Commission.

He received his B.S. degree in business administration in 1970 from Drexel University, Philadelphia, and his Ph.D. degree in management in 1975 from the University of California, Los Angeles.

In addition to serving as president of ASTD in 1984, Dave was president of the International Federation of Training and Development Organizations from 1985 to 1986.

Julie O'Mara is president of O'Mara and Associates, a full-service human resource development consulting firm formed in 1972. A part-time faculty member of the University of California Extension, Berkeley, and John F. Kennedy University, she writes and publishes *The Developer* newsletter.

Julie and her associates provide a wide variety of management and human resource development consulting services and products. These include the design and implementation of systems-oriented human resource and career development programs; advice to managers on human resource development issues and strategies; needs assessment; strategic planning; management, leadership, and sales effectiveness; organization development; programs for special populations; and design and delivery of training programs.

She previously was director of communications for The Marmon Group, a privately held, billion-dollar international conglomerate of heavy industrial firms based in Chicago. Before that Julie was supervisor of marketing communications for Whirlpool Corporation, Benton Harbor, Michigan. At Whirlpool she was part of the team that introduced the Trash Masher compactor and was Whirlpool's consumer spokesperson for radio, television, and the printed media.

She received her B.S. degree from the University of Missouri in 1969, has earned numerous professional and leadership awards, and is listed in several biographical directories.

PART I

Beyond "One Size Fits All" Management

❝_Building a new, more diverse workforce and making it tick will be one of Corporate America's biggest challenges in the decade ahead._**❞**

—"Human Capital,"
Business Week,
September 19, 1988

Tom Johnson has been managing for years, yet only recently has he begun managing women, people from different ethnic groups, and much younger workers. He's been a good boss. He tries to be fair, but he can't really relate to some of his employees' needs. He's torn between requests his people make for different work assignments, hours, and special time off, and his company's policies—which he's supposed to uphold. Recently, a couple of his employees complained about his "management style" to his boss. He doesn't know what this means, let alone what to do about it.

Martha Tolbert was promoted into management five years ago. She had been taught well, was highly competent, and was happy in her management role. She felt responsible for the work of her department and maintained good controls. Recently, many of her employees have been asking for some additional meetings to help keep them more informed, and for more opportunities to participate. She's sympathetic, but is not sure that doing these things would be seen as "good management" by her superiors. She's afraid of hindering her career, after working so hard to get where she is.

The private school Bill Parker's son attends starts at 9:15 each morning. When he asked his boss if he could shift his hours to share in carpooling responsibilities, his boss snickered, mumbled "Your wife should do that," and said no.

When Sue McNamara graduated with her Ph.D. in economics, she never expected to "pay her dues" again by being uninformed, closely directed, and ignored when decisions were made. She is bored and knows that she is working nowhere near her capability. Her boss is disappointed in her work and makes comments to others about young Ph.D.'s not being "all they're cracked up to be."

Mary Smith, a cashier at a supermarket, is part of a dual-career couple and has one child. She is frustrated by child care difficulties and the number of benefits she gets that duplicate her husband's. She and her husband are working hard to get ahead—despite the lack of support they receive from their organizations, which seem to be out of touch with their needs.

Mike Hawkins is constantly experiencing difficulties with his staff. Some employees are beginning to question departmental *goals he's set or are differing with his decisions, which he thinks is very inappropriate. Two of his staff formally protested their last performance appraisal as meaningless, yet he's required to use the company's system. One employee never seems to understand what she's told, so he constantly needs to "supervise" her. Mike's caught between what should be working, what is— and isn't—working, and what his organization will allow.*

Cheryl *Nakada, an account executive who is single, is frustrated by what she perceives to be inequitable pay and by company benefits she can't really use. Life insurance, paid maternity leave, free attendance for spouses at trade shows, and tuition reimbursement for children of employees certainly don't meet her needs. She's looking for a company that understands and a boss who will do more than just tell her to stop complaining.*

⬛

These and similar scenarios are all too common in organizations today. While they don't represent every manager's or employee's experience, they do represent some of the many variations that exist in workplaces today. We may see a mismatch between what an organization offers and what people want, managers who are struggling to do a good job in the face of constraining policies, employees who believe they're not being heard, and managers who simply reject any need for flexibility.

In organizations, managers often speak of the need for different styles or approaches in solving problems. They recognize that there is more than one way to achieve a goal, but they then strive to create systems, policies, and practices that encourage the same or similar ways to work. Our assembly line thinking has caused us to seek sameness in the interest of reducing costs and operating more efficiently. This is often done under the guise of streamlining, which it's argued, will help achieve a competitive advantage. Most contemporary thinkers, however, argue that the competitive advantage lies in maximizing the talents of individuals; to do that, one must value differences and use those differences advantageously.

People are different from one another in many ways—in age, gender, education, values, physical ability, mental capacity, personality, experiences, culture, and the way each approaches work. Gaining the diversity advantage means acknowledging, understanding, and appreciating these differences and developing a workplace that enhances their value—by being flexible enough to meet needs and preferences— to create a motivating and rewarding environment.

Meeting the needs of the changing workforce is not only beneficial from the standpoint of harmonious working relationships; it also makes good business sense. Organizations that are able to flexibly meet the needs of the workforce will be at a competitive advantage in recruiting and retaining the highest-quality workers. These organizations will be more attractive to today's workforce and more practical for the mix of workers that exists.

1

The Challenge and Opportunity of the Changing Workforce

DAILY, MANAGERS ARE confronted with new, complex challenges as they try to balance the wants and needs of a highly diverse workforce. Laws and organizational policies may constrain managers' options, dictate ineffective action, or simply make it too difficult to try new approaches. The times create so much frustration, stress, and defensiveness that many managers would like to return to the stability and sameness of the past. And that can't happen.

Employees, on the other hand, grow increasingly alienated from organizations that don't seem to value them, understand their needs, or care about their quality of life on or off the job. Employees who are not part of the majority of the workforce have struggled for years with subtle demands to adapt and fit in, sometimes not-so-subtle biases and discrimination, and a general lack of appreciation of their viewpoint. Still others have grown frustrated by the apparent inability of organizations to respond to their changing lifestyles.

Situations such as these create an adversarial climate between management and employees. Perhaps even more critical, managers and employees alike are experiencing an escalation of frustration—often over the same issues.

From Similar to Diverse

We have moved from an era in which large portions of the workforce were assumed to be similar, and those who were different were expected to adapt, to an era when the workforce is composed of many different individuals, each of whom wants to be supported and valued. In the past, there was a dominant majority in the workforce. Attention, policies, and management practices were all focused on the "average" worker—the white male with a homemaker wife and children. Today, as the sheer numbers of nontraditional workers grow, so does their impact and influence.

Today's workforce doesn't look, think, or act like the workforce of the past, nor does it hold the same values, have the same experiences, or pursue the same needs and desires. The workforce has changed significantly from six perspectives: age, gender, culture, education, disabilities, and values.

It is increasingly common for people of different ages to be working side by side. Women have entered the workforce at a rapid pace, resulting in a near majority. Expanding from only a few visible ethnic groups in the past, many culturally diverse groups from around the globe are today spread throughout the American labor force. There is great variety in educational levels, ranging from the illiterate to the highly educated. Many people with mental, physical, and medical disabilities are finding opportunities to move into or stay in the workforce. Shifts in attitudes and values have resulted in a wider variety of lifestyles, motivations, and choices. The workforce has already changed significantly, but the real impact is yet to come.

The Challenge

Managers are forced to do their best to represent the organization, even when they know that the organization is out of step with the needs of its employees. Although they may have some amount of control over what the organization does, they are often constrained by outdated policies and management systems. Personnel laws developed to "right" the inequities of the past are today a driving force against flexibly responding to employees' requests. Many management/union relationships still contain restrictive work rules—another force that hinders individualizing the management of people. There is no doubt that managers are faced with constant challenges; nevertheless, the need to manage the changing workforce differently is now more pressing than ever.

A new model is needed—and needed soon—before the workforce becomes even more discouraged, potentially creating further declines in productivity. In these times of slower labor force growth, competent, high-demand workers are choosing to move to organizations that accommodate their individuality through the work itself, through policies and systems that support their lifestyle requirements, and through management practices that enhance their dignity.

The challenge is great: As managers unlearn practices rooted in an old mindset, change the way organizations operate, shift organizational culture, revamp policies, create new structures, and redesign human resource systems, they will assist in gaining the diversity advantage.

The Opportunity

Although solving these problems will be difficult, there are great opportunities at hand. By valuing diversity, we can gain greater potential and creativity from the synergy of the workforce, recapturing commitment and unleashing pent-up talent. In short, we can turn the tide of employee dissatisfaction and put the work ethic back to work.

The good news is that many innovative organizations are leading the way—at first as a quiet revolution, and now as a strategic priority. Organizations like US Sprint, AT&T, Steelcase, Security Pacific Corporation, Merck, Stride Rite, and many others mentioned in this book have been sensitive to their employees' changing needs and have pioneered new ways of valuing diversity and supporting and managing their human assets. They help us to find great hope and optimism, as well as unexpected benefits, in transforming the workplace to one in which people are valued as individuals, their diverse viewpoints are supported, potential is fully used, quality of life and lifestyles are high, and performance is at its competitive best.

The Manager's Perspective

Although managers are not yet as diverse as the rest of the workforce, they are still very different in their styles, beliefs, and practices—and they have lived through a wide range of experiences as the workforce has changed, both as managers and as employees of the organization. For some managers, shifts in the workforce have been threatening, producing anger and defensiveness. This reaction comes, at least in part, from a concern that much could be jeopardized by altering a management approach that has been so successful in the past. Managers may also respond slowly if they are afraid that they do not have the skills or the ability to manage differently.

Other managers have biases so deeply rooted that they find themselves either rejecting people who are different from themselves—insisting on traditional male and female roles or penalizing women at work who have young children, for example—or rejecting nontraditional values, such as a better balance between work and home life or the desire for increased autonomy on the job. For these managers, the workplace is increasingly stressful. They may have the power and control to continue forcing their opinions on their employees for a while, or they may begin to withdraw from threatening employees or situations. Neither strategy is effective in the long term.

Of course, not all managers are resisting change. Some try to be different, even though they may experience confusion and feel a little overwhelmed. This may be because they're not particularly clear about the scope or nature of the differences present in today's workforce. Or they may not be sure exactly how they need to manage differently. Perhaps they're confused about why management practices taught in the past— that worked so well for so long—are now obsolete. Managers would like to initiate changes that will be effective; they're just not sure where to start—and they may still need a little convincing that sweeping changes are necessary.

Finally, some managers are making changes with excitement and optimism. These managers have long been frustrated by organizational constraints. They remember well how unhappy they were with the lack of organizational support they had on the way up, and they may have been aware of and responsive to workforce changes all along, perhaps even managing their units with "underground flexibility." These managers welcome the changing workforce. They look forward to the opportunity it provides to bring about "freeing" changes in organizational policies and systems and to operate with management practices that are in alignment with the needs and preferences of those who are being managed.

The Employee's Perspective

Nonmanagement employees are also living through a spectrum of new experiences. Some employees have felt devalued or discriminated against in the past. They may react with cynicism, caution, or guarded optimism as changes unfold. Some feel threatened, worried about how current and coming changes will affect their jobs and career goals. Others see the new flexibility as unfair; it wasn't available when they were "fighting the system" and suffering through employment/life/preference issues without organizational support. Still others see the current and coming changes positively. They gain new hope as they see greater diversity resulting in a wider range of organizational response.

Beyond ''One Size Fits All''

It is important to understand the differences, their impact on the workplace, and what is needed to move beyond the "one size fits all" model of management. The opportunity exists to utilize the richness that is inherent in variety and to tap unused potential. Innovative management approaches and the flexibility to use many of these approaches simultaneously will be required to take advantage of this opportunity.

Flexibility is the password for managing the changing workforce— flexibility to make necessary adjustments and to individualize treatment of the workforce. This could involve changing an individual's work hours to accommodate a child or elder care schedule, rewarding someone with time off rather than money, or redesigning a job to fit an individual's competencies as well as the organization's requirements.

A Shift Is Needed

A fundamental shift in attitude is needed. This shift must recognize the interdependencies among an organization's policies, systems, and practices. It must acknowledge the need for both individual and organizational change. And it must understand that individualizing means paying attention to differences and providing options and choices.

Conventional approaches have been lacking in four ways. First, under the banner of "affirmative action," and more recently under the banner of "diversity," the focus has been primarily on ethnic groups and women in the workforce. Today's workforce incorporates many more differences and requires a broader view.

Second, many early approaches tended to isolate those who were "different" and provide them with training designed to help them assimilate into the white man's world of work. Later these "different" groups and other nontraditional workers were provided with training in skills they had lacked the opportunity to develop in the past. Even recent popular waves of diversity training, focusing on all people, still address the problem as one of individual change. While training is a valuable and needed component, as a solitary effort it does little to change the organization.

Third, until recently, all matters related to the changing workforce were considered to be personnel or human resource issues rather than management issues. However, dealing with these issues should be an important management priority, because they affect the way organizations are designed, staffed, and operated and, ultimately, the bottom line.

Last, a systematic approach to help managers has been lacking. There have been isolated programs and piecemeal policy changes, but little progress has been made in linking individual and organizational components.

A Managerial Crossroad

Now more than ever, it is increasingly difficult to manage. On one hand, solving business problems has become technically complex, requiring more sophisticated skills than in the past. On the other hand, paying attention to people means focusing on a wide spectrum of options and choices. Although at times this makes managing feel like an uphill battle, it is also a great opportunity.

Managers today are at an important crossroad. One path leads to accelerated movement toward a new organizational paradigm that allows managers to recognize a variety of managerial approaches and to exercise flexibility in executing them. The other path leads to continued slow, even resistant, movement that can only prolong the status quo.

Following the second path could be very dangerous. Some employees are already being driven by impatience to see change happen and happen fast. As their reaction to no or slow change intensifies, and as other employees' frustrations with their unfulfilled needs grow, greater alienation and poor performance will result. Multiple, fragmented subgroups will begin positioning themselves to compete for an organizational response and could develop adversarial relationships with each other.

Following the first path—changing the way managers may have been managing for years, despite the obstacles—is the challenge. By meeting this challenge, managers will have the opportunity to supervise a more integrated, satisfied, and productive workforce and to benefit from the richness of strengths it contains.

A New Organizational Paradigm

By taking a systematic approach to planning for and managing the kinds of changes required by the new, more diverse workforce, a new organizational paradigm is created that is both obtainable and desirable.

The leading innovators, who have already begun aligning policies, systems, and practices with their changing workforce, are showing us why and how. We have utilized their experience, in the form of examples, together with the FLEX-MANAGEMENT model, to provide a roadmap that will help organizations and managers think and act differently, systematically modify procedures at individual and organizational levels, and move beyond rhetoric.

At the heart of the FLEX-MANAGEMENT model is the need to individualize the way we manage—accommodating differences and providing choices wherever possible. This approach is distinctly different from the more paternalistic approaches of the past. Then, everyone was viewed through the same lens, and one set of choices was made for all.

FLEX-MANAGEMENT is not another "program" or quick fix. The concept focuses on three areas that are under the control of those who work in the organization and that can be modified by them: policies—the published rules that guide the organization; systems—the human resource tools, processes, and procedures; and practices—the day-to-day activities. It can help managers to develop a fundamental, systematic plan to reshape these guidelines, tools, and practices.

If organizations can meet the challenge and capitalize on the opportunity, what might the new organization look like and do differently? While this is yet to be seen in its entirety, there are early indications from pioneering organizations and some visions of the desired "end state."

In the "new" organization, function, department, or role structures vary in type, levels, spans of control, and permanence, depending upon the specific work to be done and the workers who are used. Policies are minimal and are focused on intent or outcomes, not on constraints. Systems that involve working with people have basic and alternative ways of operating; they focus on outcomes and provide a variety of tools to aid managers. Management practices are based on accepting individual differences, valuing people, and providing choices.

People throughout the organization have high multicultural awareness and understand how to use the strengths found in diversity. They feel appreciated and have a high commitment to the mission of their organization. They are able to influence the type of support they receive, the way they are rewarded, and the way their job is designed and carried out.

People at all levels have the opportunity to participate in planning, problem solving, designing, and other activities related to change. They understand the larger goals of their organization and can move among jobs as their skills, preferences, and life situations require.

In the "new" organization, people have worked out a balance between work and home and have good support for handling issues that might keep them from being at work and being productive. If they need assistance, training, or special help, they can find it easily. When people in different roles work as colleagues with equality and collaboration, they have the opportunity to use their potential, contribute, and feel rewarded.

Copeland Griggs Productions, producer of the "Valuing Diversity" video series, describes the future organization in this way: "In the valuing diversity organization, issues of the multicultural work force are not relegated to the Personnel Department or the International Division but are integrated into all management functions and championed by top leadership. Employees are hired, not on the basis of quotas, but for their talent (and talent is recognized as not limited to one group). Institutional policies and practices—formal and informal—are shared with *all*, but they are flexible and changed to nurture differences and the advancement of people who contribute to the organization whatever their gender or ethnic identity. Power is shared and all managers are held accountable for valuing diversity. Most importantly, change is planned and diversity is *deliberately* managed: in most cases, this involves policy change and system-wide retraining to change old attitudes and ways of behavior" (Copeland Griggs Productions, n.d.)

In the move toward the new organization, systematic action must be taken to analyze the profile and characteristics of the workforce, investigate implications of change, and identify individual and organizational modifications that are affordable and desirable.

Today's diverse workforce provides critical challenges and significant opportunities for organizations in areas such as (1) attracting and retaining talent from a shrinking traditional labor pool and a generally slower-growing labor force, (2) motivating across a wide spectrum of employees, (3) rewarding people for their contributions, and (4) supporting them in new and varied ways that recognize their individuality. Answering these issues and other related questions is the strategic priority for the 1990s.

2

Portraits of Diversity: Today's New Workforce

THE CONTEMPORARY WORKFORCE doesn't look like, think like, act like, or have the same desires as the workforce of the past. Workforce 2000—and the workforce of today—is significantly different in its age distribution, increasing equality of men and women, cultural diversity, range of educational levels, inclusion of persons with disabilities, and mix of values and attitudes. These characteristics translate into portraits of diversity—a workforce of individuals who bring different resources and perspectives to the workplace and who have distinctive needs, preferences, expectations, and lifestyles.

Workforce 2000 could easily be renamed *Workforce 1990*. Diversity, at least by gender, race, ethnic background, and age, is already an organizational fact of life (Towers Perrin and Hudson Institute, 1990).

The Workforce of the Past

Prior to the 1970s, there was a very different profile in the workforce, in both demographics and attitude. It was more homogeneous, with a large dominant majority and a few visible minorities. Individuals who were "different" were either assimilated into the workplace, isolated from the majority of workers, or ignored.

The average member of the workforce of the past was male, white, approximately twenty-nine years old, and with fewer than twelve years of education. These men were usually married to homemaker wives, had children, and worked within their region of birth. A high degree of similarity and a generally less liberal society led to a prevalence of commonly held beliefs and values about such topics as work, men, women, minorities, age, authority, and family.

The man of the family held a job; women generally worked in the home or in a few acceptable types of jobs. Only certain jobs were open to ethnic minorities. It was understood that people received a fair day's pay for a fair day's work. People worked hard to get ahead; they delayed gratification and saved for future goals. Loyalty to one's employer was expected and authority was obeyed. Older workers were considered smarter because they were more experienced, and younger workers needed age and experience—they were expected to "pay their dues"—before others would listen to them.

In the past, most women who worked outside the home had traditionally "female jobs," such as teaching, nursing, or clerical positions. A few minority groups were visible in the workplace in limited roles. People with disabilities generally were not found in the workforce. Many workers had high school or college degrees, although a significant portion did not. Some workers held nontraditional values and beliefs, which were considered to be deviant. However, these relatively few exceptions paled in numbers and influence compared with the massiveness of the predominant workforce and the almost universal profile of those who managed and made decisions: older white males.

Workforce 2000

It is common knowledge that changes are taking place in America's workforce: The working population is aging, many more women are working, ethnic diversity is growing, more people with disabilities are employed, an increasing gap exists between highly educated persons and the large number of persons who cannot read and write well enough to hold simple jobs, and employees' values are becoming more personal and more divergent. Although the statistics are often dramatic, they are not as important as the reality of identifying and managing the implications of these changes to today's workplace.

Some of these implications are still unclear, confusing, and distant to many managers and organizations. A large number of managers don't recognize or have little time to deal with the implications of workforce demographics; engrossed in day-to-day problems, they are not concerned with future implications. And, in fairness, some demographic changes are not applicable to certain jobs, industries, and geographic areas—at least, not yet.

It becomes important, therefore, for organizations to chart their own demographic and attitudinal profiles, draw conclusions about the specific implications of their situation, and take appropriate action. For example, McDonald's Corporation saw a declining number of younger workers—long the labor pool for their entry-level jobs—and took action by tapping into the pool of older workers.

While it's true that each organization will have its own, sometimes unique, situation to manage, there are clear national trends that are being felt by large numbers of managers. To better understand these trends, the workforce can be broken down into the six separate dimensions of age, gender, ethnicity, education, disability, and values. Each dimension provides a different perspective; when they are considered together, these perspectives form the basis for the portraits of diversity that make up today's workforce.

The Aging of the Workforce: The Young, the Old, and the Bulge in the Middle

The median age of the workforce is increasing. In 1970 it was approximately twenty-eight and will climb to nearly forty by the year 2000, with the forty-five-and-over contingent increasing by a whopping 30 percent. In a recent survey by Towers Perrin and the Hudson Institute, 26 percent of companies reported that between 30 and 40 percent of their workforce was over age forty, another 20 percent reported that their over-forty population constituted 40 to 50 percent of the workforce, and 15 percent already had over 50 percent of their working population over forty years of age (Towers Perrin and Hudson Institute, 1990). This increase is being created by three phenomena: the Baby Boom, the Baby Bust, and advances in health care.

Baby Boomers—those born between 1946 and 1964—have consistently been a dominant force in our society. From the growth in the number of elementary schools to the burgeoning of colleges in the 1960s and 1970s, Boomers have left their mark. Now numbering 76 million, they constitute about one-third of the U.S. population. Baby Boomers represent the bulge in the middle of the workforce.

The Baby Bust generation, consisting of those born during the ten years following the Baby Boom, has only half as many members as its Boomer predecessor (Deutsch, 1988). This period of lower birth rates has led to a decline in the number of sixteen- to twenty-four-year-olds, who are relied on by many organizations for filling entry-level positions, and is a contributor to the anticipated slower workforce growth rate between now and the year 2000. It is projected that the labor pool will increase by only 1 percent annually during the 1990s (Johnston and Packer, 1987, p. xix)—the slowest growth rate during any time in U.S. history, except for the Great Depression.

Advances in health care, including awareness of health-related issues, breakthroughs in medical technology, and a more active pursuit of wellness, are extending the average life expectancy. As a result, people are able to work over a greater number of years than was possible in the past. An increase in the number of older workers, together with the aging of the Boomers and the smaller number of Busters, adds up to the "middle-aging" of the workforce.

By the year 2000, the bulk of the workforce will be middle-aged; 51 percent will be between the ages of thirty-five and fifty-four. The number of workers aged sixteen to twenty-four will continue to decline to approximately 16 percent. The senior workforce, those over fifty-five years of age, will remain fairly stable—approximately 11 to 13 percent ("Human Capital," 1988).

Implications

While all the implications won't be known until history writes its script, there are some early indicators of possible consequences.

More older workers.   Middle-aged and older workers will be the core of the workforce. The dimension of aging may have many important implications, such as the following:

- The increasing number of over-forty workers will mean that motivations for working will change. What seems motivating, challenging, or stimulating to people in their twenties may look very different to them in their forties or fifties.

- The workforce may be more stable and experienced, but perhaps less adaptable or mobile. Older workers may have strong ties to their communities and families and may be less willing to relocate.

- Younger persons will manage older persons to a greater extent than ever before, reversing the traditional older-to-younger mentoring role.

- Career opportunities at the top levels of organizations will decline, which may cause a reconsideration of organizations' hierarchical structures.

- Part-time roles will be more useful as people shift their use of time.

- The workforce will be more concerned with retirement security and planning.

- There will be an increased emphasis on health care and wellness.

- Views on the value of experience will change—some will covet experience while others may see older workers as outdated.

- Reward systems will reflect the values of economically stable older workers, who may prefer sabbaticals, perks, and time off to salary increases or other financial incentives.

Fewer younger workers.   What might the decline in the number of younger workers mean?

- Competition to attract and retain entry-level workers will be fierce.

- Recruitment efforts will be revamped, particularly for jobs that are considered undesirable and those traditionally held by youth.

- Nontraditional workers, such as people with disabilities, retirees, immigrants, and women who are not currently in the workforce, will be in demand.

- Organizations may begin to offer the different amenities and compensation options preferred by the shrinking number of younger workers and the new nontraditional workers who will be entering the workforce.

- Organizations that relied on lower-paid, younger workers may need to redesign their jobs and work schedules.

The bulge in the middle.   The increasing number of Baby Boomers may have far-reaching effects:

- The interests of these middle-agers will be a strong influence on policies related to issues such as dependent care, wellness, and family.

- Fewer positions will be open in management for qualified persons on their way to the top. The inability of organizations to absorb these people may result in shock, frustration, heightened competition, and a growing interest in self-employment.

- With reduced promotional opportunities, many employees' careers will plateau and their aspirations may decline.

- Career development will become more lateral than vertical.

- It may be necessary to have more than one career in order to advance or to increase satisfaction.

- There could be some distrust of management's ability to distinguish among employees for limited promotional opportunities; this might increase grievances and accelerate the use of the court system.

Concern about the aging of the workforce has been low to date, with small percentages of organizations responding with programs such as retraining older workers, gradual retirement, retiree job banks, or elder care referral services. Wellness programs appear to be the most popular response as the 1990s begin (Towers Perrin and Hudson Institute, 1990).

As change continues into the 1990s, organizations that respond to the aging of the workforce will use more older workers; accommodate these workers' range of needs and lifestyle preferences; accept the challenge of managing a potentially less adaptable workforce; and rethink careers, progression, and strategies for recruiting and retaining entry-level workers.

Women in the Workforce

John Naisbitt, author of *Megatrends* and coauthor of *Reinventing the Corporation* and *Megatrends 2000,* has said that the changing role of women in our society is the most significant change in this century (Naisbitt, personal communication, January 1990). While some may not agree on the degree of significance, most would agree that the increase in the number of women in the workforce has had wide-ranging effects.

More women are entering the workforce than ever before. Women will approach 50 percent of the workforce by the year 2000 ("Human Capital," 1988), when six out of seven working-age women will be at work. Almost two-thirds of the new entrants to the labor force between 1985 and 2000 will be female (Johnston and Packer, 1987), increasing dual-career families to 75 percent from 55 percent in the late 1980s ("Managing Now for the 1990s," 1989).

In a cross-sectional survey of companies, 73 percent already report that 30 percent or more of their workforce is female. A whopping 47 percent have a greater than 50 percent female population (Towers Perrin and Hudson Institute, 1990).

Three-quarters of all working women are in their childbearing years. More than half of all mothers work, even those with young children, and many are returning shortly after childbirth. In 1988, 60 percent of all school-age children had mothers in the workforce, up from 39 percent in 1970 ("Human Capital," 1988). Women with children under six years of age are the fastest-growing segment of the workforce ("Human Capital," 1988).

Women have also been entering previously nontraditional positions and are moving up within their organizations. Between 1975 and 1985, the number of women professionals and managers increased by 77 percent, while the number of males in those roles increased by only 6 percent (Selbert, 1987). The male-female pay gap is closing and is much narrower among younger workers. Women represent an increasingly larger percentage of the executive, administrative, and management workforce population in the United States—35 percent in 1987 (Selbert, 1987).

Implications

With the significant increase of women in the workforce during the 1970s and 1980s, sociologists, anthropologists, business authors, researchers, and journalists have had a field day speculating about whether or not women and men work in the same ways or, if they differ, how they differ. They have hypothesized about what strengths each sex brings to the workplace and how management styles might change as a result of the influx of women.

A decrease in the number of younger workers and appropriately skilled workers will prompt organizations to explore new ways of recruiting women, especially those who are educated but not currently working. In addition to the possibility of bringing new skills and styles to the workplace, increased numbers of working women may have the following results:

- Men and women will work together as peers or in nontraditional boss/subordinate and collegial relationships. It will become increasingly common for men to be working for women and for women to be working for other women.

- As more women enter the executive ranks, and as more emphasis is placed on the family, organizations will see different styles of management emerge and different perspectives on what constitutes success.

- Managers and executives in dual-career families may be unwilling to relocate without significant incentives and support.

- Benefit needs will vary among women who head single-parent households, those who are part of dual-income families, those who are childless, and those with children.

- Leave policies will be revamped. As more women work, there will be increasing pressure for both parents to be given leave for childbirth, child-related emergencies, school-related activities, and elder care.

- There will be an expansion of child care arrangements using providers outside the home and family.

- There will be more pressure on organizations to create part-time, flexible, shared, and work-at-home jobs.

Felice Schwartz, president and founder of Catalyst, a national non-profit organization that works with businesses to effect change for women, sums up the issue of attracting and retaining high-performing career and family women in this way: "The price you must pay to retain these women is threefold: you must plan for and manage maternity, you must provide the flexibility that will allow them to be maximally productive, and you must take an active role in helping to make family supports and high-quality, affordable child care available to all women" (Schwartz, 1989, pp. 71–72).

The authors of *Workforce 2000* go further by suggesting: "What is needed is a thoroughgoing reform of the institutions and policies that govern the workplace, to insure that women can participate fully in the economy, and that men and women have the time and resources needed to invest in their children" (Johnston and Packer, 1987, p. xxv).

Mixing Cultures at Work

In the past, white males comprised the one dominant, visible ethnic majority and blacks, Asians, and Hispanics made up the visible ethnic minority groups. Today we have many cultural groups represented in the labor force. There are a wide variety of Asian cultures such as Japanese, Chinese, Thai, Indian, many from western and eastern Europe, and a mixture from the Middle East including Greek and Arab cultures. The traditional majority is becoming a minority in many locales, and U.S.-born people of color and immigrants are expected to comprise 43 percent of new entrants to the workforce between 1985 and 2000 ("Human Capital," 1988).

The minority share of the workforce will continue to grow from approximately 17 percent in the late 1980s to over 25 percent by the year 2000 (Kutscher, 1989). In 1990, 25 percent of surveyed companies reported that their minority workforce had already topped 25 percent (Towers Perrin and Hudson Institute, 1990). In some regions, the minority workforce will approach and even surpass 50 percent. For example, in California, a significantly culturally diverse state, it is estimated that by the year 2005 more than 50 percent of the population will be composed of people of color who will be speaking more than eighty languages, and the white workforce will drop to approximately 50 percent (Leo Estrada, personal communication, June 1990). Between 1988 and 2000, blacks are projected to grow from 11 to 12 percent, Hispanics from 7 to 10 percent, and Asians and other races from 3 to 4 percent of the workforce (Kutscher, 1989).

Approximately 600,000 legal and illegal immigrants per year are expected to enter the United States through the end of the century, primarily from Latin America and Asia (of immigrants entering before 1969, 79 percent were from Canada and Europe; since 1970, 78 percent have been from Latin America and Asia). Two-thirds or more of those of working age are likely to join the labor force (Johnston and Packer, 1987). Some ethnic groups are also growing faster than others. It is estimated that the number of Hispanics will grow by over 4 percent a year to the year 2000, compared to less than 2 percent for blacks and only 1 percent for whites ("Human Capital," 1988).

Hispanics have experienced considerable growth momentum, with a 34 percent increase between 1980 and 1988 and an estimated 45 percent increase by the year 2000. The median age of Hispanics is considerably lower than that of other Americans (twenty-six versus thirty-two years of age) and their birth rate is 50 percent higher than the average. These factors, coupled with continued Latin American immigration, fuel their unprecedented growth (Valdivieso and Davis, 1988).

In some parts of the country, such as California, the Asian population is growing at the fastest rate, with an estimated increase from 9.7 percent in 1990 to 12.7 percent in 2005 (Gardner, Robey, and Smith, 1985).

Implications

The proliferation of cultural backgrounds at work brings to the surface many varieties of values, work ethics, and norms of behavior that are ethnically and culturally rooted. Attempts by managers to work together with employees of different backgrounds are likely to be hampered by communication issues, insensitivity, and ignorance of each others' motivation.

One way in which managers have effectively supervised people from different cultures is by studying those cultures and adjusting management practices accordingly. While this process is useful, the increasing number of ethnic groups that are supervised often translates into a lack of time or resources to study each culture and adapt appropriately.

The increasing number of ethnic groups and the increasing proportion of these groups in the workforce will result in the youth labor force that fills most entry-level positions being composed predominantly of workers from a myriad of cultural backgrounds. In fact, if job expansion outstretches the shrinking pool of new workers, there could be an increase in job opportunities for various cultural groups at many levels within organizations.

The challenge will be to look for ways to integrate—not assimilate— the increasing number and mix of people from diverse cultures into the workplace. Because of this, organizations may take the following steps:

- They will learn how to deal with the frustrations of encountering differences.

- They will increase cultural awareness training.

- They will rethink communication techniques to account for some employees' unfamiliarity with the English language.

- They will emphasize training for service jobs that require verbal skills.

- They will provide remedial education for those groups that were previously disadvantaged.

- They will design jobs and utilize new technology in which a command of the English language is not critical.

- They will rethink what is meant by participative management and what the participation mores are for each culture represented in the organization.

- They will establish rewards that are valued by different cultural groups and will be flexible about holidays, time off, and leaves.

- They will create special career development programs to better match people with jobs that fit their skills, wants, needs, and values.

- They will reward managers for successfully blending a diverse workforce.

With the increased proportion of people of color and immigrant participants in the workforce, coupled with related educational and linguistic issues, organizations will be challenged to match people with jobs. This is of particular concern since job growth will be predominantly in the service sector, where higher technical and communication skills are often required.

While concern about workforce diversity is high, it has generally not been matched by action. The number of companies with specific programs to address diversity issues is relatively small. Few report involvement in support groups, mentoring programs, or English as a Second Language training, and only slightly over 25 percent are training supervisors to effectively manage a diverse group of employees (Towers Perrin and Hudson Institute, 1990).

The Great Education Gap

The United States currently has the most highly educated workforce in its history. More people are completing high school, going to college, and entering continuing education programs. In 1964, 45.1 percent of workers had high school diplomas. By 1984, the percentage had risen to 59.7 percent. As recently as the mid-1980s, 86 percent of twenty-five- to twenty-nine-year-olds had high school diplomas (Lawler, 1986).

People who grew up in the fifties, sixties, and seventies have become used to being informed and educated. Television and other media have prompted a massive information explosion, more and more people are returning to school for continuing education courses, and bookstores are filled with "how-to" books. These Baby Boomers and the younger Baby Busters are increasingly working alongside or supervising older counterparts with less education and technical competence than they have.

However, the number of less educated people in the workplace is increasing, as is the number of people who are considered functionally illiterate—that is, who have not mastered basic skills well enough to meet individual goals and societal demands such as holding a good job, balancing a checkbook, and understanding a newspaper (Chisman and Associates, 1990). It is commonly estimated that approximately twenty million people comprise this functionally illiterate category. This group does not consist only of the growing number of newly arrived immigrants who are functionally illiterate in English; it also includes the increasing number of youths who drop out of or fail in the U.S. educational system.

Among eighteen- to twenty-one-year-olds in 1988, 13.6 percent dropped out of high school. Dropout rates were even higher among minorities, who make up a large segment of new entrants to the workforce. For blacks, the rate was 17.5 percent; for Hispanics, 23.9 percent. In some major cities with high concentrations of minorities, dropout rates range from 35 to 50 percent. It is estimated that as many as 25 percent of those who do graduate cannot read or write at the eighth-grade level. According to a 1988 *Business Week* article, "Most 17-year-olds in school cannot summarize a newspaper article, write a good letter requesting a job, solve real-life math problems, or follow a bus schedule" ("Human Capital," 1988, p. 129).

Implications

More highly educated workers. Baby Boomers and others with advanced educational backgrounds are likely to have certain requirements:

- They want a creative, stimulating work environment.
- They would like to have a high level of involvement, less control by supervisors, and more self-management.
- They wish to be better informed.
- They want to succeed in organizations and be compensated for that success.

Less educated workers. It is likely that the available workforce may not meet the rising demand for people with appropriate job skills. Therefore, the growing number of dropouts, U.S.-born illiterates, and immigrants must be successfully integrated into the workforce. As a result:

- Organizations will become more involved in community education systems.
- Organizations will also be required to increase training efforts in basic education.
- Managers will more closely supervise the less educated populations to help them improve their job skills.
- Different motivators and rewards will be required.

The higher-education end of the spectrum is likely to be a seller's market. The best and brightest are apt to go to organizations designed and operated in ways that are motivating, satisfying, and responsive to this population's needs. The less educated in the workforce will struggle to find matches with jobs requiring ever-increasing skill levels, while they compete with an influx of nontraditional workers for the remaining low-skilled, entry-level jobs.

Workers with Disabilities

As we move into the 1990s and are affected by the shrinking of the traditional workforce, a slower rate of labor force growth, and an increase of nontraditional entrants to the workforce, the mainstreaming of workers with disabilities becomes even more important. "The survey of disabled Americans found that two-thirds of all working-age disabled persons are not working, even though a large majority of this group say that they would like to work. Disabled persons are, therefore, much less likely to be working than any other demographic group under sixty-five, including black teenagers" (International Center for the Disabled, 1987, p. 1).

While federal law requires companies that have federal contracts over $2,500 to provide equal employment opportunities to persons with disabilities, it is still believed by most that persons with disabilities often encounter discrimination (International Center for the Disabled, 1987, p. 23). Accordingly, in 1990, the Americans with Disabilities Act (ADA) was signed into law. This act bans all forms of discrimination against physically and mentally handicapped workers in the hiring and promotion process and requires many companies to make special accommodations for disabled employees and customers.

Most persons with disabilities are far more capable than nondisabled persons are aware. "There's often a disparity between how a person looks and what he or she is capable of accomplishing," says Gordon Burkhard-Schultz, director of AID (Advancement and Independence for the Disabled) Employment, an Alameda County, California, agency that helps place the developmentally disabled with employers.

In addition to people with physical and mental disabilities, there are large numbers of people at work with disabling illnesses and addictions. Advances in medicine have helped these people remain at work longer. Today, many people with heart disease, cancer, multiple sclerosis, AIDS, and drug and alcohol addictions are working.

Ninety percent of people with AIDS are adults aged twenty-five to forty-nine years, the most vital segment of the workforce (Emery and Puckett, 1988). The Centers for Disease Control conservatively estimate that 1 million Americans now carry the AIDS virus. It is projected that in 1993 AIDS will claim 65,000 lives and 80,000 new cases will be diagnosed—there will be 172,000 patients requiring medical care at the cost of $5 billion to $13 billion (Centers for Disease Control, personal communication, October 23, 1990).

Disabilities can be broadly viewed as physical, mental, and medical; they can be either permanent (as is often true of physical disabilities), temporary (such as disabilities resulting from injury or severe stress), or progressive (as is often the case with AIDS, cancer, and alcohol addiction).

The large numbers of people with disabilities and the shrinking number of new entrants to the workforce indicate that an increasing need exists to hire and fully utilize workers with disabilities.

Implications

With larger numbers of disabled workers, organizations will respond by making special accommodations with regard to the work environment, equipment used on the job, or the nature of the job itself. However, the majority of these changes are similar in most ways to those that will be made for other nontraditional workers. For example:

- Recruiters will learn to tap into new sources to locate workers with disabilities.

- Managers will have to be educated about the excellent performance record achieved by workers with disabilities and the generally low cost of accommodating their special needs (International Center for the Disabled, 1987, p. 9).

- Managers will learn how to recognize the work competencies of persons with disabilities.

- Professionals specifically trained to work with persons with disabilities may need to be hired to administer programs and to assist both those with disabilities and managers in the mainstreaming process.

- Nondisabled persons will receive training and assistance to become comfortable working with persons with disabilities.

- Awareness education will be needed for managers and co-workers to help everyone understand the facts versus the myths related to disability liabilities, safety issues, and rights and responsibilities.

- Special career development efforts may be required. "People with disabilities who have been socially isolated for a good portion of their lives often lack the sophistication to successfully negotiate the system once they are employed; therefore, they remain in entry-level jobs and do not seek promotion," says Elisa Lederer, placement director of the International Center for the Disabled.

- Work-at-home and other flexible options will be expanded.

- As employees with progressive disabilities become less able to perform previous job duties, their jobs will be continually redesigned.

- Organizations of all sizes will have policies and processes in place for dealing with disabling illnesses such as AIDS.

- Organizations will collaborate with legislators, health care providers, and special agencies for education and support.

- Enhanced and expanded employee assistance services will help keep employees from becoming or remaining disabled.

People with various disabilities will increasingly be part of the workforce. The challenge will be to learn how to match people with jobs and provide the special kinds of support these diverse workers will need.

Old Rules, New Rules, Changing Rules

"**Y**ou can't judge a book by its cover" is an old saying that is even more relevant today when it is applied to knowing a person's values. An older person doesn't necessarily have traditional values, nor does a young person automatically have a "new age" philosophy. Just because a person lives in the Midwest or in New England doesn't guarantee that he or she has values stereotypical of that region. Yet organizations and managers regularly make assumptions about individuals' values— and often arrive at the wrong conclusions.

Today's workforce is characterized by a mix of values. Some employees will primarily value their home and family life, others their career. Some will value loyalty to their company, others loyalty to their profession, and still others loyalty to themselves. Sometimes men and women will share identical values; at other times their values will differ. Often, what people may have been lacking, such as money, respect, or control, will be most highly valued. Values may change with significant life experiences or simply with age.

Persons with differing values frequently work side by side; managers must be careful not to make assumptions about employees' values that might be incorrect. When managers accurately understand the values in a particular workforce, they can guide the organization to appropriately motivate and reward employees.

Although individual values will vary greatly, research, observation, and practical experience can help to identify widely held values and recognize trends. Not all studies and articles agree on the assessment of value shifts and trends; many show contradictory results, particularly on issues such as loyalty, obedience to authority, job security, and money.

In order to help bring some clarity to this most confusing area, a widely diverse group of managers, human resource professionals, and organization development practitioners was surveyed.[1] By virtue of their work and previously expressed interest in the changing workforce, each of these resources was a legitimate observer of current trends in the workplace. The results offer an interesting picture and provide some initial guidance into the values of large numbers of people.

Participants in the survey were asked to identify the work-related values that they believed were most important to the majority of people in their workforce now and that would continue to be important in the near future. Some traditional values received negligible to minimal support. Being seen as a loyal member of the organization and pursuit of money (accumulating wealth and possessions), for example, were virtually unsupported. Interestingly, job security received some support but fell into the lowest category.

The top tier of responses provides the most valuable guidance. Nine values stand out, having been identified by the majority of the respondents:

1. *Recognition for competence and accomplishments.* People want to be seen and recognized, both as individuals and teams, for their value, skills, and accomplishments. They want to know that their contribution is appreciated.

2. *Respect and dignity.* This value is focused on how people are treated— through the jobs they hold, in response to their ideas, or by virtue of their background. The strong support for this value indicates that most people want to be respected for who they are. They want to be valued.

3. *Personal choice and freedom.* People want more opportunity to be free from constraints and decisions made for and about them by authorities. They want to be more autonomous and able to rely more on their own judgment. They wish to have more personal choice in what affects their lives.

4. *Involvement at work.* Large portions of the workforce want to be kept informed, included, and involved in important decisions at work, particularly as these decisions affect their work and quality of life at work.

---

[1]Since 1983, we have accumulated a list of approximately 350 managers and human resource professionals who work with changing workforce issues. They came from our consulting and professional network, and from attendance at various conferences, presentations, and workshops we've conducted. This list was combined with a list of approximately 200 graduates from the Master of Science in Organization Development program at Pepperdine University, which includes both managers and internal and external consultants in change. Both lists were widely dispersed around the United States. Eighty-four persons responded to this survey on values.

5. *Pride in one's work.* People want to do a good job and feel a sense of accomplishment. Fulfillment and pride come through quality workmanship.

6. *Lifestyle quality.* People pursue many different lifestyles and each person wants his or hers to be of high quality. Work policies and practices have great impact on lifestyle pursuits. The desire for time with family and time for leisure were strongly emphasized.

7. *Financial security.* People want to know that they can succeed. They want some security from economic cycles, rampant inflation, or devastating financial situations. This appears to be a new variation on the desire for money—not continual pursuit of money, but enough to feel secure in today's world, enjoy a comfortable lifestyle, and ride out bad times.

8. *Self-development.* The focus here is on the desire to continually improve, to do more with one's life, to reach one's potential, to learn and grow. There is a strong desire by individuals to take initiative and to use opportunities to further themselves.

9. *Health and wellness.* This value reflects the aging workforce and increased information on wellness. People want to organize life and work in ways that are healthy and contribute to long-term wellness.

These values should be taken into account in designing organizations and jobs, making decisions, setting policies, managing people in general, and motivating and rewarding employees in particular. However, it is most important not to assume that specific trends are accurate for a particular workforce without first thoroughly identifying the specific values that are represented in each organization.

Although other values did not receive such strong support in this survey, they nonetheless exist with varying intensities throughout the workforce. Some that were identified and are worth noting for their possible impact on the future include (1) improving one's standard of living, (2) working with technology as a partner, (3) developing quality relationships, (4) being part of a socially responsible organization, (5) making a meaningful contribution to society, and (6) having fun at work.

Implications

It is perhaps most important to understand that values have proliferated; older ones have not necessarily been replaced by others. More values are represented and they are more widely dispersed. Managers are challenged to balance the wishes of the majority of people with the need to recognize and value individual differences.

There are numerous other implications:

- With a wider array of values, the potential for differences, incompatible values, and conflict will be higher.

- With greater diversity in the workforce, but little diversity in higher levels of management, those at the top will need to be particularly sensitive, expand their ideas of what is "right," and listen to their subordinates.

- Motivation and rewards will be linked and both will use values as a base.

- Reward and recognition systems and practices will contain more options.

- Opportunities for self-management will expand.

- Personal and career development as well as advancement goals will be based on diverse values.

- Compensation, benefits, and financial services will be looked at in terms of how they contribute to financial security, lifestyle quality, and long-term well-being.

- Helping people to be healthy at work and away from work will become more important.

- Workforce involvement and participation in decisions will be widespread.

- Paying attention to people's feelings about their work and accomplishments and helping to increase their job satisfaction will be important for morale and productivity.

- Integrating people's work with the rest of their life will require greater flexibility in their psychological "employment contract."

Portraits of Diversity

Describing the workforce from six perspectives—age, gender, ethnicity, education, disabilities, and values—only scratches the surface in illustrating what this changing workforce wants and needs and how it behaves. Individuals must be viewed as portraits of diversity—mixtures of different demographic categories and value sets. For example, consider the following individuals and think about how they might perceive employment differently; have different requirements; operate from different sets of values; and have different expectations, desires, and ways to approach their work life:

- The single, middle-aged, highly educated female with responsibility for her elderly father's care

- The single, young, black male who uses a wheelchair

- The older, widowed, Hispanic male

- The young, single-parent female

- The highly educated immigrant from Southeast Asia

- The middle-aged, dual-career, professional married couple with children

- The middle-aged, divorced, highly educated male whose children live out of state

- The older, married female with grown children

These examples serve as a reminder of how diverse and complex the workforce has become. It is important not to stereotype or make assumptions based on only one or two factors, such as age or cultural background. Values, needs, and preferences vary within and across demographic categories.

Today's portraits of diversity are individuals who should be treated as such, not lumped together in groups. There must be more focus on understanding their differences, broadening the range of options, and expanding the versatility needed to manage effectively in the 1990s and beyond.

3

Toward a New Management Mindset: An Introduction to Flex-Management

THE REALITIES AND BELIEFS of the past shaped management's mindset—its orientation to what management means, is, and does. These realities and beliefs were based on years of experience with a predominantly homogeneous workforce and form the underlying foundation of management today.

It is not difficult to understand how the mindset of the past may have developed. Consider the following scenarios:

- With a growing labor force adding new bodies to the pool of workers and a capital-intensive emphasis on plant and equipment, people could be seen as expendable or replaceable—as an expense needed for production. Consequently, labor costs, wages, benefits, and investments in people were minimized.

- When relatively younger and less educated workers were supervised by older, more experienced, high-seniority, and sometimes more educated males, disparities in status and knowledge could actually grow. Management practices such as giving direction, supervising closely, and delegating little responsibility were natural outgrowths of this system. The attitude "Managers think and workers do," or the statement by a supervisor to an employee, "You're not paid to think, you're paid to work," were statements consistent with these differences in age and experience.

- Because information, knowledge, experience, and age resided in the management hierarchy and not in the employees, the separation of "thinking" from "working" became strongly ingrained and the concept of "managing" and controlling work and employees could flourish. Scientific management, widely practiced at the time, broke all work into its smallest, most routine components. There were set methods for completing work, and employees were isolated from interaction with other workers or tasks. All planning, scheduling, and decision making were management responsibilities. Thus, employees were placed in a more passive role and were forced to follow the rules inherent in a high-control orientation.

- The vast majority of the workforce was homogeneous, and those who were different were forced to adapt and assimilate; therefore, an understandable "one size fits all" mentality developed. There was no perceived need to pay attention to differences or to identify individuals' requirements: They were presumed to be known.

- With little influence from women or employees with diverse cultural backgrounds, only the white male mentality of the time was available to create the values and behavior of the work culture. As a result, importance was placed on being tough, macho, competitive, militaristic, and paternal.

Policies, systems, and practices are reflections of management philosophy that institutionalize the mindset. They are developed, reinforced, and embedded in organizational culture. Management transfers, rewards, and acculturates them until they become "the way we run the organization and manage our employees." As a result, the mindset of the past produced

- Narrow and tightly defined jobs
- Narrow spans of control
- Layers in management for approval and monitoring
- Rigid demarcations between functions
- One-way communication systems
- Evaluation, promotion, planning, and decision-making systems controlled at the top
- Policies that tightly monitored work hours, time off, good behavior, disciplinary processes, and work rules

The mindset of the past has increasingly become out of synch with today's workforce and the organizational demands of the nineties. As the workforce has become more diverse and demanding, the old mindset isn't working. Needs aren't being met, frustrations are growing, and performance often suffers. Ultimately, productivity, job satisfaction, and hiring and retaining competent employees are at stake. As employees have greater voice, they will choose to work in organizations that at least attempt to meet their needs and preferences. Organizations that offer greater flexibility will also have a competitive advantage when it comes to recruiting and retaining the highest-quality employees.

The Flex-Management Model

FLEX-MANAGEMENT is a new mindset—a different philosophy of management. Based on a set of core values, it provides a framework for action.

At the heart of FLEX-MANAGEMENT is a deep appreciation of individual differences and the understanding that equality does not mean sameness. Although diverse needs and wants are equally respected, they are not met by treating everyone the same. Instead, FLEX-MANAGEMENT recommends creation of more individualized policies, systems, and management practices.

In the new mindset, managers recognize people as assets to be valued, developed, and maintained. They understand that the new workforce is highly diverse and should be managed, not as a set of groups, but as a collection of individuals, each with unique needs and preferences.

The FLEX-MANAGEMENT mindset is also based on the value of greater self-management, which leads to providing more options that people can select for themselves. This aspect of the concept is built on a fundamental shift from paternalistic control (with high reliance on rules and close supervision) to greater autonomy (with employee empowerment, commitment, and accountability).

FLEX-MANAGEMENT is the mindset of flexibility. It is the antithesis of a "one size fits all" viewpoint. This concept is not a replacement of one paternalistic system with another; instead, it recognizes that one system cannot work across today's diverse workplace.

"At Pac Bell, it's 9 to 5 'if it works for the individual,'" states the headline of a *Business Week* article, "How the Next Decade Will Differ" (1989, p. 154). The article describes how an account executive, a single father of four sons, now saves two hours a day by working out of a satellite work center near his home rather than commuting to a downtown Los Angeles office. Dori Bailey, a Pacific Bell spokesperson, stresses that Pac Bell is interested in "what works for the individual."

The above example illustrates the FLEX-MANAGEMENT concept. It requires management to tune in to people and their needs, create options that give people choices, and balance diverse individual needs with the needs of the organization. Successful use of this model can motivate, challenge, and reward employees; improve their performance; and increase their job satisfaction.

The FLEX-MANAGEMENT model shown in Figure 1 graphically relates the dynamics of three components of management—policies, systems, and practices—to four strategies for individualizing—matching people and jobs, managing and rewarding performance, informing and involving people, and supporting lifestyle and life needs.

The model provides a framework for action. The goal is to use policies, systems, and practices to create options and flexibility within the four strategies so that the strategies can be individualized within the workforce.

The Management Components

Policies

All too often policies become shackles. They force sameness when customizing is needed. With a long history of developing policies from the top, managing with a control orientation, and investing little authority and trust with middle- and lower-level managers, upper management used policies as a central tool. What is needed is fewer, broader policies that aid in individualizing, provide wider latitude and choice, and support desired organizational and employee values.

Figure 1. The FLEX-MANAGEMENT model.

In the past, rigid, single-option policies were used—for example: "The corporate-wide standard performance appraisal form shall be completed twice each year in April and October for each employee." Policies should focus on intent and have either more options or less specific parameters. An example might be: "Performance planning and management discussions are valuable to improve and maintain productivity and performance. A process should be developed for each employee with at least one such discussion annually."

Other considerations for more flexible policies include offering a specified number of holidays instead of naming five holidays off or providing a set amount of money to "buy" an individualized benefits package instead of giving everyone the same insurance and vacation. Similarly, policies relating to transfers or rotations could encourage internal mobility and exposure rather than restricting movement by requiring numerous approvals or by limiting who can participate in transfers or rotations. Information-sharing policies could be more open, complete, and regular, instead of being restrictive, which keeps employees uninformed.

Systems

Human resource systems and programs—the organized, "formal" tools, processes, and procedures provided by the organization for use in managing people—have long followed the "sameness" or "one size fits all" notion. They should be redesigned to have a less prescriptive focus and to allow more options, adaptations, and avenues of implementation. For example, there should be variation in the way goals are set, the number of goals implemented, and the time frames used; management should be free to customize rewards and should be able to create special opportunities to "try out" jobs. Systems are often tied to policies, so change in one of these areas usually goes hand in hand with change in the other.

It is particularly important to add greater flexibility to compensation and classification, benefits programs, reward options, performance planning and evaluation, recruiting and assessment, orientation, job evaluation and design, job descriptions, and training. These systems need greater versatility with less cumbersome procedures in order to be customized for individuals.

The FLEX-MANAGEMENT approach supports this customization. It also can help employees and managers design the best programs for both the individual and the organization.

Practices

The day-to-day practices of managers working with both individuals and groups require a great deal of flexibility today. A manager must tune in to many different people, understand their perspectives, and use more judgment in relating to them.

Some employees may require more direction, whereas others may perform better with greater autonomy. Even though they allow greater participation, managers may still need to control some aspects of work. Questioning and listening to employees will be important in trying to understand their differences, as will versatility in coaching, training, and development. The face-to-face work of managing diversity will involve negotiating, arbitrating, and facilitating, and, in all situations, managers will still need to balance production with compassion.

The Flex-Management Strategies

The four strategies briefly discussed in this section offer great latitude in individualizing management and in designing policies, systems, and practices for flexibility. The strategies are discussed more fully in the following chapters.

Matching People and Jobs

The focus of this strategy is on ways to match a variety of different individuals, their skills, and their work preferences with real job characteristics and demands. Matching involves paying attention to both the objective and subjective sides of work and people in order to individualize job profiles, assessment methods, orientation, and careers. It is used to provide better information about jobs, obtain data about individual strengths and styles, and orchestrate a variety of methods to aid employees and the organization in an ongoing process.

To do this, policies and systems related to transfers, promotions, rotation, job posting, job designs, and descriptions may have to be changed; career development systems may need review; and management practices of interviewing, recruiting, development planning, and career coaching may demand new emphasis.

Managing and Rewarding Performance

This strategy recognizes that people don't work in the same ways and are not motivated by the same methods or incentives. It is used to consider different approaches to planning work goals, managing the process of work, and rewarding people in meaningful ways. Variables that can be individualized include choosing the work to be done, the people who participate, the amount of time they spend on a project, and the steps or approach they use to perform the work tasks. To customize this strategy, the approach to performance coaching, mentoring, and feedback, as well as the use of monetary and nonmonetary rewards, can be varied.

Policies related to performance appraisal, disciplinary processes, and rewards are also candidates for greater flexibility. Performance appraisal forms and the rigidity of their use, as well as the question of who is involved in the process and in what ways, are all part of managing performance. In order to be effective, practices such as regular coaching, written evaluations, informal feedback sessions, and structured development meetings will vary greatly as they are applied to different people.

Informing and Involving People

This strategy recognizes the significant desire among people to be more informed about and involved in their workplace. It also appreciates that some employees may not wish to be highly involved and that some persons who come from different cultures may find it difficult to participate with their bosses present or to assert their views in a group setting. Therefore, this strategy creates opportunities for people to choose to participate, develops vehicles for the flow of information, and keeps people informed.

Policies may deal with the use of work time or the establishment of participation groups. Flexible systems using ongoing and temporary groups can be set up. Suggestion systems, attitude surveys, or focus groups can be used to offer flexibility in input, and everyday practices, such as delegating, asking for ideas, or running staff meetings, can be varied among individuals.

Supporting Lifestyle and Life Needs

Life needs and lifestyle preferences vary greatly. Issues include ways of getting to work, productivity at work, work-time flexibility, meeting satisfaction of life/family needs, and use of nonwork time. This leads to other questions, such as how time is structured and scheduled, which benefits count, and the need for support to care for dependents. This strategy identifies people's needs and interests and, where possible, creates supportive options—ways to obtain needed assistance, such as child care or substance abuse counseling, or to meet lifestyle preferences related to such issues as work hours, fitness facilities, or leave options.

New positions designed to assist people, new benefits policies, special interest networks, and community service referral systems, as well as supportive and creative managers, are resources that can help people to obtain individualized assistance.

An Integrated Approach

FLEX-MANAGEMENT integrates much of what we have known, but rarely used, in a systematic way. Its essence is in rethinking what can be controlled—policies, systems, and practices—as they relate to the four strategies to be used in the management of people.

The three components and the four strategies of FLEX-MANAGEMENT are not mutually exclusive; in fact, they have many interconnections and can reinforce each other. Because of this, FLEX-MANAGEMENT should be looked at systematically, rather than piecemeal. One of the most common mistakes made by human resource professionals and managers is to try to solve complex problems with simple solutions that ignore these interdependent connections.

It's not enough to train only those who manage employees from different cultural groups to improve cross-cultural understanding and opportunities for advancement; outdated career progression systems or co-worker prejudice could still hinder the outcome. It's not enough to promote women into management positions and ignore their support and development or to hire a worker with a disability without helping to build his or her relationships with co-workers. Effective management of the changing workforce will require new practices, policies, and systems.

FLEX-MANAGEMENT's four strategies are connected and reinforce each other. For example, improvements in the matching process also aid in performance management: Intrinsic rewards are more likely to occur when people are in well-matched jobs and are involved in meaningful ways. One area of possible involvement is that of performance-related issues. Informing employees about performance results often helps to improve performance. Appropriate support in this area minimizes lost time, stress, and negative attitudes toward the organization.

There are also many interrelationships among policies, systems, and practices. Policies often relate to some formal process that directs the manager's practices. Sometimes practices are not aligned with any policies or systems, a sign that they are not appropriate.

Managing with a FLEX-MANAGEMENT mindset can enable managers to develop inspiring organizations in which people are valued, supported, and satisfied as individuals; high performance is a way of life; and employees are committed to their work and workplace.

PART II

Matching People and Jobs

" *The basis of any effective human resource process is matching people and jobs so the organization and its employees benefit.* **"**

—C. Thomas Dortch,
"Job•Person•Match"

Peggy Boyd disliked her secretarial job. She thought about quitting, but she liked the company. In the midst of this dilemma, she attended her company's career development workshop. There, during a work values clarification exercise, she realized how much she disliked sitting behind a desk. After talking with someone in the human resource department, she switched to an installer's position. Now she is happily installing telephones in customers' homes. She no longer sits behind a desk all day—in fact, she doesn't even have a desk. Peggy found a job she loves and the company retained a good worker.

Steve Pointer, a chemist, was facing mandatory retirement at age sixty-five. With only two months before retirement, he knew he couldn't finish the exciting project he was working on, a project that might make an important breakthrough to his company's competitive position. He wanted to be part of that achievement, but he had promised his wife he would retire. Then he read a newspaper article about retiree job banks. He talked with several of his company colleagues who were also near retirement age, and they proposed that the company set up a retiree job bank that would allow them to continue working on a contract basis. He would be happy, his wife would be happy, and the company would benefit from his experience and commitment to the project.

Sally Middleton, a single parent with three children, loved her job as a computer hardware engineer, but it didn't pay enough. The only way she could achieve greater financial security was to go into management, which would force her to give up her technical work and travel more; this was impossible for her. Fortunately, her company initiated a two-track program. High-performing engineers can now move up a technical ladder in responsibility, challenges, and income. Sally is staying with her company, working hard to move up the technical ladder, and enjoying every minute of it.

Len Supolo was brilliant with numbers and reports but less comfortable managing groups and making presentations. Alice Worthington was excellent with people and groups, yet really hated the documentation and paperwork needed in her job. Both of these people managed similar types of projects within their large data processing division. Together they redesigned their jobs, shared work on all of their projects, emphasized their *preferred tasks, and agreed to cross-train each other on their less preferred ones.*

━━━

These vignettes show what happens when organizations are flexible enough to match people with jobs that meet their needs. Both employees and their organizations win. Too many people work in jobs that don't fit them: They lack some skills, are not interested, or are unhappy. Often employees are trapped into such situations by the organization's culture, traditional career paths, or reward systems. But motivation, productivity, and morale depend, in part, on the fit between the demands and characteristics of the job and an employee's competence, needs, interests, and values.

When issues of age; gender; ethnicity; educational level; values; and physical, mental, and health limitations come into play, it can be a challenge to match people and jobs so that employees are satisfied and job requirements are met. Organizations and managers may be less experienced with this issue and may be following systems, policies, and practices that were established before the workforce evolved into its present form.

Traditional selection and promotion practices don't allow for the complexities of the matching process. All too often people are matched on the right *objective* criteria—education and previous experience—but not on the right *subjective* criteria—preferences, interests, and values. People are selected, placed, or promoted based on what the organization needs without balancing these requirements with the individual's skills and preferences.

Consider the following personal characteristics: attention to detail, ability to learn and communicate, tolerance of ambiguity, need for structure, need for information in decision making, desire for challenge, and slow work pace. Jobs have certain characteristics and requirements along the same lines. For example, some demand rapid decision making with little information, some require employees to work in groups, some are slower paced and more methodical, some require regular written or verbal communication, and still others are always changing. These more subjective aspects often contribute to success, productivity, and satisfaction, or to stress, failure, or sickness. Everyone loses in a mismatch.

C. Thomas Dortch, developer of the software products used in Job•Person•Match, says that effective job/person matches require more than matching a person's skills and abilities to the content of the job. The job shouldn't be the fixed element and the person the variable element. All aspects of the match—job content and required behaviors as well as the individual's skills and preferred behaviors—are variables that must be considered before achieving a successful match (Dortsch, 1989).

In today's workplace, it is even more critical to face the subjective issues of matching. These issues don't go away; instead, they remain inside the person, surfacing later in poor performance or turnover. The strategy for effectively matching people and jobs revolves around three key premises:

1. Both the objective and subjective aspects of jobs and people are important considerations.

2. People today have a wider range of preferences, skills, motivations, and needs. They usually know their own attributes or can be helped to understand them.

3. Organizations must provide more accurate, realistic information about job characteristics to help employees make more informed choices.

Managers can put these premises into practice by taking the following actions:

1. Be informative and creative when describing jobs and recruiting employees.

2. Help people develop careers they want.

3. Change jobs and work hours to meet employee needs.

4. Hire older and temporary workers.

Chapters Four through Seven provide guidance for taking these actions and give examples from organizations that have successfully done so.

4

Be Informative and Creative When Describing Jobs and Recruiting Employees

THE REALISTIC PORTRAYAL of a job includes accurate descriptions of such characteristics as work hours, skills, co-worker relationships, decision making, and supervision. It is equally important to assess the candidate's preferences, style, needs, values, and goals. In today's world, this often means exploring nontraditional sources to find job candidates and going to greater lengths to ascertain both objective and subjective matching information.

Apple Computer, Inc., which develops, manufactures, and markets personal computer systems, does go to great lengths to hire the right person. "Recruiting Apple employees is a long process. Sometimes up to fifteen interviews take place to make sure the candidate understands the environment he or she will be working in. A match between company values and individual values is critical to success," states Debbie Biondolillo, vice-president for human resources for Apple USA, the marketing division of Apple Computer, Inc.

Go Beyond Traditional Job Descriptions

Most people have difficulty with job descriptions. "It's too much trouble to write the description, because it just changes anyway," they say, or "I just do what my boss tells me. He never follows the description," or "We don't have time to write job descriptions. We're too busy doing the work." Most job descriptions list the duties and the experience and credentials required to do the job. Sometimes the list includes skill and knowledge, but these are usually assumed to be synonymous with experience and credentials. Descriptions commonly reflect the way jobs are designed—in rigid, hierarchical ways (it's no mistake that organizational charts show jobs in boxes). Generally, job descriptions don't specify the actual behaviors or characteristics needed to do the job. In addition, managers are sometimes reluctant to tell the truth about a job; they may shade the truth about hours, work group dynamics, level of skill required, reputation of the work group or organization, and productivity.

When jobs are designed with flexibility, they can be described in ways that more accurately reflect the actual job situation. Here are some workable suggestions:

- Use a menu of outputs to describe the job rather than just listing duties. *Outputs* are the products, services, or information "people are paid to produce for or deliver to those they serve" (McLagan, 1989, p. 15). For a human resource development professional, outputs could include the transfer of development or career planning skills to the learner, implementation of change strategies, and facilitation of group discussions. Outputs provide a clearer picture of the job than descriptions that include attending staff meetings, visiting plant locations, or serving on a policies task force.

- Use plain English and be especially sensitive in the language you use if English could be the second language of the candidate.

- Accurately state the degree of commitment in terms of the hours to be worked and the work pace expected.

- Accurately describe the norms and culture of the work group —how people work together, socialize, help each other, and become accepted.

- Describe the relationships that are important to getting the job done. A job that requires working with senior levels of management is very different from one in which the employee will work with colleagues or customers.

- Create job profiles, also known as "user-friendly" job descriptions. One version, from Atlanta Resource Associates' Peggy Hutcheson, includes complexity of key outputs (or skills), characteristics of the work environment (alone, in a group, or with customers), special expectations (travel, overtime, or deadlines), and key relationships.

Make Job Information Readily Available

Job posting is an effective strategy to fill jobs that are vacant and to provide a way for employees to learn about the company's openings and the requirements that are needed to qualify for other jobs. Without job posting or some other easily updated system of job profiles, employees may not know what positions exist and if any might suit them better.

A number of companies have come up with creative job posting systems. For example, at Tandem Computers Incorporated, a manufacturer and marketer of large computer systems and networks for online transaction processing, employees have access to job openings companywide by using the internal electronic mail system. Managers who are hiring simply send job specifications to a job opportunity coordinator, who posts the openings on the system. Employees can pursue these jobs electronically.

Merck & Company, the world's largest pharmaceutical company, has a Job Opportunity Program that helps management become aware of all employees who may be interested in vacancies and encourages employees to apply for jobs for which they feel qualified. Announcements of vacancies are posted for five days on centrally located bulletin boards. Employees may submit an application for any job to a human resource representative. The hiring manager interviews those who most closely fit the job qualifications and the name of the successful candidate is posted for three days. Candidates who are not selected can receive feedback on their own qualifications by requesting the reasons for the decision.

Security Pacific Corporation, California's second largest banking and financial institution, realizes that employees want a variety of career options, including part-time work, career changes, and relocation. Their newsletter, *Career Opps,* which lists job openings throughout the company and its subsidiaries, is distributed to all employees. It gives employees the opportunity to apply for jobs first, before they are advertised externally. The twelve-page newsletter lists all nonexempt and most exempt positions in the corporation by grade, salary level, and company.

Employees interested in a job send an application to the recruiter filling the position. Those who are selected for an interview compete with other candidates for the position. The process is handled confidentially, although employees are encouraged to discuss their career plans with their supervisors.

The Career Opps program was set up to help employees become actively involved in their career management. Employees are also encouraged to seek career information or direction from their supervisor or personnel officer.

The company also offers an employee referral award program, called The Superscout program. All bank retirees and regular full-time, part-time, and temporary employees are eligible to participate. For each qualified referral an employee submits, whether or not that person is hired, the employee is entered in a quarterly drawing for up to $500. If the person referred is hired, the employee may receive a cash award ranging from $25 to $1,500.

Exercise Sensitivity in Recruiting and Transfers

Don Smith, national sales manager for paper chemicals at American Cyanamid Company, a chemical manufacturer, puts a high priority on recruiting people from colleges. "When you look at the job, you can understand why. Our salespeople need to have a science or engineering degree, the personality to sell, a willingness to work sixty hours a week, and the ability to travel three or four nights during the week. It's a tough job to sell and a tough job to fill. That's why I don't delegate the recruiting responsibility to our personnel department. My regional managers and I develop relationships at key colleges through presentations to chemistry and engineering clubs as well as through ongoing contact with professors. This greatly increases the probability of getting top students."

Don considers the geographical preferences of his college recruits. "Although initial assignments may be anywhere in the country, careful consideration is given to geographical preference prior to assigning a sales territory. We make adjustments when our college graduates tell us they want to live and work in a certain area. Some will relocate only under certain conditions. If we want top people, we have to be flexible."

The needs of dual-career couples are another important factor organizations must address in recruiting or transferring an employee. According to Peter Drucker—author, economist, and respected management expert—"People aren't moving anymore." In the two-paycheck professional family, "today's young professionals have to take into consideration the career possibilities of the spouse." For example, Drucker's son, a physicist in Chicago married to a banking vice-president, turned down a promising job opportunity in Ithaca, New York, "because he realized that Ithaca would offer zero opportunities for an up-and-coming female banking executive" (Shaw, 1989, p. 17).

If organizations do not address the career needs of the spouse, they risk failing to recruit or transfer an employee. Merck responded to this need by offering two options for employees who are members of a dual-career family. When possible, the company provides employment for the spouse. In any case, spouses have access to a computer-based dual-career job bank sponsored by the Home Buyers Assistance Corporation. The job bank coordinates a network for exchanging resumes in northern New Jersey and New York.

Gail Tiwanak, R.N., director of administrative services at The Queen's Medical Center in Honolulu, Hawaii, faces several challenges that are rather unique to the process of recruiting and screening. "First of all, because of our location we get between 2,500 and 3,000 inquiries per year with as many as 300 inquiries in a month. We spend a lot of time screening both written and telephone inquiries. Second, because Hawaii has only two schools of nursing, we are dependent on out-of-state recruitment efforts to meet our staffing needs," says Tiwanak.

One creative solution was to offer up to $3,000 in financial and temporary housing assistance to nurses who relocated. However, some nurses were attracted to Honolulu for reasons that weren't consistent with the hospital's philosophy and professional values. "We had to revise what we advertised to be sure we attract nurses who are prepared to make a significant cultural shift and who are committed to the field. That meant eliminating the dollar amount from the description of our Relocation Assistance Program," adds Tiwanak, "playing down the 'fun in the sun' idea in our ads, and preparing a list of questions that assess a candidate's likelihood of making a commitment to the position.

"Some of our new R.N.'s have never been more than 100 miles from their families. These candidates need to display a certain level of maturity about how they would handle the cost of relocation, the cultural adjustments, and the distance from their family. We now have fewer single nurses far from home among our staff and have an increased number of couples and families."

Retention among The Queen's Medical Center nursing staff has increased over the past two years because of a combination of factors, including higher salaries, better recruitment strategies, and innovations such as schedules designed for couples that allow them to have the same shifts at the hospital. "We have hired about a dozen married nurses in the past year," says Tiwanak. "When they both apply, we see it as an opportunity to gain two nurses instead of one and try to be accommodating. Our managers are alerted that a couple is being considered and we do our best to find them positions in different units in their areas of expertise and interest."

The pre-employee training program at The Queen's Medical Center recruits employees and also increases job retention. Dan Rutt, vice-president for personnel services, describes a twenty-hour workshop that offers immigrant job applicants the chance to learn in advance what a housekeeping aide's job entails. "Our housekeeping aides tend to stay because they have a solid understanding of what the job is before they are hired," says Rutt. "We are able to recruit and screen employees from Indochina, Thailand, Japan, and Korea; present an accurate description of the medical center and the job; and hire only those applicants who like and can do the housekeeping aide's job."

To effectively take action in these areas, an organization needs to develop a flexible combination of policies, systems, and practices. *Policies* should favor recruiting internally before going outside and should make transfer options available. *Systems* and *processes* should be designed to facilitate job posting and assessment options, to encourage the use of realistic job descriptions, and to establish training in interview and assessment techniques.

5

Help People Develop
Careers They Want

A CAREER DEVELOPMENT SYSTEM,
according to Zandy Leibowitz,
Caela Farren, and Bev Kaye,
is "an organized, formalized,
planned effort to achieve a
balance between the individual's career needs and the
organization's work-force
requirements" (Leibowitz,
Farren, and Kaye, 1986, p. 4).
A system may include a variety
of programs and activities,
including policies, human

resource planning, workshops, counseling, outplacement, training for managers in conducting career discussions, and incentives for having or supporting career plans. The most important feature of such a system is an organizational strategy that links its various components together. When information from and about employees is linked with information from and about the organization, career management becomes an intricate part of employee and management practices. With a highly diverse workforce, a career management system can play a significant role in effectively matching people and jobs.

Implement Flexible Career Management Systems

Brad Bills, quality assurance (QA) manager for Ethicon, a Johnson & Johnson company that manufactures medical supplies, understands the value a strategic career development program brings to a diverse workforce. "The workforce population in San Angelo, Texas, is quite a melting pot," comments Bills. "Hispanics make up 67 percent of the plant population; blacks and Asians about 10 percent. Educational levels range from high school to doctorate."

Ethicon's QA managers put together a career development vision statement for all its plants that linked business strategy and long-range plans with career development and job opportunities. The program's components include self-assessment, research into career fields at Ethicon, identification of experts to contact for information, career coaching for supervisors, and a four-session career discussion between the employee and supervisor.

"The career discussions were tremendously beneficial to our employees and myself. We learned that our employees were especially concerned with the company's direction and how it would affect their career opportunities in QA. We also learned to appreciate their individual talents as well as their cultural heritage. I heard firsthand about the language barriers that existed in the company and felt it was my responsibility to learn Spanish so that I could build rapport with Hispanic employees and assist with their career development. Employees were able to develop short- and long-term career plans, including identification of job rotations or other developmental opportunities.

"One of my third-shift supervisors, Molly Guevara, really reaped the benefits of our career program. Because of our cultural differences, I felt personally challenged to get to know Molly. She was very timid and shy during our first meeting. During subsequent sessions, I was able to develop a good rapport with her and learned that she was bilingual, had put her-

Until recently, managers supervising Ventura County, California's, 6,500 employees had to contend with high turnover, over 700 job vacancies, and good personnel being lured away by higher salaries. To make matters worse, in an area where housing costs are the second highest in the state, attracting and keeping young professionals seemed nearly impossible.

Then came an innovative shift in policies, benefits, and incentives led by personnel director Ronald Komers. The results of his efforts to prepare for a changing workforce are the Career Development Program and the Educational Incentive Program, which aim to retain current county employees. These programs motivate employees to pursue advanced education, help pay their tuition, and reward them monetarily for their effort.

Keith Turner, director of the county's planning department, is structuring the benefits of the Educational Incentive Program to meet his department's needs. He submitted a budget request to exchange one professional planning position with two paraprofessional positions in the coming year.

"I expect to fill the paraprofessional positions with clerical staff who have some experience in the planning department. It will also be a transitional position that requires employees to take some university extension courses and attend seminars to become grounded in the planning profession. After they complete this training, they can pursue a formal education and the county will pay their tuition and fees through the Career Development Program. With an appropriate degree they can compete for the professional positions within the department." A career counseling and development program is also provided so that the county can ensure the employees' success.

Both the Educational Incentive Program and the Career Development Program are gaining management support. "Our managers have been reoriented to convey the message that a broad general education is important to us and that we are willing to form a partnership with employees to help them achieve their goals," says Komers.

self through college while raising four children, and desired an international career with Ethicon where she could use her language skills.

"We laid out a career plan, and I encouraged her to begin networking with certain people in the company who could assist with her career goal. Several months later we were able to arrange a job rotation for Molly at one of our plants in Puerto Rico as a lead supervisor. She is also going to do our career planning workshops while she's in Puerto Rico.

"The career discussions really unleashed Molly's potential. She is markedly more confident and now calls me by my first name, which means we've broken down some of the cultural barriers that existed early in our relationship. I see a bright future for her with Ethicon as an international auditor."

Career development is still a relatively new idea. Few organizations have systems in place or specialists on staff to address this issue; for many years the career development of employees has been left to chance. Some managers will do everything in their power *not* to promote a high-performing employee, in order to hang on to their star performer. Although most will agree that this is a losing strategy in the long term, the practice persists. In conversations with the authors, Peggy Hutcheson, president of Atlanta Resource Associates, said, "Employees have the ultimate responsibility and should initiate career development activities, managers should support and facilitate employee initiatives, and organizations should provide information and structures for sharing and using data."

A good example is 3M, a diversified manufacturer serving ten major markets including office, training and business, industrial production, and health care. Its Career Resources Department provides services to meet individual career planning needs as well as systems for internal placement.

The department consists of three functional areas: Career Development, Career Transition, and Career Information Systems. The Career Development group provides employees with career and organizational information, testing and assessment, and individual counseling, as well as a variety of workshops and seminars. Employees are encouraged to attend a two-hour orientation before participating in workshops or individual counseling. The orientation introduces them to the basic concepts of the career planning process and enables them to decide which services are most appropriate for their individual needs.

The Career Directions Workshop provides a fourteen-hour structured experience in which employees gain information about their values, interests, skills, personality type, and learning style; analyze their current job as a basis for their next career step; and then identify and prioritize options and set goals.

Seminars and workshops covering career decision making, transitions, resume development, and interviewing techniques are also offered. A career resource library offers publications on general career fields and job information specific to 3M.

The Career Transition group assists 3M management in identifying and planning the services needed in redeployment of employees. Its Unassigned Status Program provides management with resources for placing people whose jobs are affected by organizational change or who decline relocation during an organizational move.

The Transition Workshop provides services for employees facing job loss. It helps them develop job-hunting techniques and addresses the emotional aspects of job loss. Employees learn about skill identification, resume writing, interviewing techniques, job search strategies, and informal networking.

Career Information Systems includes an internal search system, which identifies manager-nominated candidates for job openings, and a Job Information System, which gives employees electronic access to current job openings and a process for self-nomination.

Pacific Bell, a Pacific Telesis company, provides telecommunication products and services to interexchange carriers, residence customers, and business customers throughout California. The company operates ten career centers throughout California, each of which is managed by an on-site career development specialist with ten months of intensive on-the-job training. In addition, the company operates two mobile vans that service the career needs of employees in outlying areas.

Employees are free to come to the center on their own. Their visits remain completely confidential. Others may be referred by their managers or a medical health services counselor.

Each center has a reference library that contains numerous printed, audio, and video resources on career planning, retirement planning, job titles, and corporate culture. Employees have access to the company's job posting systems and a computerized, self-guided career-life planning program. All of the center's resources are linked to the corporate business plan.

The center's staff also provides workshops on resume writing and interviewing, group interpretation of career assessments, and career planning.

Employees can make an appointment with the career development specialist, who will help them examine their skills, interests, abilities, and values and identify appropriate choices. The counseling process helps employees answer the questions: Who am I? How am I seen? Where do I want to go? How do I get there?

The specialist will assist the employees to research career options within the company, or outside, if necessary, and help them to realistically appraise their skills and abilities against the job requirements. Personal issues affecting career options are considered and are incorporated into each employee's individualized plan. Specialists also provide ongoing support while employees are making job changes and transitions.

Brian Cowgill, the career counselor who provides clinical supervision to the northern California centers, states that the centers were created in response to the changing work environment and its effect on employees' values and needs.

"Pacific Bell has changed its corporate mission to be more focused on the customer," says Cowgill. "As a result, job descriptions and job duties have changed for many employees. They are challenged to examine their interests and abilities in order to keep up with the changing work environment. The career center provides a safe haven for them to do so."

Also evident is a shift in employee values. Younger employees are challenging old assumptions about work and are feeling the need to explore all the options open to them. A recent decrease in loyalty and commitment has been observed in new employees who have highly sought skills and knowledge. A flattening of organizational structures leaves these employees with fewer opportunities for advancement, and they are actively making themselves available to the highest bidder.

Career development and planning processes link the needs and desires of individual employees with corporate business planning efforts through effective capitalization of human resources. "By attracting, retaining, developing, and motivating quality workers, we satisfy customers, shareholders, and employees," says Cowgill.

Enable People to "Try Out" Jobs

Although job rotation has been a strategy used by organizations for many years, it takes on a new look when it is used with the changing workforce. Temporary opportunities can be created to help people try out jobs to determine the ones in which they do best and are most comfortable.

Gannett, the nation's largest newspaper group with eighty-three daily newspapers, provides some of its local reporters with the opportunity to report national and international stories by assigning them to the staff of *USA Today* for a two- to three-month period. During this cross-training opportunity, the local Gannett paper pays the reporter's salary and *USA Today* provides lodging plus a cost-of-living stipend.

3M Corporation, which spends more than $650 million on research and development yearly, allows its researchers up to 15 percent of their time each week to work on projects of their own choosing. An inventor whose idea is not compatible with a division's product line is free to promote the idea elsewhere in the company. If another division is interested, the employee and product transfer to the new division. 3Mers are also free to recruit marketing professionals from other divisions to assist them.

Hallmark has changed the way it develops a new employee's artistic abilities. In the 1960s and 1970s, specialization was encouraged. Today, the emphasis is on diversification of techniques and breadth of skills. During their first five years, employees are developed through job assignments, creative workshops, and continuing education. An employee who enters the company as a cartoonist, for example, may later be exposed to assignments such as nature illustration or photography used as a design tool.

"Providing on-the-job experience via job rotations has been one of the best ways I've found to develop employees," says Marcia Hyatt, director of staffing and employee development of the Minneapolis-based utility Minnegasco.

"One of my employees, a management development specialist, took a job rotation in Operations to learn workforce planning and work flow. She was able to return from a six-month assignment with the necessary skills and experience to be promoted to a staffing supervisor's position that had just become vacant.

"Another employee, a compensation specialist, wanted to broaden her human resource experience. She was very extroverted and felt confined in her job. The human resources manager was able to create a rotational assignment for her as a safety specialist and later as a training specialist. After the assignment, she was able to secure a permanent position in the training department. The training specialist she replaced took the job in Safety. The compensation position is being filled with an external person.

Celia Currin of Dow Jones typifies a manager of the changing workforce. As director of operations support for eighteen printing plants of the *Wall Street Journal,* Currin manages a full array of employees ranging from technical writers with master's degrees to machinists with technical degrees and mailroom clerks with high school diplomas. Differences in age, gender, education, and culture as well as job function result in a very diverse department.

"No matter what their age, gender, or educational background, people in today's workforce have limited opportunities for vertical job movement and can plateau very early in their careers,"

says Currin. "Cross-functional or lateral job rotations give my employees an opportunity to 'try out' a new career or develop a new skill. These assignments also help people to develop new perspectives and stay fresh in their jobs."

Currin currently sponsors six-month internships within her sixty-two-person department. Staff can self-select their rotations, working two half-days on the rotational assignment and the rest in their current job. The rotations also help to cross-train people in the department. "Teaching new skills and exposing people to new responsibilities puts energy and vitality back into the department," says Currin.

"The long-term development of our employees is important to Minnegasco's future," says Hyatt. "Our flexibility in providing assignments where the employee's experiences, interests, and personal goals can be applied to new developmental opportunities keeps talent within the company. Job rotations increase our chances of keeping valuable employees as well as rejuvenating employees who have plateaued."

Create Alternative Career Paths

Traditionally, a key way to increase one's salary has been to move into management. However, many people are just not suited for management positions. They would make a greater contribution to their organizations if they could remain in a technical or specialist's position and receive increases in compensation equivalent to those that come with managerial positions.

At 3M, scientists who prefer to stay in the lab receive promotions in a system parallel to that for managers and, like managers, they receive profit-sharing benefits related to the performance of their division. A similar promotional system has been set up for the sales organization.

Tandem has dual career ladders in place for technical employees. As technical professionals grow in their careers they have the opportunity to pursue managerial positions or to follow a technical expert path. This philosophy has helped Tandem to retain and improve its excellent technical resources.

To more closely match the motivational and career needs of technical employees and other individual contributors, National Semiconductor, a Silicon Valley electronics company, has created a technical career track that is parallel in terms of competence, responsibility, influence, and rewards to the traditional managerial track.

Recognizing that the individual can make valuable contributions to organizational success, the company has designed and implemented career paths that build on innovative ideas, technical aptitude, and entrepreneurial spirit.

"The innovator should have as great an opportunity to contribute to organizational success as a manager," states Milan Moravec, corporate human resources manager.

Effectively using career paths can provide more meaningful jobs for both individual contributors and managers. As employees move laterally or from one level to another, they recognize that they are making career moves based on their particular contributions, qualifications, and interests.

During the 1960s and 1970s, Hallmark experienced tremendous growth and assembled America's largest creative staff under one roof. However, when it came time to promote creative staff employees into management, the company encountered resistance. Employees weren't willing to let go of their creative roles. In an attempt to develop artists, writers, and photographers while honoring their creative value, Hallmark designed a dual-track career advancement system.

Most creative employees begin their careers as an Artist 1, then move up to Artist 2 and Artist 3 (levels 1 to 3). At that point they can advance to either Designer or Designer Supervisor (level 4) and then progress to either Senior Designer or Senior Design Supervisor (level 5).

At level 6, employees can move into a Master Artist or Stylist position, where they will conceptualize designs, work with the business side of the organization to design new lines, and make presentations to clients. The focus of this track is on artwork.

Other level 6 jobs include the Design Group Manager, who focuses on managing, mentoring, and developing the craft skills of other artists, and the Creative Product Development Manager, who is positioned in an individual business unit to approve and direct product lines to work with business plans.

Level 7 jobs include Consulting Stylist, Senior Design Group Manager, and again, Creative Product Development Manager.

Employees can move into and out of managerial positions. Some managerial assignments are six to eighteen months long, giving employees an opportunity to function as managers on a temporary basis. This meets the company's needs and develops the employees' knowledge of business operations.

To implement these kinds of actions an organization must create systems that include career development, alternate career paths, and temporary moves, as well as policies that allow mobility, support individual career planning, and offer nonmanagerial career tracks. Managers also must place more emphasis on career discussions, coaching, and feedback to find the best matches between positions and employees.

6

Change Jobs and Work Hours to Meet Employee Needs

IN THE PAST, job duties were fixed, and people were asked to adapt. If someone didn't exactly fit the requirements of the job, the person was required to change. Today, the best actions may involve changes in the job structure or hours, not the person. It is becoming increasingly clear that nontraditional jobs and flexible hours benefit not only employees, but customers and management as well.

In addition, the use of flexible work hours and workplaces enables employees to balance family and work responsibilities, or to retrieve some time from commuting and use it for more valuable pursuits. Employees on flextime or flexplace may have different starting and stopping times with common core hours during each day or week; core days at work with some days when the employee works at home or at nearby facilities; a compressed work week—for example, four ten-hour days—or some other configuration created by the organization.

Interest is growing for part-time, flexible hours and stay-at-home jobs (Johnston and Packer, 1987). Many project-oriented and computer-based tasks can be done from small field offices or in the home. The search for affordable housing has taken many people farther from central, city-based offices, and telecommuting, at least part of the time, is a viable alternative. Many older workers may also welcome more flexible hours. While the compressed work week has some drawbacks, it is also credited with improving morale, reducing turnover and absenteeism, and aiding in recruitment (Berkman, 1989).

Use Changing Work Hours to Benefit All Players

Wells Fargo Bank, the third largest full-service bank in California, has changed its hours to meet many needs. "Extended banking hours and our flex schedule teller positions came about as the result of our customers' changing lives. Traditional banking hours didn't meet customer demand any longer. We needed to be open longer hours and have a more flexible workforce that could meet our scheduling needs," says Una Stephens, vice-president of personnel. "Initially, we wondered if we might find it difficult to locate people who wanted to work short, flexible hours, but it has proven not to be a problem at all."

Service managers at each branch are responsible for recruiting and have found that personal contact with a variety of nontraditional recruiting sources works well. They've contacted day care centers and PTAs to locate women with young children who may be interested in part-time work; teachers' organizations for people interested in positions in the summer or after school hours; retirement organizations; college placement offices; arts, orchestra, and theater groups to locate people who might have some daytime hours available; and self-employed people who might want to supplement their income. "We find that these positions are perfect for some people and not for others. They are not career opportunities. They are, however, great for people who are interested in this degree of flexibility and who don't want to work a traditional forty-hour work week," adds Stephens.

Employees, both women and men, find that sometimes their job schedule just doesn't fit in with school schedules, orthodontist and doctors' schedules, and the remaining few retail firms that insist on being open ten to four, Monday through Friday. At Procter & Gamble, employees at the general offices in Cincinnati may alter their work schedule by one hour on either end of the work day to attend to family or personal needs that occur regularly.

In response to this frequent clash between daily demands and work demands, Merck offers flextime at many of its locations. The objective is to help employees meet personal obligations while at the same time maintaining their total number of work hours. Employees may begin as early as 7:00 A.M. or as late as 9:30 A.M. Merck has found that the flexible approach reduces absenteeism, tardiness, and the need for personal time off.

At Minnegasco, flexible work scheduling has allowed a training manager to pursue a master's degree in organization development at Pepperdine University in California.

As her duties and interests moved her into the organization development arena, Ginny Belden felt that an advanced degree would be a good career move as well as providing her with a wider skill and knowledge base.

Minnegasco created a part-time position in organization development that allowed Ginny to attend periodic courses in California as well as to focus her job duties on an area that interested her.

Sabina Sten, formerly an international banking officer and manager at First National Bank of Minneapolis, knows how to show flexibility as

Hewlett-Packard Company is an international manufacturer of measurement and computation products and systems. Art Young, HP's corporate benefits manager, believes that flexible scheduling improves morale by demonstrating the company's confidence in its employees.

Hewlett-Packard's system of flexible work hours has no formal mechanism for monitoring hours. Most employees—whether they are in office or manufacturing jobs—work on the honor system. Flexible scheduling allows employees to control their own work pace if their performance does not depend on the presence of other workers. The system helps employees deal with long commutes, medical appointments, or the demands of their home life.

The flextime approach has also been successful at plant locations. Employees are given the choice of arriving any time between 6:00 A.M. and 8:30 A.M. and leaving eight hours later. Plant management offers similar flexibility for shift workers as well.

Since manufacturing jobs typically require an entire team to be present at once, HP restructured certain jobs, enlarging their scope to allow employees to perform independently for portions of the day. First-line supervisors received special training to help them adjust to these changes.

a manager. She managed a diverse team of five (two Europeans, one Filipino, and two Americans).

"One of my employees, Vita King, wanted to enroll in a master's program for an economics degree. She was one of two analysts in the bank's international credit department. As a team we were responsible for the financial analysis of our foreign customers as well as for the political and economic risk assessment of some twenty-five countries where we had credit exposure. Our work was subject to deadlines, often at very short notice.

"I worked with Vita and the rest of the team to accommodate her needs, the team's, and the bank's. The bank cooperated by placing Vita on part-time status. Work was redistributed, and Vita's hours were adjusted so she could attend classes and work thirty hours per week—frequently evenings and weekends—as her schedule permitted. Vita was a solid worker; her thirty hours of quality work equaled some people's forty hours of work. Her reduced schedule did not negatively affect the team's work at all."

This type of change relies heavily on appropriate policies and on management flexibility. The manager's role is to be supportive and coordinate with other employees so that the work is done with minimum disruption.

Create Job-Sharing Opportunities

Another option for changing the job structure is *job sharing,* a situation in which two or more employees share the responsibilities of a particular job, meeting frequently with each other to coordinate tasks. *Job splitting,* on the other hand, refers to merely splitting one job into two part-time positions, which requires far less coordination. Job sharing works for a wide variety of positions including many support, teaching, program administration, and repair functions.

A survey conducted by the Commerce Clearing House and the American Society for Personnel Administration (ASPA) and reported in *Training* magazine ("A Look at Alternative Work Schedules," 1988, p. 74) found that the majority of firms using job sharing were in either human services or manufacturing. "The respondents identified seven factors that led them to institute job sharing. In order of importance, they were: to strengthen employee motivation, to reduce turnover, to increase performance, to strengthen employee attitudes toward their jobs, to attract potential employees to the organization, to strengthen employee attitudes toward the organization, and to improve morale.

"The biggest advantage of job sharing, as perceived by respondents whose companies used it, was that the company could accommodate working parents. Employees who shared jobs were perceived as having high

Steelcase, Inc., the world's largest manufacturer of office furniture, offers job-sharing opportunities to all employees except those with supervisory or budgetary responsibilities. Employees with at least one year of full-time service and the endorsement of departmental management are eligible.

Once an employee gains management approval, the human resource department helps arrange the work team by posting the matching position.

Each job sharer receives half of the regular benefits. Vacation and sick leave are based on each participant's current status. Merit raises, seniority, and advancement are preserved.

Typically, job sharing is used by women to ease back into the workforce after the birth of a child. It is also requested by both men and women who wish to continue their education, accommodate health conditions, or phase into retirement.

Steelcase believes that job sharing increases employee productivity and loyalty; reduces the time and expense of recruiting, hiring, and training new employees; and retains a trained employee base for full-time positions in the future.

job satisfaction (5.5 or greater on a 7-point scale), as it pertained to hours of work, leisure time and their overall level of organizational satisfaction. Management also was well satisfied (5.5) with job sharing."

Flexibility and teamwork are key to job sharing, according to Susan Simeola and Lorraine O'Brien of BayBanks, Inc., in Burlington, Massachusetts. The two working mothers share a full-time executive secretary position in the training department.

"I'd been working in the training department since 1982," says Simeola. "When I got pregnant two years ago, I knew that I would want to work only part time when I came back from my maternity leave. Lorraine and I make our job-sharing arrangement work by leaving notes for one another and spending an hour and a half each week going over current projects."

"I was very happy to have the opportunity to job share with Susan," says O'Brien. "I had been employed part time for nine years and had lost my job due to a reduction in force. Having job shared in the past, I knew the arrangement would require me to be flexible."

Their boss, training director Maryann Renzi, says that the job-sharing arrangement is advantageous for both BayBanks and the employees. "By being flexible and professional, Susan and Lorraine can satisfy their personal and work goals and we can benefit from their experience and talent."

Redesign Jobs to Adapt to Changing Needs

Sometimes people's needs and goals change, yet they're still valuable to the company. Redesigning jobs or hours can often help.

Patricia A. McLagan, CEO of McLagan International, advocates the use of flexible job modeling, a practice that helps to assure that the work an individual does is the best mix of responsibilities, given the organization's needs and the individual's skills. Employees take on responsibilities based on their competence to perform and contribute to the organization, rather than on artificial requirements such as years of experience or attendance at the right school. This process transcends age, ethnicity, culture, disabilities, gender, values, and even formal qualifications. The relevant factor is the individual's ability—regardless of where or how it was acquired—to do the job. In *Productivity in Organizations* (McLagan, 1988, p. 369), the advantages of flexible job modeling are discussed. According to McLagan, flexible job modeling

- Systematically forecasts future organizational requirements.

- Views the organization as an open social system that is constantly changing in response to outside influences. That is, human resource management cannot be designed for the status quo.

- Focuses on outputs (products, services, programs, information) as the major building blocks of organization design, rather than positions, organization structure, or type of technology.

- Identifies both the job performance requirements and the individual capabilities needed to produce the outputs of a job.

- Views job design as a process of assigning or reassigning outputs to jobs based on (1) the organization's current and future needs; (2) the current capability, motivation, and development priorities of individuals; and (3) the current capabilities, motives, and development priorities of others in the organization or work team.

- Supports a view of job evaluation that places individuals in broad salary bands based on the overall types of outputs they produce. This allows maximum flexibility in job design without requiring constant adjustments in the compensation structure.

- Treats a description of performance goals as the job description, thus eliminating the traditional job description process and allowing for job design flexibility.

- Provides a conceptual framework for integrating all human resource functions related to organization and job design, development, performance management, selection/placement, and career management.

- Provides managers and the workers themselves with the information they need to fully participate in defining their jobs, managing performance, and guiding development.

- Is easily updated as organization strategies and conditions change.

Kevin Kennedy, who has a congenital eye disorder, was hired as a design engineer by the Aluminum Company of America in 1985. "Kevin was very open about his condition upon hire," comments Phil Bretz, Ph.D., his current manager. "Alcoa was fully aware of Kevin's visual impairment and the fact that he would lose total eyesight within a ten-year time frame.

"From the onset, we always had to be mindful of the type of assignments Kennedy was given," Bretz says. "A process design engineer's job responsibilities typically involve the operation of large industrial machinery. Without peripheral vision, Kevin was at a distinct disadvantage performing this aspect of his job. We made sure that Kennedy was accompanied by another employee when he made operating plant visits."

This arrangement worked for three years. In early 1990 Kennedy approached Bretz with a concern about the progression of his disease and the changing nature of his work.

Bretz says, "Kevin's project had moved from a developmental phase to an implementation phase that requires more routine plant visits and operation of heavy machinery."

Anticipating total blindness in three to five years, Kennedy was concerned about his future career at Alcoa and how he could best use the next few years to position himself. His immediate concerns were how to carry out job tasks in the safest manner possible.

Bretz responded by shifting Kennedy's job responsibilities to fundamental research and development in process modeling, which concentrates on computer simulations, requires limited plant visitations, and matches his career interests and training.

Kennedy was also appointed to a half-time, two-year position as a quality facilitator. This position gives him a broad exposure to laboratory teams in an office environment while at the same time meeting his need for a safer work environment. The new assignment as a facilitator does require frequent visits to the Alcoa Quality Training Center a mile away. Transportation arrangements have been made with a co-worker.

"Although Kevin's disability is unique to Alcoa Laboratories, it provides us with valuable insight into how we can best adapt the work environment to meet the safety needs of all employees," Bretz says. To this end, Kennedy was appointed to the division's safety committee.

"Kevin has not requested much in the way of special equipment to date," explains Bretz. "We have provided special lighting in his work space as well as a magnifying lens for reading." The human resource department is working with Kennedy to look at other ways in which his work space can be adapted as his condition progresses. These may include a large-screen computer and a software program for text conversion.

"Kevin and I agree that it is no longer safe for him to conduct experiments in the lab alone," shares Bretz. "We have blocked off a small area just inside the lab for Kevin to inspect his work. This is a safe, low-traffic area where Kevin can look at his specimens and speak with technicians." Alcoa is also considering installing video cameras in the laboratory with a monitor in Kennedy's office so that he can observe his experiments.

Gary A. Foss, senior vice-president for human resources at Maryland National Bank, has used flexible job modeling in several departments in the bank. "The financial services industry is undergoing massive change, and our bank is no exception. In the past, jobs in banking have been based on hierarchical models that foster traditional thinking about how jobs and the organization should be structured. To be successful in the nineties we are taking a fresh look at designing jobs. Performance goals based on flexible job modeling will provide a mechanism to help us match people and jobs by focusing on the competencies of individuals, not credentials. It's a much more powerful way to evaluate people for jobs," explains Foss.

When Hannaford Bros. Co., a food and drug retailer headquartered in South Portland, Maine, decided to open a 439,000-square-foot warehouse in East Schodack, New York, they were determined to hire a more diverse workforce.

"Our typical warehouse worker was a primary wage earner who relished physical work," says Walt Stilphen, director of labor relations. "We felt we needed to hire a more diverse and experienced workforce in New York by selecting employees who wanted to work in a team environment. We asked for more than physical requirements; we wanted employees who would apply their hearts, souls, and minds to these jobs," he added.

The company created light-weight and heavy-weight sections of the warehouse so that employees with modest physical capabilities could perform some of the work. "That enabled more women and older workers to compete for and perform these jobs," says Stilphen.

The role of warehouse worker was also expanded to include tasks that were not usually performed by these workers, including paperwork duties. "And we wanted to create an environment where people worked together as a team, supporting each other in getting the work done. We don't have a traditional organization. We've flattened the hierarchy and there are no managers. Various team members are responsible for managing the work," adds Stilphen. "We want high performance and high commitment. We want team members who can take care of problems at the point at which they occur, and we desire a self-governing environment."

Applicants who are interested in a job spend about fourteen hours in the recruiting process. They take several tests and are interviewed by six people using structured questions that are designed to determine if they have the ability to work in this culture. In addition, they watch a twelve-minute video that describes the plant environment by emphasizing twenty-two tasks employees must be willing to do. Applicants also participate in a two-hour simulation of how they would act as a self-managed team discussing the way they would sell a product to a customer. "We want to have team members who understand the bigger purpose of the business and the day-to-day operations. The video is a realistic job preview that advises potential employees to ask themselves if they'd feel comfortable working in this environment," Stilphen adds.

Apparently, people are feeling comfortable. In the first three months, of the 140 persons hired, there were no Workers' Compensation injuries, no accidents, and only one person who left. "And that person left on his own because he realized that the group norms of team and commitment were not for him," adds Stilphen.

Make Special Arrangements for Successful Matching

Creating special arrangements for persons with disabilities makes sense to The Prudential Insurance Company. "We have an expense analyst who is a wheelchair user and has speech and muscular impairment," says Debbie Gingher, director of human resources. "When he was hired ten years ago a special phone was installed to accommodate him. After a while, employees became familiar with his speech pattern and were more than willing to listen carefully to him. He was also given the latitude to communicate with other employees through his personal computer.

"At one point during his career, his department was consolidated with another, requiring relocation for all employees. We allowed him to stay in the building so he could continue to van pool with an employee who also worked there.

"As he progressed in his career, job assignments were tailored to meet his skills as well as to accommodate his disability. The company promoted him purely on his technical abilities rather than on traditional supervisory and managerial skills. Breaking a job into essential and non-essential functions allows persons with disabilities to excel in their specialty, and the benefits are mutually rewarding," adds Gingher.

Jocelyn Tilsen, executive director of Parents Anonymous of Minnesota in St. Paul, supervises a sixty-seven-year-old program coordinator. Tilsen recognizes that her employee, who will retire at the end of the year, likes to do things her own way and is resistant to certain changes. In one instance, when Tilsen asked the employee to learn to use a different typewriter keyboard, the woman insisted that the keyboard she had used before was better. Tilsen acknowledged her employee's discomfort and resolved the issue by finding a used model of the preferred typewriter for the office.

"She knows things her own way very well and is extremely bright. My job has been to help her use her skills without putting limits on her or making the program revolve around her. For example," says Tilsen, "I've been flexible about her working between thirty and forty hours a week since she came here four years ago. Now that she gets tired after six hours of meeting with people, she works thirty-two hours a week."

Tilsen's small organization also pays her employee's insurance premium on a private policy because she is ineligible for group insurance. "As a manager, I believe that these adjustments are part of supporting a valued employee."

Consider Telecommuting

For the first time in his management career, Brian Monahan, manager of the media relations department for AT&T Bell Laboratories in Short Hills, New Jersey, is supervising an employee long distance using a telecommuting relationship. Donna Cunningham lives in the Green Mountains of Vermont and is in regular contact with Monahan and the other members of the Bell Labs media relations department through electronic mail, fax machines, and the telephone.

Cunningham feels that the move from the New Jersey office to her home-based arrangement was crucial to her staying with the company. It is working out well due to "enlightened management and the right office equipment." Monahan emphasizes that the shift has been manageable because he knows her work and has tremendous confidence in her.

Although both admit to missing the social aspects of working in the same environment, Monahan recognizes that Cunningham's work is ideally suited to telecommuting. "Other than missing having coffee with her, I know she is instantly available by telephone or by computer. She comes here about once a month and everything else gets handled very well electronically."

7

Hire Older and Temporary Workers

COMPANIES ARE BEGINNING to creatively match the needs and interests of an older workforce with their organization's requirements. Organizations will no longer be able to satisfy labor needs by employing only workers aged twenty-five to fifty-five. Instead, they must consider the diversity of goals, interests, and needs that exists among the older and retired worker population and take advantage of the availability of a more temporary workforce. The career and financial needs of a fifty-five-year-old middle manager, for instance, differ greatly from those of a sixty-five-year-old on Social Security who is looking for part-time work.

Coopers Animal Health, Inc., a manufacturer of animal pharmaceuticals located in Kansas City, Missouri, brings back some of its retired employees on a temporary basis. The employees who want to participate in this program actually work for a temporary agency and are assigned to the Coopers account. The amount of time an employee works is based both on personal preference and on the organization's need. Retirees may fill in after an unexpected resignation, add expertise to a project, or simply help out when the company's workload is more than the full-time employees can manage.

According to Diane Heffner, director of personnel, Coopers has found that retired employees are fantastic at training and have more patience, time, and desire than many other employees. One bilingual employee was brought in to handle a Latin American account after their only other bilingual employee suddenly resigned. The retired employee, who had become bored at home, was ecstatic to come back to work for a while. Another employee, a seventy-year-old with a doctorate in microbiology, works three hours a week as a consultant on a number of projects. Employees value his feedback and guidance in this particularly complex area.

Capitalize on Older Workers' Skills

Project Resources, based at Middlesex County College in Edison, New Jersey, assists people over fifty-five who are seeking employment by offering guidance, counseling, training, and direct job placement. The project was initially conceptualized for retirees, but has been expanded to include skilled older workers who have lost their jobs as a result of corporate restructuring or downsizing. The diversity of talent represented by participants is exemplified by the corps of volunteer peer advisors who share their expertise in job development and counseling. Project Resources found that because older workers come from a generation in which employment stability was rewarded, they may lack skills in resume writing and interviewing. The Project Resources job search skills training program addresses this need with a monthly one-day workshop. Area employers conduct the interviewing portion of the workshop, giving participants an opportunity to be involved in "mock interviews."

Through recruiting efforts in the community, Project Resources maintains an active job bank of hundreds of employers, which is updated every day. It has also published a manual for hiring older workers, accessible on the ERIC Clearinghouse data base for junior colleges.

Days Inns of America, Inc., in an effort to curb the effects of a shrinking traditional labor force, has actively recruited senior citizens to work in its reservations centers since 1985. Older workers make up 30 percent of the staff in both the Atlanta and Knoxville reservations centers. In addition, many Days hotels across the country hire older workers for the front desk, food and beverage operations, housekeeping, sales, and general management.

Days has seen many benefits in hiring seniors: Turnover is low (1 percent among seniors, compared with 40 percent among other employees), absenteeism and tardiness are virtually nonexistent, guest satisfaction with service is higher, and health care costs have not increased.

At corporate headquarters in Atlanta, a Senior Citizens' People Circle has been organized. This employee group provides input to management on a variety of issues including morale and attendance.

The international hotel chain is the only company ever to organize a job fair on a national basis specifically for senior citizens. Held annually in May, the Senior Power national job fair attracts over 1,000 businesses and 10,000 older workers. Days hotels host the event, inviting businesses such as Kelly Services, Wendy's, Kmart, and Sears to join them in interviewing senior citizens.

American Cyanamid Company has used the technical abilities of other retirees to implement statistical process control (SPC) training programs, supervise clean-up programs, and contribute to other technical operations efforts. Rick Tabakin, who manages the Warners Plant in Linden, New Jersey, has successfully retained the services of several retired employees to manage special projects. "Time constraints and workloads often make it difficult for plant personnel to take on special projects," says Tabakin. "Retired Cyanamid employees are a perfect fit. Already familiar with our plant and its operations, they possess the technical expertise and pertinent job experience needed to step in and handle a project with minimal or no extra training. They enjoy working on a part-time basis and can be flexible about a project's time requirements."

Tabakin hired back a retired personnel manager to coordinate a community relations program mandated by the federal government's Superfund Act. "His excellent writing skills and public sector contacts made him the best candidate to notify state and local agencies about the plant's chemical releases and waste reduction programs," offers Tabakin. "Our program has been widely recognized as exemplary and many other companies have borrowed our approach on this issue."

A retired process engineer was hired to implement an SPC training program. He was familiar with plant product lines, possessed good communication skills, and had some SPC background. After attending an orientation program, he was able to train and facilitate process action teams

McDonald's Corporation is acknowledged as a corporate leader in systematically attracting older workers. Long-range planning, plus an honest commitment to employing older workers and developing a hospitable working environment, is critical to the success of the company's rehiring efforts.

"Seniors have to feel that they're welcome," explains Stan Stein, personnel vice-president.

"We have to break through the image that we're just for young people. Advertising accomplishes this by showing images of younger and older employees working together."

McDonald's also attracts older workers through formal relationships with senior citizen's organizations and local governmental agencies. Through its McMasters program, older workers are trained by an appointed McDonald's Job Coach. The Job Coach closely supervises and typically trains eight to ten McMaster's employees a month.

The McMasters program is a partnership between McDonald's and a contracting government agency, such as a state Department of Aging. Each partner contributes money for the program's administration and operation, which includes the Job Coach's salary.

McDonald's did not have to significantly alter its policies or practices to accommodate older workers. The company provides extensive guidance to owner-operators on all aspects of recruiting and managing an older workforce. Sensitivity training includes videotapes featuring seniors describing their work experiences.

The company emphasizes flexibility and responsiveness in all aspects of employment. Seniors may choose to work in a specific job or to rotate among different jobs.

(PATs). Under his leadership and guidance, there are presently six PATs functioning at the Warners Plant.

Tabakin sums up the role of retired employees by saying, "When temporary staffing requirements arise, you want someone who is reliable, can do the job without a great amount of additional training, and is familiar with the plant and its operations. Retired employees score high on each count. They have already proven their reliability and knowledge. They know us and we know them. We've benefited from valuing their experience and dedication."

Set Up a Pool of Temporary Workers

The Travelers Companies of Hartford, Connecticut, previously introduced a job bank for retirees, initially codirected by two Travelers retirees aged seventy-two to eighty years. In 1990, The Travelers expanded its retiree job bank into an in-house temporary agency called TRAV Temps—a move designed to help the company meet all of its temporary needs through an in-house pool.

TRAV Temps, which began operation January 1, 1990, is recruiting workers from outside the company to bolster its temporary pool of retirees. In 1988, The Travelers used outside agencies to fill more than one-third of its temporary needs. TRAV Temps is expected to reduce Travelers' reliance on outside agencies and save the company about $1 million annually.

"The retirees in our job bank have done an outstanding job assisting the company," said Tom Helfrich, senior vice-president of corporate human resources and services, "but our needs are too great to be met by the retirees alone. By augmenting the retirees with other temporary workers, we'll be able to fill in the gaps in a more cost-effective manner."

When TRAV Temps began operation, there were 403 Travelers retirees and 297 outside retirees registered as temporaries in the job bank. In a given week, 150 Travelers retirees and 80 outside retirees are likely to be working in temporary jobs with the company, equivalent to roughly two-thirds of the temporaries the company uses. After six months in operation, Travelers' retirees filled 36 percent of temporary needs, outside retirees filled 22 percent, and the new group of TRAV Temps filled 35 percent. This means that dependency on outside agencies was reduced to less than 10 percent of temporary employment needs.

A special benefits package is offered to temporaries who work at least 500 hours over a six-month period. The package includes medical and dental coverage, free life insurance, paid holidays, commuter bus pass discounts, in-house training, and access to the company's job posting program and employee fitness center.

"We're also implementing a consistent salary approach with annual increases," said Florence Johnson, assistant director of career and temporary services. "When temporaries first enter the program, we establish an hourly rate based on their skills and experience. They then are placed in jobs that allow them to use their skills effectively."

PART III

Managing and Rewarding Performance

66 *There's no question that it's easier to manage people who are the same, but we are not—and it is not our similarities that cause our problems.* **99**

—J. Braham,
"No, You Don't Manage
Everyone the Same"

Maria Santiago was new to the workforce after moving here from Honduras, where she had been a full-time homemaker and mother. She and her husband now needed two incomes. Her new employer ran special training for people who had not worked; topics included the basics of how the organization worked, time management, and working in teams, among others. Maria was given a planned series of rotations through different jobs in her department, with specific learning and performance goals. Her new supervisor scheduled weekly meetings with her to answer questions, review her work, and help her plan her career. She feels very lucky.

Herman Wambolt had been with his employer for thirty years. He was a loyal, solid performer, but he was less energetic than his enthusiastic, recently hired co-workers and was becoming discouraged. Herman's boss worked with him to set new performance goals. They developed a special project that used Herman's experience to rethink departmental procedures and improve overall quality and service. He became very interested in the project and developed twenty key changes that included redesigning forms, changing workflow, and generally improving efficiency. Before his retirement the following year,

the entire department attended Herman's first, last, and best training program, where he shared his wisdom. The dinner celebration honoring Herman was a highlight of his life.

Leon Martinet, a Ph.D. engineer, works on many projects at the same time. This gives him the variety he enjoys. He sits down with his boss twice each year to review new and old projects, set goals, and discuss expectations and continuing education needs. In between, they consult each other as needed. All of Leon's work carries his name. He's known throughout the company and feels appreciated. For his good performance, he was recently given something he had wanted for a long time—a two-week field tour to study the engineering practices of similar organizations in Sweden.

Colleen Johnson was partially disabled in an automobile accident. Her mobility was limited, but not her talent. She and a co-worker, Tom Richards, teamed up to share their two jobs, structuring tasks to use each person's strengths and recognize their limitations. Her boss loved the idea. They hold three-way planning and evaluation sessions three times each year. Colleen and Tom have weekly feedback sessions *with each other. Both people feel that they are doing the work they like and they are valuable to each other. It must have been a good idea. They have been performing at a higher level than any other two people in the office.*

David Pham is young, bright, and conscientious. He and his boss get together each quarter to discuss goals, expectations, problems, and development. They look at his work, the organization's needs, and important priorities. They develop agreements and write them down. They also each write a brief evaluation of the past quarter's work, including their ideas for improvement and for other skills David might want to learn. David is challenged, involved, and valued. He feels that the organization is investing in him.

These scenarios give a glimpse of the ways in which flexibility can be used to plan, manage, and reward performance, and of the results possible when managers pay attention to individuals and their differences. New expectations about performance are surfacing daily. What moti-

ivates people? How can performance be managed effectively? What is considered rewarding by employees?

In this second key strategy for managing the diverse workforce more effectively, the concept of individualizing is central. It is increasingly important to recognize that managers are no longer managing *groups* of similar people but *individuals* with differences.

In the drive to eliminate discrimination and prejudice, treating people equally or fairly came to mean treating them the same. Today—because it is recognized that people have different needs—they sometimes must be treated differently to be "equal" or "fair."

New techniques cover the entire range of activities involved in what is commonly called performance management. However, the important message is not to develop *one* new performance management system, but to create flexible options that allow for greater individualizing—to have policies, systems, forms, and practices that will allow managers and their employees to focus on performance *and* on individual differences in styles, needs, preferences, motivators, and rewards.

The basic components to work with are
- Setting goals and standards for work

- Clarifying tasks and roles
- Observing and/or coaching performance
- Providing feedback and performance evaluation
- Identifying training and development requirements
- Rewarding good performance

This strategy can be achieved by taking the following actions:

- Train managers and employees to value diversity.
- Enable persons with disabilities to meet performance challenges.
- Individualize—don't standardize—performance management.
- Align rewards with employees' values.

The actions described in this section of the book offer a multitude of opportunities to individualize performance management. With this strategy we create winning situations in which the individual is satisfied and productive, rather than fighting an old system, and the organization gains greater value from its employees. The "one size fits all" approach hinders overall productivity and reduces the real potential, as if we were flying with one engine turned off or driving a car with one cylinder poorly timed. Managing and rewarding performance is yet another way to pay attention to differences, expand options, and provide individual and organizational success.

8

Train Managers and Employees to Value Diversity

ONE WAY TO IMPROVE the performance of both managers and
co-workers is by providing
information and experiences
that will awaken people to their
individual strengths and unique
perspectives. This approach seems
to be spreading across organizations. In addition to training,
some companies also provide
awareness workshops, networking opportunities, and orientation sessions.

Merck began a massive educational program in 1979 that was designed to raise its employees' awareness of attitudes about women and minorities. "Merck's philosophy on affirmative action and equality is that individual employees must take responsibility for their views and expectations of others," says Art Strohmer, executive director of human resources.

During 1983 and 1984, Merck's 17,000 U.S. employees participated in a one-day training program, in which they watched a thirty-minute film that depicted real-life situations and discussed their own views and stereotypes. The program is now integrated into ongoing management training; it emphasizes how policies and systems can be tailored to meet changes in the demographics of the workplace.

Procter & Gamble has been a leader in developing programs aimed at valuing diversity. Some of the company's initiatives include multicultural advisory teams, minority and women's networking conferences, and "onboarding" programs to help new women and minority employees become acclimated and productive as quickly as possible.

Procter & Gamble has implemented "valuing diversity" programs at the plant level as well. At one plant, a mentoring program has been developed to raise the retention rate for black and female managers. At another, all new employees are involved in a day-long diversity workshop. Susan Wilke, manager of affirmative action and work/family coordination, says that Procter & Gamble's goal is for every employee to be a champion of diversity and to be empowered to object to racism, sexism, and classism.

Raise Awareness and Inspire Action

The three-day diversity program at Folger Coffee Company, a subsidiary of Procter & Gamble, is focused on increasing the awareness of all employees. Through role-playing exercises, people begin to recognize, understand, and appreciate the differences each person has. In one segment, assumptions are made about whites, blacks, males, and females after reviewing information that contributed to the socialization of white, black, male, and female children. In the role play, people play roles different from theirs so they can experience walking in another's shoes.

Martha White, training coordinator, describes the underlying purpose of the program as "to learn to work effectively together, build on our common goals and values, and create advantages from our differences." The plant manager, Mike Story, captured the essence by stating: "The learnings were excellent! All of us participating in the training were profoundly affected by personal insights on how we are programmed from early childhood to put value judgments on differences in people. The lost synergy

In late 1985, Ortho Pharmaceutical Corporation identified a need to do a better job of accommodating and managing an increasingly diverse workforce. The company's concerns were based on the recognition of high turnover rates and a scarcity of women and people of color in upper management.

The strategy that evolved from both internal and external analysis was a top-down management initiative called "Managing Diversity," which was designed to foster a process of cultural transition within the organization.

The training began early in 1986 with the board of directors, then extended to all managers and supervisors. A typical three-day workshop consisted of twenty to twenty-five employees, including white men and women and men and women of color. Participants gained awareness of their attitudes about race and gender, examined how these attitudes influence decision making and other behaviors, and developed action plans to help them integrate newly learned principles and skills into their daily activities.

To signal management's ongoing commitment and to provide continuing guidance for the process, a Managing Diversity Committee was formed in the fall of 1986. The eighteen-member advisory committee, currently chaired by Ernestine Thrash, director of selection and training, acts as an independent observer of what goes on inside and outside of Ortho with respect to diversity, and serves as a liaison to the board of directors.

"Each member serves as a 'champion' to his or her own organizational unit in looking for ways to remove barriers to the full participation of women and people of color," says Thrash. "Members also serve on Managing Diversity task forces to coordinate programs at the division level."

Today, Ortho continues its three-day managerial workshops. Since November 1989 a two-day workshop focusing on racial awareness has been put in place for nonexempt employees and exempt employees who do not manage others. "The inclusion of nonexempt employees means that everyone is on board with some awareness of diversity issues. In essence, all employees are reading from the same script," says Thrash.

A situation management program was incorporated into the Managing Diversity curriculum in response to supervisors who wanted to improve their coaching and counseling skills. The two-day program is designed for individuals who manage a diverse workforce.

To keep the momentum of employee awareness up, Ortho sponsors quarterly symposia during which an outside expert speaks on an issue related to diversity in the workplace. All employees are invited to attend the one-hour session, which addresses such topics as managing diversity in the 1990s, communication issues of the Asian workforce, and ways for women to succeed in male-dominated organizations.

As an outgrowth of the Managing Diversity process, Ortho has recently embarked on a company-wide cultural change process designed to retain the best elements of its present culture and to eliminate or replace the barriers identified with new cultural norms. The new culture will facilitate upward mobility for all employees irrespective of race or gender.

"We have already made excellent progress in terms of our integration of women and people of color into middle and upper management," says Thrash, "but the next two to three years will really tell whether our objective of changing the culture has been realized."

and productivity encountered when we do not appreciate and build on our differences can be crippling to an organization."

King-Ming Young, manager of the Professional Development Group at Hewlett-Packard's corporate education, headed up a team that designed, developed, and institutionalized the Managing Diversity Program. In early 1989, the program went worldwide with the help of over 100 internal trainers.

HP's program has four objectives: (1) to raise employees' awareness of diversity issues, (2) to increase their understanding of HP's philosophy that diversity can be an asset if it is recognized and managed appropriately, (3) to increase employees' skill in dealing with different kinds of people, and (4) to improve their understanding of legal/EEO issues.

The emphasis in the HP process is to make managers aware of their own biases and assumptions. "Many decisions managers make are based on unconscious values, attitudes, and perceptions," says Young.

For instance, a manager who doesn't understand an Asian's respect for modesty and authority may misinterpret the employee's reluctance to speak of his or her accomplishments as a lack of competence. "Managers today must demonstrate a larger repertoire of behaviors to get the most out of each employee," Young adds.

"The whole emphasis of managing diversity is that it takes us away from the mindset that either a woman or a minority is deficient in some way. We need to recognize that every person is different and not necessarily better than others."

The module-based program addresses HP's philosophy and attitude toward cultural diversity, affirmative action, gender, age, race, and disability. The program is distributed on computer diskettes, which facilitates local adaptation by divisional training staff. It uses various learning techniques such as lectures, discussions, case studies, simulations, and videotape analysis.

Young points out that although the program's goal is to heighten awareness about cultural tendencies and values, it is important for managers to recognize that these tendencies vary from individual to individual.

Hallmark's "Valuing Diversity" program addresses culture and gender on three levels—personal, interpersonal, and organizational. Minority and nonminority managers are brought together in small groups for a day-and-a-half-long workshop to discover their own personal biases about race and gender and to learn how their behavior affects their employees and the organization. The workshop's primary objective is to communicate to managers the value of cultivating a culturally diverse workforce. In addition, several times a year Hallmark offers informal after-work gatherings called Minority Forums. The forums, designed to help minority employees grow professionally and personally, allow employees from every area of the company to network, exchange ideas, and share experiences. During these forums, employees have the opportunity to discuss ideas with senior management staff, outside authorities, and public figures; to ask questions; and to tap into career advancement opportunities. Hallmark's Minority Scholarship Internship Program is open to college students entering their senior year in the fields of art or writing. Recipients are awarded scholarships as well as paid summer internships.

Provide Language and Communication Training

English as a Second Language (ESL) training has been conducted at many organizations for years. Because this training, when it is conducted effectively, contributes significantly to increasing self-esteem as well as communication, it becomes an important part of an organization's program.

Northeastern Products Company, a division of Campbell Soup Company, established an on-site ESL program to meet the needs of Hispanic and Asian employees, who represented 36 percent of its workforce. The course, offered in two-hour modules twice a week, was designed to assist employees in everyday activities, such as comprehending food labels, applying for credit cards, reading road maps, and communicating in the work environment.

A buddy system has been set up at Ore-Ida Foods of Boise, Idaho, a subsidiary of H. J. Heinz Company, to address the language barriers and cultural differences of Hispanic and other culturally diverse employees. A buddy translator is assigned to new employees during on-the-job training and continues to assist them with communication problems. The "buddy" is a worker who is proficient in his or her job and has the ability to demonstrate it. The company also sponsors voluntary ESL classes and offers a tuition aid reimbursement program that covers the expense of Spanish classes.

"Culture is a significant factor in building good communication," says Rudy Santos, Ore-Ida's employment manager. "Many misinterpretations can be prevented if it is realized that emphasis must be placed on such things as being on time for the shift change, maintaining safe and clean working conditions, and other details."

"My success as food service director depends on the front-line worker who interfaces with the patients on a daily basis," says Larry Hill, director of food service at Memorial Medical Center in Savannah, Georgia.

Hill's biggest challenge is to provide good service with a staff that has minimal education. "To achieve a level of productivity that the hospital expects involves teaching reading, writing, and basic work value skills to my employees," he says.

In 1986 Judy Riggs was hired by San Francisco–based apparel company Esprit De Corp. to teach English at the company's distribution center in San Francisco. Her students, employees of Esprit, came from around the world to form one of the most culturally diverse workplaces in the area. It was not uncommon to have Cantonese, Spanish, and Tagalog speakers working in the same area. Employees and supervisors were both experiencing frustration as language differences interfered with meeting company and departmental goals. Riggs's task was to create classes and seminars that met the language and business needs of the distribution center so that a team with a common language and common vision could be established.

Riggs, who has fourteen years' experience in training foreign-born employees, began her project by speaking personally with managers and supervisors about their frustrations with the language and cultural differences. Then she spoke with foreign-born employees about their frustrations within the workplace. She also spent time on the floor of the distribution center learning job tasks and terminology. Being on the floor and learning about job tasks allowed her to meet people, build relationships, and understand the intricacies of business practice. These experiences would find their way into the design of the classes and the content of each presentation.

The next step of the process was to test each interested student to obtain his or her language, listening, and grammar levels. From this point, course design, internal marketing, and enrollment were the focus.

The initial class offerings for both supervisors and floor employees included beginning, intermediate, and advanced conversation classes. Through practice exercises, class discussions, and role playing, employees gained not only a command of the English language but also an understanding of American business practices including interviewing skills, participation in meetings, time management, performance evaluations, and corporate culture.

Business skills were embedded within the classes. These included effectively using upward, downward, and lateral communication; giving instructions; organizing and delegating tasks; training new employees; facilitating performance reviews; and managing conflicts.

"When poor food service was reported by the nursing and medical staff last year, I organized my management staff within twenty-four hours to examine the problem and decide on an action strategy," says Hill. "My challenge was to change the perceptions of doctors and nurses about the service we provided.

"With the help of my management team we set up on-the-job training that standardized the procedure for delivering food trays. We focused on 'leading by example' and had each manager team up with a service worker to deliver food trays to patients and demonstrate the importance of smiling and saying 'good morning' to each and every patient.

"After a two-week training period, in which I was personally involved, we surveyed the patients, as well as the medical and nursing staff. The survey comments were overwhelmingly positive. My most vocal critics have now become my most vocal supporters."

Northern Telecom's move to self-directed work teams in 1986 made it necessary for the company, a global supplier of fully digital telecommunications switching systems, to retrain some 500 employees at its Santa Clara manufacturing facility. Because of the ethnic and cultural diversity of its manufacturing workforce, an improvement in basic communication skills was essential. Therefore, a curriculum was designed to expand the skill base of employees in both technical and interpersonal areas.

The ESL program provided the foundation of the interpersonal skills training, supplemented by training in problem solving and team building.

The technical components covered Total Quality Control, Statistical Process Control, and the Just-In-Time manufacturing process. Employees were also trained in various manufacturing processes that would enable them to be cross-trained on different jobs.

Along with the retraining came a move from tenure-based pay to skill-based pay for hourly flow line employees. As employees demonstrate proficiency with a particular skill on the flow line, they receive a pay increase. They can receive up to two advances in pay per year if they choose to learn two new skills.

Northern Telecom received state funding for half of the program budget to train hourly employees and their supervisors.

Use Varied Training Methods to Meet Varied Needs

Another aspect of today's diversity is the entrance of the "Baby Busters" into the workforce. They are the generation just now making the transition from college to work life, and they come with their own particular expectations and needs.

National Semiconductor Corporation of Santa Clara, California, recognizes that the Baby Busters have different expectations from those of graduates of a few years ago. They aren't wedded to their jobs; they value independence and are more willing to put their careers at risk. Yet, in moving into the workforce, they also need to be able to work as team members.

National has set up a special orientation program for all new college hires. The College Club, which is made up of previous college hires, helps new employees meet people, sets up monthly outings to acquaint the new hire with the area, and promotes networking.

The club is part of National's College Hire Assimilation Program (CHAP), which begins about three months after the employee has begun work. The program includes a peak performance workshop; a day of networking and team building; strategic seminars on technology, human resources, business issues, and leadership; and assignment of an advisor.

The retail staff development department of Wells Fargo Bank uses an individualized approach to its training and development programs. "Our instructional process recognizes that today's workforce brings a wide variety of experience, education, and learning preferences to the job. We design our programs in a flexible way so that the learner can truly individualize his or her approach to the training," explains Roger Addison, manager. One program, Map, is a self-paced curriculum for key positions in the bank such as branch managers, service managers, and sales officers. It contains modules covering what a person holding that position must know to be proficient. This design allows an employee to concentrate only on the skills that he or she actually needs to develop. Modules on skills that have already been developed can be skipped.

"CHAP eases the graduate's transition to work life, providing focus on career, work, and personal objectives in a positive way," states Milan Moravec, corporate human resources manager. "It also helps the new employee build peer and professional networks and provides a working understanding of National's business and its customers."

In these skill- and experience-enhancing actions, the focus is on targeted development, communication networks, and special resources for nontraditional workers. These organized programs not only provide inclusion and career enhancement for employees, but also provide feedback to management on practices that could be improved.

Shell Oil Company in Houston, Texas, uses interactive video in manufacturing, sales, service station, and financial management courses to train nontraditional and new members of the workforce. Interactive video is a training method in which a learner, using a computer terminal interfaced with a videodisc player and a touch screen, works alone through a self-paced lesson. Instructional material is presented and followed by questions. If the learner responds with the correct answer, the lesson proceeds to the next segment. If the learner responds incorrectly, the point is repeated in another way. Gene Hahne, manager of training, says that because interactive video enables a learner to learn at his or her own pace, it is particularly helpful for persons with language and learning disabilities.

A course called "Basic Manager Survival Skills" is part of the orientation of new managers at Apple. The focus of the three-day training is to communicate the Apple way of managing: Provide people with a productive environment to work in by supporting and coaching individual performance.

"The focus of training and development at Apple is employability— maximizing the individual's potential," comments Debbie Biondolillo, vice-president for human resources. The basis for employee training is identifying and developing the skills and knowledge needed to stay at the top of the profession. "We recognize that Apple employees demand more flexibility in their career development. They don't value security and structure as much as the opportunity to be innovative and creative."

As the examples in this chapter illustrate, education, awareness, and skill development, together with appropriate policies and supporting systems, are important actions. They help managers and co-workers to better understand differences, increase sensitivity, and more flexibly manage and reward performance.

9

Enable Persons with Disabilities to Meet Performance Challenges

SOCIETAL AND HEALTH ISSUES such as chemical dependence, substance abuse, and acquired immune deficiency syndrome (AIDS) are creating another kind of diversity. Organizations are developing greater understanding and skill in working with people with these problems and are creating guidelines for managing their performance.

Many organizations are using educational programs to increase people's understanding and flexibility.

Educate About AIDS in the Workplace

Pacific Gas and Electric Company, a San Francisco–based utility, began its AIDS program in 1984 in response to PG&E public service workers who feared that they would become infected by going into the homes of people with AIDS. To reduce their fears about casual contact with individuals infected with human immunodeficiency virus (HIV) or AIDS patients, PG&E developed a three-step approach to educating its workforce about AIDS. The approach involves communication, education, and a commitment to providing employees with the most current information available.

At the heart of PG&E's AIDS education program is a one-hour formal presentation involving the Employee Assistance Program administrator, prominent AIDS specialists, psychologists, social workers, and counselors. The seminar includes a video presentation and a question-and-answer session.

In addition to noontime seminars, AIDS education is incorporated in the company's safety and supervisory training. All employees receive literature on the topic and have access to an AIDS hotline, which is staffed by human resource personnel. The educational emphasis has shifted from providing basic medical information to helping employees deal with working or living with HIV-infected co-workers or loved ones. Topics such as grieving, loss, and living with a long-term illness are addressed in training. PG&E also works closely with the San Francisco AIDS Foundation and other community agencies. Its formal policy and guidelines for supervisors are revised when significant medical developments occur.

The company takes the position that employees afflicted with HIV do not present a health risk to other employees under normal working conditions. Employees with HIV disease are subject to the same working conditions and performance requirements as any other employee. Employees with AIDS are entitled to all company benefits.

The State of Florida currently has a number of programs designed to address the AIDS epidemic. The Florida AIDS program, sponsored by the Department of Health and Rehabilitative Services, coordinates the state's efforts. Emphasis is placed on surveillance, information and education, counseling and testing, and health education and risk reduction.

The department has produced a videotape entitled *Florida Responds to AIDS,* which assists managers, human resource administrators, and trainers in planning and implementing AIDS education programs for their

Digital Equipment Corporation, which with 125,000 employees is the second largest computer company in the world, has what is probably the country's most comprehensive AIDS strategy. Digital is the only corporation to establish a full-time office devoted to managing the issues of AIDS in the workplace.

Digital's AIDS Program Office was created in December 1987 to oversee the design, development, and implementation of educational programs; consult with management and personnel to identify trends in the epidemic so that the company would be prepared for all contingencies; and serve as a liaison with other companies, community organizations, and government agencies.

The AIDS Program Office also works with Digital's corporate contributions and community relations departments to recommend funding for AIDS-related programs.

According to Paul Ross, corporate manager of the AIDS Program, "Digital's educational programs aim to protect the legal rights of all employees, prevent work disruption based on misinformation and fear, support the physical and emotional well-being of all employees, and ensure fair treatment of all employees by modeling behavior consistent with Digital's core values."

Educational efforts are focused on managers, who in turn collaborate with personnel to educate their employees. A typical half-day managers' seminar has four components: an explanation of corporate commitment, medical information, an examination of human factors, and a description of Digital's policies as they relate to AIDS.

Digital's business rationale for implementing AIDS education is presented by the AIDS Program Office manager, a senior personnel professional, or a line manager. The business rationale concerns the larger business, political, human resource, and community issues surrounding AIDS.

Medical facts about the disease— what it is, what it is not, how it is transmitted, protection, prevention, testing, symptoms, and cost—are addressed by a health professional from the Digital staff or an outside health agency.

The section on human factors is a critical component of the managerial seminar. The subjects covered include prejudice, homophobia, sexuality, grief, death, dying, and the politics of AIDS. Formats for this section range from group exercises to interactive dialogues with persons living with AIDS.

Digital's program emphasizes the psychosocial aspects of living and working with a long-term chronic illness and of relating to other employees who have AIDS or the HIV virus. Participants discuss company policies on dealing with employees with HIV, who are encouraged to work as long as they can if they are able to meet acceptable performance standards. Also covered are the company's guidelines for providing reasonable accommodation to the changing needs of such employees.

Through its Employee Assistance Program, Digital offers counseling to employees whose lives have in some way been affected by AIDS. The company also plans to institute seminars for families that are dealing with death and dying.

Digital recognizes that the company reflects the strengths, weaknesses, and problems of society as a whole. How Digital responds to an issue such as AIDS directly affects its position as a world-class employer and a corporate citizen of the communities in which its employees live and conduct business. Digital believes that societal and health issues require a collaborative response from all sectors of society, including business.

employees. State legislation requires that state agencies and departments provide information about HIV and AIDS on a yearly basis to current and new employees.

In 1983 Wellcome Animal Health, a manufacturer of animal health products now owned by Coopers, was faced with its first AIDS case. Diane Heffner, director of personnel, knew that the situation had to be handled well. Although little information was available on AIDS in the workplace in 1983, Diane researched what there was. Working with her management and the employee's supervisor, she decided to treat this AIDS case in the same way she would treat any other medical disability.

The company did not isolate the employee and did not change his work responsibilities. He was allowed to work as long as he could. The supervisor handled the situation particularly well; this reduced co-worker anxiety. In fact, as soon as it was clear how the company was going to handle the situation, employees began to support their co-worker. Because the rules were clear, employees were better able to handle the situation.

Management felt no need to create a special AIDS policy, because they already had a policy for medical disability. As the employee's condition deteriorated, Diane treated his partner in the same way the company would treat a spouse. When the employee's partner contacted her to discuss health and other benefits matters, Diane was called upon to be as empathetic and supportive as she would be with a spouse. She insisted that her personnel staff do the same, even though that might be contrary to how they felt about AIDS and homosexuality.

Handling sensitive situations of all sorts is a particularly important skill in working with people of diverse backgrounds. An IRS case shows how it can be done. According to Joe Meade, Employee Assistance Program administrator, AIDS education in the workforce is important to the IRS. The IRS sponsors a course, "AIDS—Manager's Role and Responsibility"; distributes a brochure, *AIDS in the Workplace;* and uses the film *One of Our Own,* which is available from The Dartnell Corporation, in addition to providing the services of an Employee Assistance Program. The IRS has also run articles by managers and friends of AIDS victims in its internal management magazine.

As Roscoe, an AIDS-stricken employee who later died, wrote in the magazine: "I didn't have any problems at work. None whatsoever. Everybody was so helpful. They acted as if they cared. There didn't seem to be many challenges to the normal work. Part of that was because my boss, Dave, was very supportive of me and made sure I got work assignments that I could handle. So that stress was lessened. As for the office, Dave and my colleagues were wonderful and very supportive. They didn't pester me. They asked how I was doing, but they didn't hang around. Sometimes you feel so down, you really don't feel like talking. I couldn't have asked for a better workplace. And I don't know whether it was because of the training everybody got or a combination of the training and that we have a more sophisticated workforce. Everyone rallied around me and I really appreciated that."

His manager, Dave, writing in the same magazine, commented: "My first reaction was concern and grief for him. Later the managerial concerns began to trigger—Who has to know about this? What does this mean regarding his continuing to work in the section? I didn't see any negative reaction or any sense of fear or concern on anyone's part. What I did see was a positive, supportive reaction to a personal tragedy. Roscoe's energy level was not always consistently high. There were periods when he was resting, but within that context, Roscoe was doing his job and providing a valuable service, virtually until the day he decided to retire." IRS's policy states that an individual with AIDS should be treated the same as a person with any other illness. AIDS is considered a "handicapping condition" under federal laws that guarantee "reasonable accommodation" for its victims. An IRS manager is expected to support the victim, to know the facts, and to provide accurate information in response to any fears or anxieties of other employees.

Address Alcohol and Substance Abuse

Alcohol and substance abuse problems have also been on the rise in our society and therefore in the workplace. This produces more employees whose "differences" must be considered in relation to managing performance.

Lawrence Livermore National Laboratory, operated by the University of California for the U.S. Department of Energy, spends about $1 billion annually on research, most of it in the area of national defense. Security and safety are vital to its 8,000 employees. To this end, the Laboratory embarked on developing a comprehensive alcohol and substance abuse policy and educational program in January 1989.

A committee made up of managers from various areas launched A.S.A.P. (Alcohol and Substance Abuse Prevention Education Program) in August 1989. This program has the following objectives for employees:

- Understand the Laboratory's substance abuse prevention policy.

- Learn to implement performance management techniques to correct deteriorating performance resulting from substance abuse.

- Learn to implement drug crisis management techniques.

- Know the Laboratory's resources and programs for helping employees.

- Learn to recognize signs of potential substance abuse on the job.

A consultant was hired who had extensive experience with the U.S. Drug Enforcement Agency and knew how to manage substance abuse in the workplace. "Credibility was essential," says Ladonna Robson, human resources project leader, "because many of the Lab employees are highly educated scientists and engineers. We wanted to be able to have an expert on hand to address the area in depth."

The consultant provided off-the-shelf training materials that were customized by the Laboratory. Video interviews featuring the Laboratory's director and representatives from the medical, security, staff relations, and communication resources departments were added to the training design.

Because of the importance of the issue, training was mandatory. More than 1,600 managers and supervisors participated in a one-day course. Line managers were responsible for identifying and scheduling their employees for the training. "This got Human Resources out of the policing role," comments Robson.

The Laboratory is now planning an employee education program for all employees to help them understand the policy and the resources available to them.

Promote Mainstreaming of Persons with Disabilities

Mainstreaming, the placement of persons with disabilities into regular school classes and workplaces, is generally considered the most advantageous accommodation for both the person with a disability and the organization. Mainstreaming usually requires flexibility on the part of nondisabled employees and managers. The following success stories attest to the positive outcomes of exercising such flexibility.

Kathy Jorgensen is an information systems supervisor for the St. Paul Companies, a worldwide property casualty insurance organization head-quartered in St. Paul, Minnesota. She has managed a hearing-impaired programmer/analyst for two years. "We treat her like everyone else. She reads lips and speaks very well, so our main job is to help her understand us. For example, she has taught us to face her directly and keep our hands away from our mouths as we speak."

Jorgensen also supervises a visually impaired programmer who recently completed his training in programming. "His PC is equipped with a voice adapter and screen reader, so he is all set to do his work. But we need to tell him where to find memos in his system and have someone read his in-basket material to him. We are experimenting with employees reading to him a half-hour each day on a rotating basis. We thought he

Cleveland Electric Illuminating Company provides a twelve-week training program for the disabled that rotates them through a variety of positions in the company—including those of customer service representative, accounts payable clerk, computer programmer, and data entry clerk—based on the participants' needs as well as those of the company. Since the program's inception in 1984, CEI has hired 50 of the program's 227 participants.

The program is operated in conjunction with Vocational Guidance Services (VGS), a not-for-profit Cleveland rehabilitation facility. A VGS counselor works with program participants and CEI supervisors to ensure a mutually satisfying partnership.

During the work experience, participants also work closely with CEI employees who act as peer counselors, helping trainees develop good work habits.

"For many trainees, this program is the individual's first opportunity to learn and earn outside of a rehabilitation facility or workshop," says Bruce Campbell, employment manager. According to Campbell, the work experience gained at CEI helps more than 50 percent of the participants gain employment in the Greater Cleveland area.

would get to know people faster this way and our employees are better equipped to answer his questions than someone from the outside."

In addition, the company's human resource department sent a Multi-Resource Center representative to speak to Jorgensen's department about attitudes toward persons with disabilities. "We are doing everything we can to anticipate his needs and questions. It helps that he is determined and motivated to be part of the problem-solving process. I expect he will be handling the same responsibilities as everyone else as soon as all systems are in place and he is fully oriented."

A Lawrence Livermore National Laboratory video on the work done by AID Employment, "I Know You Can Do It," vividly portrays what can be lost if managers assume that persons with disabilities cannot take on full responsibility. In AID's employment program for the developmentally disabled at the Laboratory, a manager working with a mentally retarded person noticed that the employee—who checks computer tapes for defects—responded slowly to verbal requests and did not appear to understand instructions. The manager was cautious about giving this employee too much responsibility until he learned that the employee had three computers at home. Not only did he use them to play games, but he performed elementary programming. At that point the manager took off the kid gloves; the employee blossomed when he was given additional responsibilities.

In these examples we can see clearly the interplay among policies, which create a framework; management practices, which are used in working with individuals; and systems of resources, which support managers and employees.

10

Individualize— Don't Standardize— Performance Management

SOME PEOPLE WORK WELL with highly structured processes, while others prefer more latitude. Some wish to have more collaboration and involvement in goal setting, while others do not. Some can work on longer-term outcomes, while others prefer short-term, specific goals; in addition, the number of goals an employee can handle may vary. Also, achievement and development goals are valued more by some than by others. These differences point up the importance of flexibility in setting performance goals.

How, when, and where managers and employees work together on performance issues; what kinds of discussions they have; how coaching is handled; how performance development is determined; and how training is done are all options that can be handled flexibly and that provide opportunities to improve employees' effectiveness.

According to Dr. Susan Resnick-West, co-author of *Designing Performance Appraisal Systems* (Mohrman, Resnick-West, and Lawler, 1989), the only predictor of success in performance appraisal systems is whether the process is customized for individuals. Factors that should be taken into account include previous experience, task competency, educational level, and preferences.

Involve Employees in Performance Management

Self-managed work teams at Aid Association for Lutherans, a fraternal insurance society serving 1.5 million members, run their own operations with little supervision, including their own performance appraisals. Many teams review their own performance, conduct peer evaluations of individual employees, and handle problems such as absenteeism and poor performance.

"Performance planning typically begins with a team development plan," says Rick Stach, director for human resource development. The team decides which additional services, based on workload and volume, it would like to provide in the future and identifies any additional staff, training, and projected costs associated with providing the new service. Individual developmental plans are generated that identify the specific competencies associated with providing the new service. An action plan is completed that outlines the type of training, either on the job or in the classroom, that must be completed by the employee.

To obtain feedback on performance, team members send feedback forms to their manager and peers that list key competencies they need. In many cases they also rate themselves. "Obtaining feedback is also a collaborative effort involving all members of the team," states Stach. "Each feedback form is specifically tailored to the employee and fits in with overall team competencies."

The final component of the process is an individual development action plan, which is the only piece submitted to the human resource department. The plan summarizes the feedback from the manager, employees, peers, and customers, and identifies the career interests, developmental needs, and specific action plans that are required.

Employees are encouraged to develop new skills in order to increase their flexibility; they typically learn how to perform three or more functions. Work teams are responsible for motivating, training, coaching, and developing their members. They may teach new skills to each other or arrange for outside training.

"As a result of the group performance appraisal system, I've seen a significant improvement in developmental planning between employees and managers at AAL," comments Stach. "Individual and group development action plans that are the result of analyzing feedback are much more specific."

At Colgate-Palmolive Company's Global Business Systems, the explanations of "1-," "2-," and "3-level" performance were vague as they appeared on the appraisal form. The form gave three or four sentences, which several secretaries felt were not enough to go on. They decided to act. Julie Zerbe, manager of organization development, encouraged them to take action in a positive way by helping them and their bosses reach a consensus on what the standards of performance should be.

"These performance standards were written for our department, although they can be applied to other departments as well. They were initiated by the secretaries and then agreed upon by the bosses. One of the key differences between their 1-level Outstanding Performance, their 2-level Commendable Performance, and their 3-level Competent Performance was the degree of initiative taken by the secretaries. This distinction made sense to all involved. One of the key outcomes," explains Zerbe, "was that the secretaries stopped focusing on 'just me and my boss' and began focusing on being a team member on our administrative support staff."

Make an Extra Effort

In Claims Operations at Blue Cross Blue Shield of Florida, Pam Haddock was transferred into a new department to supervise the second shift. One of the employees in the department was Bruce, a claims examiner who was deaf. Bruce's production at the time was extremely low, although his quality level was excellent. He had virtually no communication with his peers and participated in no formal departmental activities. During group meetings he would frequently read a book or simply daydream because he was unable to read lips or understand what was being said. Had Bruce's performance continued at that level, he would have received no merit increases and might possibly have been identified as a "productivity problem," resulting in a demotion to a lower position or even termination.

Soon after she was transferred, Pam learned that Bruce was deaf and decided to learn sign language in an attempt to communicate. Ini-

Coaching can sometimes take the form of caring confrontation. One human relations manager at a major aerospace company recalls a particularly emotional situation involving a seriously ill employee.

Both the quantity and the quality of a design engineer's drawings were deteriorating. His supervisor knew that something was wrong but did not know exactly what.

The health services organization had previously determined that the symptoms could indicate multiple sclerosis. MS causes lessening control over one's muscles, and since he was a drafter, this was a particularly significant disability for him. The employee was not able to face his physical situation and openly discuss it.

Since he had not told the supervisor about his illness, the supervisor had a very difficult situation to face. After consulting with several people in the human resources organization, he decided to meet with the employee, put the situation on the table, and offer support.

The supervisor, the human relations manager, and an employee assistance counselor told the employee that they were aware of his condition, were concerned for him personally, and thought his illness was affecting the quality of his work. The meeting was very emotional. The employee said that he appreciated their concern and that he was having difficulties doing the work and facing his condition. With this basic truth telling, they were able to go on to work out solutions to this difficult situation.

tially Bruce taught her during spare moments, but she also attended a class at a local college. Within a matter of weeks, Bruce and Pam were able to communicate using sign language. Subsequently, two other employees and one trainee who were deaf and who were experiencing similar difficulty, were transferred into the department.

In a span of two years, through the ongoing efforts of Pam and other employees, Bruce's productivity increased 1,000 percent. Currently his productivity is routinely more than twice his nightly goal and his quality is still excellent. One of the other deaf employees has been promoted to senior examiner and the other is being considered for a similar promotion. The trainee has also maintained acceptable levels of both productivity and quality since being hired. Together, the four employees and their supervisor attribute their success to their increased communication, participation, and interest.

Specifically, the employees who are deaf now participate in group meetings, and their peers and supervisor translate their sign language for the benefit of those who have not yet learned to sign. Overall, the department is a very positive example to other employees and represents a successful blending of handicapped and nonhandicapped people working together.

Jocelyn Tilsen, executive director of Parents Anonymous of Minnesota in St. Paul, manages a female employee in her forties with a college degree, who left the workplace twelve years ago and has returned to work in an entry-level clerical position. "I used a supportive and available management style with her. We met two to three times a week to set priorities and clarify expectations.

"Helping her improve her attitude about herself and the work she does is a big part of my job because she is unhappy about making the same money she made when she was twenty years old. I give her opportunities to succeed and assign work that progressively moves her toward higher-level tasks, because I know that's important to her. At the same time, I work with her to keep her expectations in line with her skills."

Facilitate the Use of Mentoring

Mentoring, the practice of coaching, guiding, and teaching the success strategies of one's field or organization on a one-on-one basis, is an effective model of learning that has been recognized for centuries, in the apprentice system of skilled craftsmen. Today's new or less skilled managers can benefit from a similar one-on-one learning relationship through a facilitated mentoring process.

The term "facilitated mentoring" was first used by Skip Everitt, manager of continuing education at Federal Express Corporation, and Margo Murray, president of MMHA The Managers' Mentors, Inc. They were looking for a term that would describe something between a formalized process of matching mentors and protégés and a haphazard process of simply encouraging mentoring and hoping that mentors and proteges would connect on their own.

The mentoring program at Federal Express evolved under the leadership of Linda Crosby DeBerry, managing director of human resource development, to meet Federal Express's changing needs. It included training mentors and protégés in the skills used in coaching and being coached, developing a process to effectively match mentors and protégés, and creating guidelines to help both manage the relationship well.

"Facilitated mentoring enabled Federal Express to individualize development, which is of primary importance to its workforce. Each person has unique training and development needs because each has a different background and experience. Facilitated mentoring is a realistic, cost-effective method to develop today's workforce," explains Murray.

Facilitated mentoring can be particularly useful when the workforce is diverse. It can help match mentors and protégés who might be uncomfortable in a close, one-on-one relationship without the structure provided by an organized program. This is particularly true when the mentor and protégés are from different ethnic groups or of different sexes.

Susan Chellino, engineering manager at New England Telephone Company in Boston, had not been in a line organization for ten years when she was selected from a Corporate Leader Program by her mentor, Ted Hatch, managing director of customer service. "He took a risk by putting me into a downtown Boston operations group where I was responsible for 75 percent of the businesses and residences," explains Chellino. "I suddenly jumped from having three people under me to having sixty-one report to me."

Ted Hatch made his decision based on a careful assessment of her background, skills, formal education, and training experience. "Her background was in human resources as a trainer and course developer," recalls Hatch. "She had previous operating experience, and she was motivated about learning. Over a twenty-year period, she had earned two master's degrees and a doctorate. I thought she could inspire others to obtain more formal education and ultimately she did. Also, I picked someone who fit into my team according to human resource development needs and requirements and organizational biases."

Her demonstrated willingness to work with her employee organization was a major factor in her successful transition. "The people I select need to be open and humble about learning from experts who will be reporting to them," says Hatch. "She had a highly skilled, veteran management group that reported to her and a strong, competent peer team to rely on for support." The combination worked extremely well for Chellino, who refers to her time under Hatch's guidance as the "Camelot of my career."

Inspired by her mentor, Chellino later used what she had learned to prepare a black female college graduate for the job she would be doing, and she adds, "Young people entering a new company need a frame of reference. If they can't see where they fit into the organization, it's going to be harder for them to understand where their job is."

Chellino reports that it took several steps to ensure her new employee's success. "First, I prepared my workforce, which consists of primarily older male engineers, to be ready to offer help and tutelage. Then I assigned her to a stable, nonthreatening neighborhood. I teamed her up with a newer engineer who had experience as a technician, and her work was checked by a more experienced engineer. To make sure she was scheduled for the appropriate technical and general management courses, I set up an orientation day with each department so that she could sit in and observe the culture and pick up the jargon before doing any work with them. As a safeguard, I identified another black female employee she could talk with if any race issues arose."

When Ralph Thompson asked for help in moving from Marketing and Corporate Planning into Operations, Ted Hatch offered him the chance to move into this very different discipline as a director. "I knew and liked

''**W**e're willing to offer jobs to people who don't necessarily have all the 'right' background and experience. We couple them with a manager who is responsible for mentoring them, which has proven to be an effective strategy for us,'' says John Major, corporate vice-president and general manager of Motorola's Communications Systems Group.

''When we hired Choonie Teh as product manager, I knew she didn't have the degree of experience tradition-ally considered necessary for that posi-tion, but she was bright and I believed she would do well in the position and add some much-needed innovation. I saw to it that she had support up and down the unit and cut back the span of control. We took some risks and they paid off,'' he adds. Choonie has been promoted twice since then and now is a vice-president in Motorola's Com-munication Systems Group.

At the time Major contacted Teh about moving from a staff to a line position, she was ready to take a risk. ''Neither of us was sure of my direc-tion in the beginning, but John gave me a charter to grow the business. It was like being given a plot of land to cultivate however I chose, but I knew I had to produce,'' says Teh.

She believes that Major's mentoring motivated her to set high standards and then exceed them. Now her depart-ment is attracting people and has shed its image as one of the least important and slowest growing businesses in the communications sector. ''I cannot duplicate John's unique style, but I can use what he taught me to help others take risks and, in doing so, to reach their potential.''

Ralph's work and felt he demonstrated the appropriate interest and moti-vation. So we put together his individual development plan—an approach I use with everyone—that outlined his goals and commitments.

"Then I selected three experts a level below him who became his support group. They designed a technical training curriculum that required Thompson to spend a day with each one of them on a rotating basis. He set aside one day a week for this in addition to holding a full-time job."

The support team was expected to give Thompson candid and honest feedback and to report directly to Hatch. This group remains important to Thompson even now that he's been in the field for a year. He calls them or drops by, or they call him with advice.

"What helped Ralph tremendously," says Hatch, "was his line experi-ence as a telephone installer and repairman, a role we gave him during a sixteen-week strike. From there, he became director of operations and brought his hands-on technical experience and already strong administra-tive and analytical skills to the job. Now he is an astute troubleshooter. Of course, his humility about learning from employees and doing whatever it takes has earned him considerable respect around here as well."

Ted Hatch mentors between twelve and fifteen people at one time. He says, "I develop all my direct-reporting people and as many others in the organization who are interested and motivated." According to Hatch, he has grown into this role by listening to people talk about what they want to do with their talent and skills. "Of course, I got some of my ideas about mentoring from my own mentor, who is now retired."

Multicultural Officers Networks (MONs) have been set up at Security Pacific Corporation to encourage the personal and professional growth of culturally diverse officers in the areas of leadership, management ability, and communication skills. Local chapters of BOSS (Black Officers Support System), HON (Hispanic Officers Network), SPAN (Security Pacific Asian Network), and MON offer programs, projects, and experiences that focus on career development and achievement.

The networks have established a mentoring system that identifies talents and provides visibility and exposure for their officers. They also encourage officers from different ethnic groups to actively assume a liaison role between Security Pacific and local ethnic communities to promote a positive corporate image.

Gail Tiwanak of The Queen's Medical Center in Hawaii utilizes a performance-based development system to individualize the orientation and management of new nurses. The Assessment Center's process is used to assess nurses entering the hospital or transferring from other departments. It evaluates nurses in three areas—critical thinking, technical skill, and interpersonal relations—and is customized to The Queen's Medical Center's policies and procedures.

Each new hire or transfer goes through a day-and-a-half-long orientation that includes a verbal assessment, a written assessment, and a video simulation exercise that depicts clinical situations and interpersonal conflicts specific to the department in which they will be working. Following the assessment, written results are shared with the manager, a perceptor, and the new nurse. This information alerts supervisory staff to the new nurse's strengths and weaknesses. Then the perceptor works alongside the new nurse for the first two and a half weeks of orientation.

At the end of this period, the nurse, perceptor, and manager meet again to discuss what additional unit-based education or training should be provided in the first three months of employment. The first performance review is held after three months.

According to Tiwanak, "the benefits appeared soon after the first six months of adjusting and streamlining the assessment process. We noticed that we were staying within our given orientation time and budget. Also, our new nurses were more productive sooner because we capitalized on their strengths and addressed their weaknesses from the start of their employment."

Performance management needs to be individualized even more with today's diverse workforce. The type of assistance, amount of direction, and form of feedback can all be varied in order to be most effective. Tailoring or customizing the processes will greatly enhance the outcomes.

11

Align Rewards with Employees' Values

WHAT IS REWARDING to different people varies greatly depending on their background, expectations, values, and needs. The value of money, response to public recognition, the desire for peer and professional respect, and the need for challenging assignments all vary according to lifestyle and culture. The importance of these rewards to individuals affects their motivation, productivity, and satisfaction. A greater variety of rewards is clearly called for.

Rewards can either be performance based or given for the achievement of other meaningful goals, such as quality, attendance, or community service. They can be tangible, such as pay or merchandise, or more intangible, such as recognition, time off, or special assignments. It is important to custom-design reward systems so that they are meaningful, credible, and available to large numbers of employees.

A report of a survey by the American Productivity Center and the American Compensation Association (American Productivity Center, 1983, p. 11) states:

> Many current compensation systems are not custom-designed to meet the needs and unique circumstances of work groups. We think organizations should rethink their reward systems, and when appropriate, redesign them, to meet the following criteria:
>
> (1) Vary the size of the reward with changes in performance and productivity.
> (2) Incorporate a measure of performance upon which the individual(s) rewarded have both perceived and real impacts.
> (3) Incorporate a measure of performance that gauges TRUE measures of success rather than measures (P&L) that are primarily driven by inflation, accounting conventions, or other factors. . . . Further, assure that measures balance short and longer term business needs, as well as unit and corporate needs.
> (4) Provide rewards that are meaningful to individuals in terms of the FORM of tangible rewards, as well as the opportunity to achieve personal goals such as career growth, autonomy, and personal growth.
> (5) Be jointly designed by management, employees, and union representatives.

Greater competitiveness and the changing needs of the workforce are resulting in the use of nontraditional reward systems (O'Dell and McAdams, 1987). Jerry McAdams, vice-president of Maritz Inc., the world's largest performance improvement company, sums up the employee perspective well: "Today's employees require information, involvement, security, and incentives. They need and want to know what is going on. They want to know how they are doing and how judgements are made. They want to be involved in solving problems and improving performance. They want to understand what determines the security of their jobs. They want a direct connection between their performance and their reward" (McAdams, 1988, p. 17).

Use a Variety of Flexible Rewards

Pay-for-Applied-Services is a new compensation system designed to support self-managed work teams set up at Aid Association for Lutherans. Descriptions of individual positions have been replaced by a team job description and individual personal assignments. The personal assignment is a listing of the services an individual performs to support the team's mission and his or her own career interests. Compensation has two components: a "valued service" payment, which increases as an employee learns and performs new services, and a team bonus. The team bonus is tied to productivity; team results determine its size and team members determine how it is to be distributed among themselves.

The basic pay scale that Steelcase factory workers receive is relatively low, between $8 and $9 per hour (about $17,000 per year). However, on top of these basic wages, employees receive incentive pay keyed to their specific performance and cash bonuses based on company profits. The average salary for 1989 was $35,000.

Apple currently employs 11,000 people worldwide. Fifty percent of its employees are women and people of color. "Apple has a 'hero system' for recognizing its employees," says Debbie Biondolillo, vice-president for human resources for Apple USA. "People who design our products will get the recognition for their work, rather than the top manager of the project. Apple is as close as you can get to owning your own business. There's a sense here of employee ownership and entrepreneurship."

Apple offers stock options to all employees. Assembly line workers through top management receive options ranging from 200 to 20,000 shares. A cash award program encourages and rewards employees who obtain patents for products developed at Apple. The awards are given to employees based on the type and number of patents issued. Apple's Restart Program rewards employees with a six-week sabbatical after five full years of continuous service.

Paul Bilello, plant manager at Dow Brands, a division of Dow Chemical, is a strong proponent of the pay-for-performance system. He has considerable latitude within the company's flexible policies to reward people individually on the basis of merit. "We have a special recognition program that allows us to award someone a few hundred dollars for a job well done. As important as the money is, I think attaching a letter to the boss stating why the employee has earned this recognition is even more important. The employee gets feedback from several levels and it builds trust in management."

Bilello likes to individualize his system of management and reward. When dignitaries visit the plant, he invites employees to join them for lunch. Sometimes he meets his boss for breakfast and brings an employee

"At Tandem, it is important to reward people fairly, which may not mean equally and in the same way," comments Debbie Byron, director, office of the president. Tandem has consequently developed a variety of flexible mechanisms to reward employees.

In accordance with the company's belief that it must provide balance in order to maintain a committed, motivated, loyal workforce, all employees are eligible after four years of service for a company-paid sabbatical of six weeks, in addition to regular vacations.

Tandem also believes that everyone should share in the company's success. Approximately once each year, stock options are awarded equally to every employee. More than 80 percent of the employees have received additional stock options for top performance and promotion. Cash bonuses are awarded to top performers at all levels of the organization. A "night on the town" is given to people who make a special contribution to complete an important assignment or project.

In a further effort to recognize employee excellence, the TOPS program—Tandem's Outstanding Performers—annually brings together 10 percent of Tandem's employees and guests in a special retreat at a resort. These retreats create a place for top performers to relax, network, become acquainted, and brainstorm on key issues facing the business. Attendees are nominated by supervisors and peers for outstanding contributions. Balance across job function, demographics, and location is also built into the program.

with him. According to Bilello, "It's okay to treat two employees differently, but I need to justify it and be consistent about how I reach my decisions."

In his annual performance reviews, Bilello includes specific feedback and offers as many supporting examples as possible. He supplements his own observations with feedback from the employee's peers. Goals and expectations are set each year, "because people want different things at different times in their careers. I need to know what they want and where they are headed."

Typically he spends two to four hours on the formal review. In addition, he believes that he owes employees day-to-day evaluations of their performance. "Through regular interactions with employees, I am in a good position to know what they have earned and reward them for their performance," says Bilello.

St. Louis-based Maritz Inc. uses a wide variety of flexible reward systems to motivate its 5,500 employees. These performance rewards include

- Merchandise awards
- Incentive travel programs
- Cash bonuses
- Honor and recognition
- Individualized awards

Every employee is exposed to an assortment of reward opportunities, all of which are contingent upon the delivery of specific performances. Sales incentive trips are not restricted to a fixed number of top performers, but can be earned by *every* salesperson who achieves annual objectives.

Nonsales personnel qualify for awards by reaching targeted goals for their business unit. Whether their work is in sales, information processing, copy writing, design, or the mailroom, the performance formula at Maritz remains consistent:

- Identify desired performance criteria.

- Communicate goals and consequences.

- Measure performance frequently.

- Provide feedback and support.

- Reward the achievement of goals.

The successful application of this performance formula can best be demonstrated in the Maritz "Bright Idea" program, during which employees working in seven-member teams generated $10.2 million in cost-reducing and revenue-generating ideas—and earned thousands of merchandise awards for themselves. The top-performing teams earned the ultimate reward: a 60-second "Run-Through-the-Warehouse," where each member gathered a cartload of television sets, videocassette recorders, stereos, and dozens of other items.

The key to managing and improving performance in the complex environment of the future lies in understanding employees' *needs* and *wants*. Cash can handle some of the needs, but the fulfillment of tangible and intangible wants is what ultimately drives performance. In fact, cash often is not an effective motivator.

Add Creativity and Fun to Rewards

Adding creativity and fun to rewards helps establish and maintain an environment that encourages employees to repeat the performance they are being rewarded for.

Wells Fargo Bank has over the past few years acquired and merged with several other banks throughout the state. Recognizing that all employees were required to put in extra effort during these acquisitions, Wells Fargo gave some special rewards to all employees following one major acquisition. "It was late in the year, the holidays were approaching, and our people were exhausted from the extra work. We wanted to do something special," says Jackee McNitt, vice-president and manager of communications services. The program was a series of surprises over a two-week period. First, approximately 20,000 employees received mugs with the inscription, "Take a Break"; inside was a letter of appreciation suggesting that they pace themselves and giving them an extra day off before the end of the year. One week later, all employees received a $100 check, and a week after that, they received an extra week's vacation for the following year.

On another occasion, after a year of record profits, the bank began its "In Good Company" recognition program. First, all salaried employees below the level of senior vice-president with at least one year of service received a $500 bonus with a newsletter emphasizing how much employees were valued. The newsletter described the values that were prized and contained stories reprinted from newsletters dating back to 1912 that recognized employees who epitomized those values. A few days later, employees received a coupon worth $35 and instructions to give the coupon to a co-worker who demonstrated these values prized by the company.

The thirty people who received the most coupons were further recognized. First, they were able to select a special gift from a list of 101 awards. "They were zany things, as well as some very nice items. We wanted to give people awards that would be fun, meaningful, and tailored to their needs. Things like six months of housecleaning or babysitting, a color monitor for your home PC, the CEO to do your job for one day. One person, a receptionist, did have the CEO do her job for a day. It was great fun and our CEO found out what a challenge that job can be," says McNitt.

The thirty winners were brought together twice to be recognized as a group. The first event was selection of their prizes—which they did in the executive dining room to kazoo music—and preparation for the second visit. The second event was a first-class reception attended by the vice-chairman, a few members of the board of directors, and the executive managers of the winners' groups. It included a presentation of the prizes by the CEO and the president. At this reception, the executives were given noisemakers and used them with vigor to loudly recognize these employees. Over a period of two months, newsletter articles featured stories on the winners with quotes from their co-workers describing what they did to deserve the awards. And ten of the thirty participated with the CEO and the president in a videotaped roundtable discussion about a variety of business and personnel issues. The tape was edited to twelve minutes and used later throughout the bank.

"We've made the celebration of successes an important part of our corporate values," says Terry Cohen, senior vice-president of human resources and corporate services for UNUM Corporation, a publicly held specialty insurance company headquartered in Portland, Maine. The company designed a three-tiered approach for rewarding performance consisting of a Chairman's Award, Individual Performance Award, and Division Award.

It is the role of every employee of Blue Cross Blue Shield of Florida (BCBSF) to strive to deliver superior service to members, groups, providers, and internal constituents who are their customers. The purpose of their "MVP" (Most Valuable Player) Recognition Program is to spotlight specific acts of employees of BCBSF who exhibit the attitudes, behaviors, and skills that enable all employees to better serve their internal and external customers. These "players" set an example in delivering superior customer service and, therefore, are helping BCBSF to succeed over its competition.

Players who meet the recognition requirements of this program have taken action that has measurably improved the service provided to customers. Examples of behaviors that meet this criterion include situations where the employee

• Took an important "extra step" to help the customer

• Maintained a positive attitude in a difficult situation

• Followed through on a challenging commitment made to a customer

• Coordinated an innovative solution to a customer's problem

• Anticipated and took action to meet a customer's need

• Prevented a customer service problem

• "Saved" a customer for BCBSF

Players who demonstrate these qualities may be recognized immediately by any member of the management council or may be nominated by any employee to their supervisor.

Those who are selected are awarded an "I'm an MVP" badge and a $20 gift certificate. Each management council member is limited to awarding one MVP per month; additional awards are available with prior approval by the director of operations. As closely as possible to the award presentation, a photograph of each MVP is taken and posted on the Service MVP wall. Management council members who award an MVP include information in their monthly activity report on who was recognized and why.

The Chairman's Award recipients are nominated by their peers. Last year five people were each awarded $5,000 in stock and $2,500 in cash gifts and were honored at a dinner with the board of directors. Individual Performance Awards are requested by managers, who need one other approval to give a spot cash award. Recipients can be nominated by their own managers or by peers and managers in other divisions.

In contrast, Division Awards are budgeted and distributed within one's own division on a quarterly basis. They are considered more a form of recognition than a financial reward. Recipients are chosen by an employee committee.

Jane Carson is one of three UNUM directors in Disability Operations who create informal ways of recognizing employees. "Because our employees are under a lot of pressure and work in a busy and stressful environment, we acknowledge their efforts with fun and spontaneous rewards," says Carson. "For example, we might decide on a Friday to let people go home at 2:00 P.M. or surprise them with refreshments like sandwiches, ice cream, or cake. We sometimes bring in pizzas and guest speakers, and we offer people a chance to share information informally. We give certificates for dinner out or present people with little gifts from our UNUM gift brochure. We recently had a barbecue at a manager's home where everyone received a humorous award. Also, the last week of every quarter, we allow people to wear casual clothes to work and, of course, say 'thanks' and give credit to employees in front of their peers at staff meetings," she adds.

"All of these informal and formal rewards stem from UNUM's corporate visions and values. Senior management has placed a great deal of emphasis on recognition, with a clear message that our most important asset is our people," says Carson.

The company prides itself on hiring highly motivated and skilled employees. At the same time, it recognizes that the opportunity for employees to move up in the organization has plateaued over the last several years, according to Carson. "You have a lot of very qualified employees applying for the same position. Obviously only one person will get the job. The challenge for management is keeping the good employees stimulated by jobs they have, in a sense, outgrown. One of the things we do in our area is to create opportunities within the employee's current job, such as projects or training responsibilities that allow the employees to continue their professional growth. More importantly, we are trying to send the message that we recognize and value the contributions these employees bring to the organization."

Effectiveness and competitiveness in the 1990s will increasingly require managers to gain the commitment and stability of a highly diverse workforce. Rewards are central to meeting employee needs and creating a motivating environment.

PART IV

Informing and Involving People

" *The most important changes for management style are those concerned with education and the desire of employees to have a say in the events and decisions that affect their lives.* **"**

—Edward E. Lawler III,
High-Involvement Management

Mary Watters serves on her company's Excellence Committee, composed of people from various levels and departments. They meet on a regular basis to identify aspects of the organization that require problem solving or barriers that impede the organization's excellence. Mary feels honored to be a part of this group, which meets quarterly with the company's executive committee to review plans and recommendations and to receive approval for actions they wish to take.

Ray Garza is his union's representative to his company's work redesign effort. Ray is receiving special training in economics, work technology, the company's organization, and other subjects that he has never been exposed to before. He's happy to be working for the kind of organization that involves its people and, in the process, helps them to develop and grow.

Yolanda Torres was recently pleased when her boss's boss called on her to assist in developing certain information and recommendations for a special report to the board of directors. She was further honored when this vice-president asked her to attend the meeting and make the presentation.

Gabe Pahinui knew that his company needed to cut costs and might have to lay people off. But instead of just informing employees of what might happen, the company asked them for their involvement to help improve the economic situation. He and six co-workers formed a special task force to review all aspects of cost and to find options other than layoffs. Through their work they were able to reduce operational costs by 10 percent and to redesign work so that attrition would eliminate the need for layoffs.

People today want greater control over their lives and are eager to participate in matters that affect their jobs. Television, computers, and higher educational levels have raised people's expectations. They want to know what's going on, why it's going on, and how it affects them. Many want more than to be informed; they want to help decide what they will be doing and determine how they can be most effective.

Employee participation not only fits in with workers' values; it is also cost effective. For example, Lawler (1986) cites the case of an American manufacturing facility that was sold to a Japanese company and converted to a participative style. Over time, productivity doubled and defects were reduced from 150 percent to 2 percent. Many major companies—such as Motorola, Ford, Westinghouse, and Xerox—have committed themselves to participative approaches. The U.S. Department of Labor runs public service ads to help employees benefit from involvement. This growing trend is geared toward improving organizational effectiveness. In particular, research has focused on the positive impact of involvement on motivation, satisfaction, acceptance of change, problem solving, and communication (Lawler, 1986).

In an earlier study, Lawler, Renwick, and Bullock (1981) identified what people want to influence. Determining how to do their own work topped the list, followed by scheduling their work; giving raises; hiring, firing, and promoting others; and making organizational policy. The differences between how much influence people felt they should have on these decisions and how much they actually did have often turned out to be quite significant. These general attitudes, coupled with higher levels of education and a more mature workforce,

help to to establish today's participative ethic.

At the heart of any effective participation program are four components: power, knowledge, information, and rewards (Lawler, 1986). Participation works when people are given the *power* to make certain decisions, the *knowledge* and *skills* to make them effectively, the necessary *information,* and meaningful *rewards* for their effort.

Most of today's workers want and expect to be involved in decision making that affects their jobs. However, some prefer to put in their "nine to five" and go home to other aspects of their life, while still others come from cultures that cause them to be uncomfortable with involvement. When organizations begin to involve employees in decision making—from items of major concern to company picnics—care must be taken to allow flexibility for those who prefer not to be involved. Care must also be taken to respect cultural and ethnic preferences.

For example, Asian cultures generally value deference to authority. Thus, Asians may find it difficult to challenge decisions made by management—even when it would be preferable to do so. This was the case at one city government organization. A group of employees didn't seem to be performing at the required level, and management requested an assessment to determine what training was needed. The assessment revealed that the deficiency was not in the employees' competence to perform the work, but in the communication between management and the workers, who were mostly Asian. Management gave rather vague instructions, assuming that the employees would ask questions or offer alternative methods. Instead they followed the vague instructions and were perceived as incompetent.

There are many ways to involve employees, provide them with information, and reward them, including these two key action areas:

- Share information and encourage participation.
- Create new ways to share responsibility.

In the following two chapters, you will learn how to put each of these key actions into practice.

12

Share Information and Encourage Participation

IN THEIR REPORT on reward systems and productivity, the American Productivity Center stated: "In order to be productive, committed members of an organization, employees need more, and better, information about their jobs, business conditions, customers and competitors. Unfortunately, managers are often reluctant to 'open the books' to employees. But without this information, employees are unable to make the best decisions in their jobs, or see the relationship between their performance, the performance of their firms, and the rewards they receive" (American Productivity Center, 1983, p. 1).

With the increasing use of print and electronic media, organizations can communicate information more easily. Many organizations are tapping into newer methods of communication and are involving employees in these methods. At Apple, quarterly teleconferencing meetings are held to keep employees abreast of new product and industry developments as well as company news. "We tell employees what's going on. This builds their trust and commitment," says Debbie Biondolillo, vice-president for human resources.

Information is also shared via AppleLinks, which employees can access with their computer terminals. Two features of the system are a bulletin board that keeps employees up to date on information and events and an electronic mail service for sending messages and discussing issues and problems.

At Security Pacific Corporation, single-page newsletters are available daily on industry, economy, the marketplace, and news about competitors, with updates on the bank's products, programs, and activities. Divisions also have their own regular vehicles for keeping employees informed.

Tandem is committed to a high level of communication with its employees to make sure that everyone understands the business and new developments. It was a corporate pioneer in setting up its own television studio (TTN) for educating and informing employees and customers. Tandem has developed a number of creative programs that are completely conducted by its executives and employees.

"First Friday," a live monthly program, uses prerecorded segments and a talk show format to share information on new products, programs, and changes in company policies or product strategies. This show is broadcast to 100 North American sites.

Another show, "Frontline Live," reports on individual product developments and marketing programs. This program is offered for Tandem's U.S. sales force and its customers and features live call-in opportunities.

In addition to the television broadcasts, the company encourages communication by holding "town meetings" on a rotating basis at all Tandem buildings (plants, development sites, and offices). This interactive forum is hosted by company executives for the purpose of hearing and responding to employees' questions, concerns, and suggestions on any aspect of the business.

Some Xerox teleconferences feature signing for hearing-impaired employees. Xerox's Teamwork Day, teleconferenced via Xerox Education Networks (XEN), its satellite broadcast system, to the major Xerox locations, features presentations of its Team Excellence Award to work teams who have made significant contributions to the corporation.

The California State Lottery's "Video Magazine," produced six times a year, helps keep its 1,200 employees, located throughout the state, up to date on lottery activities and changes. The twenty-minute magazines contain several vignettes that feature changes in policy or direction, product information, stories on departments or individual employees, sales projections and results, and other topics. Periodically, magazine supplements are produced. Most departments schedule showings during staff meetings. Other employees view the magazine during open showings and some borrow the video for home viewing.

"The magazine's quality equals that of a commercial broadcast," says Wayne Appleman, chief of staff and organization development. "We believe that our quality—content and production—needs to be equal to what people see as today's standard. The high quality of the magazine models the high-quality performance we want from all employees.

"The benefits are many. Because it's more personal than written communication, it ties people to the organization by literally providing an opportunity for people to see what's important. People in the field love it. Management is able to communicate messages in more subtle ways. For example, just by consciously showcasing our ethnically diverse workforce, we show all employees that we value our diversity. People today want to know more about their organization and the video is just one of twenty-five to thirty tools we use. It seems that employee appetites for information are never satisfied," adds Appleman.

Keeping people informed shows respect for them and provides them with more information to use in carrying out their job, thereby enhancing their capability to be effective. Some of the methods involve company-wide systems and all of them change traditional management practices on informing people.

Facilitate Top-Down and Bottom-Up Communication

Both top-down and bottom-up communication are important to implementing FLEX-MANAGEMENT. Many organizations are making special efforts to assure that quality, two-way communication takes place.

The Boise, Idaho, branch of Argonaut Insurance Company, a Workers' Compensation insurance company headquartered in San Mateo, California, recently set up an Advisory Board Committee. After hearing of its success in other branch offices, Hugh Phillips, division manager, took the lead in providing a forum for employees to bring their complaints and suggestions to management. The committee is made up of the division manager, the human resources manager, and three other employees who were randomly selected and are neither managers nor supervisors.

Ore-Ida Foods established a "Fellows Program" in 1982 as a strategy to encourage innovation among employees by freeing them from corporate red tape. Each year the company allocates $200,000 to be split among five "Fellows," who can reduce the red tape of corporate bureaucracy. They are approached by employees (known as "Idea Champions") who are looking for funding, seed money, or advice on how to proceed with an idea. Fellows may accept or reject ideas as they see fit and may provide funds for the various projects.

The Fellows themselves are selected from different company locations for two-year terms. They are typically managerial employees, who are chosen by the other Fellows and approved by the management board on the basis of their knowledge of the workings of the company and their accessibility to other employees.

In the program's seven-year history, twenty-four different Fellows have disbursed a total of $910,000 to more than 420 projects by enterprising employees.

Phillips feels that the committee is long overdue and benefits him as much as the employees. "I see this as an excellent way to get candid feedback from employees without management interference. As a manager, if you don't know how employees think and feel, you are more likely to make mistakes that cost you down the road."

He also thinks that there is less risk for managers who back employee-initiated ideas. "I firmly believe that if you make employees part of the decision-making process, the entire company is likely to be more successful." Phillips's role as a member is to redirect and/or inform the committee of its limitations. "I'm also there to lend management credibility to employees' ideas, which helps them feel that their efforts are worthwhile and their suggestions are legitimate."

Ensuring top-down as well as bottom-up communication is important to national retailer J.C. Penney Co., Inc. At corporate headquarters in Dallas, Texas, senior management holds quarterly participation meetings to share information on organizational activities as well as to listen to employee concerns and suggestions.

"JCPenney is a very participative organization," says Betty Ann Catanzaro, manager for human resource development. "Since our founding, involvement at all levels has been encouraged throughout the company. The participation meetings are just one vehicle for two-way communication with JCPenney associates."

Typically, a senior manager meets with ten to fifteen staff members on a quarterly basis. Meetings are informal and run without an agenda. Managers have the opportunity to discuss issues of importance to their department and the company as a whole and to solicit input from participants. These meetings are a two-way process—top down as well as bottom up. Employees have the opportunity to share concerns and receive immediate feedback from their manager. Questions or concerns that cannot be resolved during the meeting are researched and answered by the next meeting.

Managers may hold as many as six meetings quarterly depending on the size of their staff, according to Catanzaro. Each quarter there is a different mix of employees, allowing them to interact and discuss issues with a variety of people. Sessions with support staff are usually held separately in order to assure an open, participative environment. The notes from all the meetings a specific manager conducts in a quarter are consolidated and distributed to anyone who attended one of the meetings.

Tandem executives want direct input from employees on how well their management is working. Employees are surveyed every six months to provide feedback on twenty key items, including their manager's performance, how they feel about their job, and their understanding of Tandem's business strategies.

Use Informal Approaches

In today's fast-paced environment there often isn't time to hold formal problem-solving meetings. Informal, quick approaches to solving problems and resolving conflicts—especially when they are done with a creative twist—are an effective alternative.

Powwows are part of Southwest Texas Methodist Hospital's pharmacy department. Powwows are brief impromptu problem-solving meetings that may be called at any time by any member of the pharmacy staff. Their purposes are to facilitate problem solving, improve patient care, increase productivity, and involve all pharmacy employees in the decision-making process. Powwows use the following policies and procedures:

1. Powwows may be called to discuss only patient care or job-related issues.

2. Any pharmacy employee who is concerned about a work-related or patient-care-related issue may call for a powwow.

3. A powwow is called by simply announcing it. The employees who are involved will complete all work that cannot wait and join the powwow.

4. The person calling a powwow is the powwow leader. The leader's responsibilities are to state the problem, lead the discussion, keep the discussion orderly, and assure that the powwow is brief and that all employees return to work promptly.

5. Powwows are always brief—no more than five minutes. If the problem cannot be discussed and resolved in less than five minutes, the powwow is not the proper forum.

6. The powwow can be a policy-making forum and may result in a change in the department's written policies and procedures. However, a powwow must be presented to and approved by the pharmacy supervisors and staff before official departmental policy is changed.

7. It is also the powwow leader's responsibility to inform a supervisor, the assistant director, or the director about the problem and the solutions that were discussed during the powwow. This information will be presented at the next supervisors' meeting and staff meeting.

8. The final results of a powwow will be presented to the powwow leader by the department's director. Any new or revised policies and procedures will be approved by the powwow leader and the department's director.

Create the Vision Together

The vision or strategic plan of most organizations usually involves the top management team and sometimes includes middle

Involving all of your employees in planning an annual company event may seem like a monumental, overwhelming task. Telephone Marketing Programs of New York City, the largest Yellow Pages advertising agency, does just that—successfully involving more than 250 people in the process.

"A series of planning meetings is held involving virtually all employees at every level," says Lucy Suarez, personnel generalist. "We involve people in preplanning meetings to brainstorm ideas and suggestions for the coming year's event. By getting many people involved in the planning process we gain insight into the issues and concerns facing our employees. This information helps management test the pulse of the organization and helps set the backdrop for the annual meeting."

Employees generate ideas for the meeting's theme as well as ways to carry it out. The 1990 annual meeting included colorful flags printed with each department's goal for growth. Since the 1990 meeting in March, a permanent Goals Committee has been set up to monitor departmental goals and departmental flags are displayed around the office as a visual reminder of these goals.

"By involving employees at all levels and providing many opportunities for input, we pulled off a very successful event and set the stage for future planning efforts," says Nancie Cheppo, director of human resources.

managers. Becoming sensitive to the needs of the diverse workforce includes involving all managers and employees in contributing to the organization's direction, vision, and values. An example is Apple's New Enterprise Values task force, which is addressing what the company will look like in the twenty-first century. It considers such topics as the organizational infrastructure and the changing role of the manager.

The County of Santa Clara, California—home to innovative Silicon Valley—has invested time and resources to encourage over 2,000 managers to focus on vision and values and to understand how the systems of the county operate. These topics were rarely discussed in the past. Now people have a better understanding of their own relationship and contribution to the organizational mission. "We've moved beyond what leaders say and write, to paying attention to what leaders do," says Bob Farnquist, director of staff development. "We learned a lot, but especially that people support what they participate in and are committed to."

Don't Forget Temporary and Contract Employees

With competitive and economic forces encouraging the use of flexible staffing, the workforce of many organizations now includes a variety of nonregular employees. Temporary workers, independent contractors, "leased" employees, consultants, and employees of outside service firms— security, janitorial, and data processing, for example—are just a few of the outside workers who become part of the company's work process.

Martin Babinec, president of TriNet Employer Group, a provider of employee leasing services, sees the fast growth of outside workers bringing an additional set of challenges to managers and organizations. "A manager cannot afford to ignore the needs and concerns of contracted workers, especially when they are performing duties right alongside a company's regular staff."

Xerox Corporation's customer and marketing education department uses contractors to work on projects for its internal clients. This enables Xerox managers to adjust the number of staff needed at any given time according to the number of projects to be done. According to Carlene Reinhart, manager of the Instructional Technology Development Group, "This process has significant economic benefit to the corporation and works well if we are sensitive to involving contractors according to their desired level as well as our needs. Some contractors would prefer to be employees and others prefer the flexibility of working on a temporary or part-time basis. They definitely need to be involved in decisions that affect their work, and we always invite them to staff luncheons and other social events. But there are gray areas, such as informal discussions on benefits and employee incentives. Since they aren't employees, we must be sensitive when discussing those matters, particularly if the contractor desires employment status."

Tom St. Clair, a project manager in Xerox's ITD Group, changed from contractor to employee status. "One of the most important considerations is to avoid making artificial distinctions between what an employee can do and what a contractor can do. Ask if it's really necessary for contractors to wear different-colored badges, for example. And managers need to be sensitive to the fact that both contractors and employees are present at some meetings. I remember one meeting where the topic of discussion was how much the success of our efforts could increase employee profit sharing. As a contractor, that was not a motivator for me, since I didn't participate in profit sharing," explains St. Clair. Other suggestions to managers include individualizing motivation for each contractor on a project, being aware and honest about project status and performance, including the contractor in team-building activities, and offering access to company recreational facilities. The organization should also consider creating a path through which contractors can become employees.

13

Create New Ways to Share Responsibility

PROGRESSIVE ORGANIZATIONS
are seeking more creative ways
of achieving participation and,
through that, greater productivity. The use of self-managed
work teams and employee
ownership plans are examples
of creative techniques that are
gaining in popularity.

Emphasize Teamwork

Self-managing work teams—an ideal option for meaningful participation—become a core element of newer organizational forms.

Ed Kur, president of Phoenix Associates, Inc., an Arizona-based consulting firm, writes, "Many organizations are fostering self management due to an increase in the level of global competition and the corresponding requirement to produce more goods and services of higher quality at lower cost. When properly designed and appropriately nurtured, these teams provide a substantial competitive advantage in the marketplace, as well as a human or social advantage in the workplace" (Kur, 1989, pp. 1–2).

A self-managing work team is a group of people who plan, control, and conduct their own work. Basically, self-management is a relative matter, with shades of autonomous decision making and problem solving. Tasks can be completed with substantial input from other management, or with little or no input.

Providing superior customer service to internal as well as external clients is a key goal for many companies of the 1990s. Ten teams of the operations support department at Dow Jones meet once a month to identify and resolve the concerns of their internal customers, which represent the eighteen *Wall Street Journal* printing plants. The teams are made up of trainers, technicians, buyers, and clerks.

"When the department was reorganized, we merged employees from five departments together," says manager Celia Currin. "My goal is to develop our own culture with new loyalties and to let people get acquainted with their colleagues and their skills.

"The Focus teams help to break communication barriers and open people's eyes to the big picture. They can see the importance of their jobs to larger departmental goals as well as gain exposure and knowledge of other functional areas of the department.

"I know that once a month all people in the department who affect the quality of our service on a particular product will bring together their individual perspectives," she concludes.

Participative management not only increases efficiency and productivity, but increases the bottom line as well, attests Gene Hendrickson, general manager for Oregon-based Tektronix. An organizational change that instituted participative work teams in a newly built factory in 1981 helped to boost plant sales from $20 million to a record $62 million in 1989.

In June 1981 Hendrickson was hired to oversee the building and operation of a new printed circuit board facility and to install a new work system. A year later a training program was begun to equip employees with the communication skills and organizational knowledge necessary to run participative work teams. "Many people didn't see the connection

From 1982 to 1986, Aid Association for Lutherans expanded its workforce by 40 percent to keep up with business volume. By 1987, the family-style organization was becoming increasingly bureaucratic—an unwanted characteristic—and the company made a commitment to participative management.

Faced with a need to reduce its workforce while at the same time speeding up the processing of insurance cases by 1,900 field agents, the company reorganized and regionalized its insurance products services division (500 employees) and field administration services division (50 employees). Formerly life insurance was handled by one section, health insurance by a second, and support services—such as billing and policy loans—by a third.

Under the new system, the insurance department is divided into five groups, each serving agents in a different region. Each group consists of three or four teams of twenty to thirty employees who together can perform all of the 167 tasks that formerly were split among the three functional sections. Team members are cross-trained to learn skills that link the once-divided functional tasks. The time required to process complicated cases has been cut by as much as fifteen days. Field agents or district representatives now deal solely with one team and develop close relationships with its members.

The team approach has enabled AAL to compress the management hierarchy and redistribute decision making to the lowest levels. As a result fifty-five jobs have been eliminated as team members have taken on additional managerial responsibilities. The displaced managers have found new jobs elsewhere in the company or have retired.

between their job and how it fit into the overall product line. The training program was designed to expand people's job focus by providing this missing link as well as to build confidence in interpersonal communication."

Sixty employees representing six different operations were elected by their peers to participate in the eighteen-day training program, which continued for over six months.

"The participants really developed an esprit de corps. They were able to take their learning experiences back to their work groups and become effective facilitators of change."

After startup of operations in the mid-1980s, work teams were charged with developing and writing job descriptions that reflected this different work style. "This was a complicated task which required the group to involve many other employees in the process," says Hendrickson.

A steering committee, made up of management and nonmanagement employees from a cross-section of functional areas, was formed to develop a new compensation system. This group formed subcommittees that documented the responsibilities and competencies for all plant jobs. A job evaluation committee was formed to evaluate each job in order to determine the relative worth of the position in Tektronix's pay grade structure.

In 1985 Ohio-based Globe Metallurgical Inc. set out to become the lowest-cost, highest-quality producer of ferroalloys and silicon metal in the United States. At the same time, the firm shifted its focus from commodity markets, such as steel manufacturing, to higher-value-added markets, represented by the ferroalloy, chemical, and aluminum industries.

The quality improvement program began with statistical process control training that same year. This training laid the foundation for a company-wide improvement system that was termed Quality, Efficiency, and Cost (QEC).

The QEC program is fully integrated into Globe's strategic planning and research-and-development activities. Quality committees exist at every level within the company from top management's steering committee to the workers' quality circles, which meet weekly.

At each of Globe's two plants is a QEC committee composed of the plant manager and department heads. The committee meets each morning to review the previous day's performance. It assesses the causes of out-of-control conditions, reviews corrective measures, evaluates suggestions made by quality circles, and addresses the broader quality issues that might be raised by the steering committee.

The QEC program has suffered no lack of good ideas for improving quality and reducing cost, many of them originating with workers. Improvement measures are carefully tracked, and the results—successes and failures—are published monthly.

Customer service is strongly emphasized. All employees meet with customers, and it is common for employees to visit their customers, tour their facilities, and gain an understanding of how Globe's products match the customer's requirements. As a result of these quality improvement efforts, customer complaints have decreased by 90 percent since 1985.

Globe received the Malcolm Baldrige National Quality Award in 1988, and today it occupies a quality niche above the competition. The company's sales in Canada and Europe, as well as its U.S. market share, have risen dramatically. In quality audits by General Motors, Ford, and other customers, Globe has received certified supplier status.

"Because of the high level of employee involvement, the project took longer than a traditional project. However, this up-front involvement facilitated a very smooth implementation of new job classifications," explains Hendrickson.

"Today there are thirty-five or forty teams representing more than 650 employees. Approximately ten of these teams are institutionalized, while the balance are ad hoc in nature. The teams receive minimum direction from myself or senior plant management. The structure of the teams is organic in nature, changing quickly and easily to focus on the business issues at hand," says Hendrickson.

"During the past nine years we've developed literally hundreds of people in the areas of problem solving, group leadership, and facilitation. My job now is to sustain the participative management effort and lobby for consistent direction with senior management."

In order for any of the various forms of employee participation to work, there must be a shift in both attitude and skills for managers and employees alike. While a policy shift may also be needed in the case of such forms as participative or self-managed teams, the two most important requirements for successful employee involvement are (1) a change in management practices and (2) training in collaboration and in ways for employees to work together in groups.

Support Employee Ownership

One increasingly popular way for people to feel more involved in their organization is to share in its successes and failures through various forms of performance-based rewards—including gainsharing plans (such as profit sharing, Scanlon, Rucker, and Improshare) and special bonuses—or through full employee ownership of the organization.

According to the American Productivity Center (1983, p. 13):

> Gainsharing is often associated with a greater degree of employee and union contribution to management decisions. Where there is gainsharing, the quality of management decisions is of direct concern to workers. Bad decisions cut the gains to be shared.
>
> Evidence suggests that linking participative work practices and gainsharing produces superior results.
>
> A [New York Stock Exchange] study revealed that gainsharing companies (with 500 or more employees) have:
>
> • A much higher proportion of Quality Circles
>
> • A greater level of employee involvement in decision-making than companies generally.

Avis, Inc., is one of the largest companies in America owned by its employees. Since the creation of an Employee Stock Ownership Plan (ESOP) in September 1987, stock values and operating profits have soared along with employee morale, productivity, and service.

"Just creating an ESOP isn't going to make you a better company. It's how you involve the employees, maintain a dialogue, listen to their input, and use it," says chairman Joseph V. Vittoria. Vittoria spends two to three days per month visiting Avis's offices, briefing employees on business development, and answering questions.

Since the buyout, Avis has organized employee participation groups (EPGs) as a conduit for ideas to solve business-related problems, as well as a vehicle for management to convey policies and identify areas needing improvement.

Omak Wood Products, a small company producing plywood and other wood products, is located in rural Omak, Washington. Previously owned by Cavenham Industries and Crown Zellerbach, Omak set up an ESOP in 1988 when it faced being put on the auction block by its owner, Sir James Goldsmith.

The buyout was led by Local 3023 of the Lumber, Plywood and Industrial Workers Union, which represents approximately 90 percent of Omak's 650-person workforce. The goals of the ESOP, which owns 60 percent of the stock, were local ownership, job security for its employees, and community stability.

A significant challenge for the organization was to help clarify the meaning of ownership to its employees. As an owner under the ESOP, each employee is responsible for company profits and productivity. Individual and collective performance is rewarded with stock ownership.

A communications committee, made up of salaried and hourly employees elected by their peers, was set up to channel information about the ESOP throughout the organization and to set up participative networks to share information.

Monthly meetings now serve as a forum where employees ask questions of the company's president. Newsletters, semiannual reports, and other publications disseminate information about the ESOP. A new logo advertises the employee ownership.

Joint committees addressing business planning, product improvement, and safety have been set up to involve employees and encourage them to share their expertise at every level, from the smallest production crew to the board of directors.

Training workshops are being held to help front-line supervisors and managers with the problem-solving, team-building, and communication skills necessary for the transition to participative management.

The EPGs are made up of representatives from each class of line worker, from mechanics to rental agents. The groups meet monthly at each of Avis's company-owned locations. The local groups also elect representatives to attend quarterly zone meetings, semiannual regional meetings, and an annual meeting.

Scores of valuable ideas have surfaced through the EPGs, which have in turn saved the company thousands of dollars. By carrying out the ideas that have been generated, management gives employees both the opportunity to assume new duties and the means to follow through with them.

Another channel for employee-management communication is the One More program. Employees who have suggestions simply mail them in on a postcard. The suggestions go directly to Chairman Vittoria and then are filtered down to the appropriate division.

Robert Salerno, field operations vice-president, claims that the ESOP participation process has changed the manager's role, calling for management to be more participative. The company has started a training program to address this issue.

In September 1988, after fifty-seven years as a family-owned business, Wyatt Cafeterias, Inc., set up an ESOP and made shareholders out of every employee on its payroll.

Creation of a 100 percent ESOP prompted the need for a deep cultural change within the organization, according to David Dostart, director of ownership development. The first part of the change process involved an intensive communication effort to educate the employees on the ESOP concept. Videotapes, posters, and company newsletters explained the principles of stock ownership as well as the benefits of the ESOP. Workers now receive quarterly statements that keep them up to date on their account balance and stock price.

Increased employee involvement was also essential to creating the new culture. All employees—dishwashers, servers, and cooks—needed to know that their performance affected company profits. Employees who demonstrate innovation or give extra service are now highlighted in a company video newsletter.

To encourage participation, each cafeteria has a committee that handles suggestions from employees and customers, and that acts as a liaison to the corporate office.

General managers of cafeterias receive training in participative management, learning about the importance of allowing relevant experts lower in the organization to make decisions and of sharing communication up and down the organization.

It is interesting to note that when ESOPs are put in place, the techniques described in this chapter and in Chapter Twelve—informing and involving employees—result in an increase in responsibility by employees and a change in the policies of the organization.

PART V

Supporting Lifestyle and Life Needs

" *The complicated lives of workers, for better or worse, will become a corporate affair with employers helping see them through personal crises or family turmoil. Such assistance will have little to do with benevolence and everything to do with the bottom line.* **"**

—"How the Next Decade Will Differ," *Business Week*, September 25, 1989

Joe and Michelle are a two-career couple. For years their two benefit programs have overlapped— Joe's health plan covers Michelle and hers covers Joe—yet they still haven't had the flexibility to meet their real needs. Now, with flex-benefits programs from both of their employers, they are able to balance their benefits: Joe takes more of the insurance, and both of them can now take an extra week of vacation. Michelle has added a financial planning service into her package, which has organized the financial side of their life and given them peace of mind about future savings and retirement plans.

When Chin Yee's company built its new headquarters, the company arranged to have its offices connected to a variety of shops and businesses. Now Chin can go to the drugstore, dry cleaners, tailor, shoe repair shop, and supermarket when he arrives in the morning, during lunch, or at the end of the workday. These conveniences are an incentive for Chin to work there, as it leaves him more free time on the weekends to spend with his family.

Bruce Jaffey was becoming increasingly irritable and frustrated. He had a long daily commute, and at work there was a great deal of noise and too many disruptions for the kind of detailed, concentrated work that he needed to do. Then he found out that flextime and flexplace arrangements were available. He established a schedule of working at home on detailed projects that required concentration, while still maintaining core hours in the middle of the week to work on team projects. On the days when he commuted, Bruce scheduled his hours so that he could avoid rush hour traffic jams and shorten his commuting time.

Naomi Shirai had to use up her sick leave when one of her children was ill and had to stay home from school. As a result of a company survey and the input of focus groups on the needs of the changing workforce, Naomi discovered that she was not alone. More than half of the women in the company had been struggling with the same issues. In response, the company changed its policies, granting employees up to ten days per year of personal leave time in addition to their sick leave allotment.

———

The fourth FLEX-MANAGEMENT strategy for aligning management

and the workforce involves supporting employees' lives and lifestyles. People have an increasingly wide array of personal obligations, such as combining work and child rearing, commuting, continuing education, or elder care. Also, with demographic and value shifts, there is now a wider array of lifestyle choices, including how to use free time, how to balance the various parts of one's life, where to live, and how much money to make.

The array varies greatly even within a seemingly homogeneous group—dual-career couples. The requirements of these couples vary according to whether or not children are present, the ages of the children, whether one or both partners have children from a previous marriage, the income earned by the partners, and the couple's skill in integrating two careers into one family life. "Employers can't ignore the work/family conflicts of dual-career couples. If couples have more stress at home, it only stands to reason that there will be more turnover, absenteeism, tardiness, and distractions, all of which decrease productivity and ultimately profits," says Joan H. Linder, a consultant specializing in the integration of work and family (Linder, 1988, p. D-2).

Underlying this strategy is the recognition that people are assets to the organization and that the world of work can never be fully separated from the rest of one's life. Organizations must pay attention to all of their employees' needs to help them work in a productive and satisfying way.

It should be clear that there are many different ways to support the employees' diverse lifestyle and life needs. Many of these approaches require the organization to make a considerable financial commitment. Every organization must balance these costs with the advantages of new programs. Increasingly, it has been shown that organizational support is a key factor in a person's decision to accept employment with an organization and that it has a significant influence on retention of employees.

Managers can take action in the following ways:

- Offer flexible employee benefits and services.

- Help employees take care of family responsibilities.

14

Offer Flexible Employee Benefits and Services

THE WORLD OF BENEFITS has been changing significantly. In some ways, it represents the most widespread organizational response to the changing workforce. Over the past twenty years, many benefits have come to be seen as entitlements, and over the next twenty years, many newly appearing benefits will become standard (Selbert, 1988). Many employers will be offering new benefits that reflect the changing needs, values, and lifestyles of their workers. For example, many workers may prefer more autonomy over more money, leading to increases in flexplace and flextime.

Many other possibilities for future benefits have been suggested or anticipated (Salisbury, 1982; Employee Benefits Research Institute, 1989), including such employee support ideas as

- More on-site well and sick child care

- Expanded options to assist with elder care

- More health and wellness programs

- Flexible arrangements concerning workplace and schedule to balance family needs

- More job and schedule designs to allow for variations on retirement (such as early, partial, or phased retirement)

- Part-time work to provide more options for expanded maternity/paternity leaves

- More financial planning assistance for work and retirement years

- Greater employer assistance with obtaining or disposing of housing

Design Flex-Benefits Programs

People's needs today vary greatly depending on their age, marital status, and living arrangements, and on whether or not they have children. Benefits programs have traditionally been designed for a principal wage earner with a wife and children at home. Now the number of single-parent and dual-wage-earner families has increased substantially and the same benefits package no longer satisfies all employees. There has been an enormous amount of duplicate coverage, leading to resentment among employees and adding to everyone's expense. Organizations have been increasingly pressured to add benefits that appeal to only a few of their employees—a practice that does not maximize benefits dollars. Flex-benefits programs offer employees choices of medical, dental, and disability insurance coverage, as well as vacation, sick, and personal leave; wellness and recreational options; parental care; retirement programs; financial planning; legal assistance; and pre-tax accounts for dependent care. People prefer to be able to make choices, to customize their benefits, and to gain more control over part of their life. By offering flexible benefits, organizations are not only responding to their employees' needs; they are also containing what would otherwise be increasing benefits costs.

Procter & Gamble's FlexibleCare Plan gives employees three options for health care. They can choose from a Base Plan or two options, depending on their individual requirements.

Under the Base Plan, an employee can choose any doctor or hospital for care, paying 20 percent of the costs after a yearly deductible has been met. The High Deductible Plan offers the same coverage with a higher up-front deductible and a rebate at the end of the year.

On the Dual Choice Plan, the employee can choose among a network of health care providers, paying a small monthly premium but no deductible for services, or can revert to the Base Plan and pay 20 percent for services.

Another P&G benefits program is FlexComp. Under this program, the employee receives flex dollars, based on salary and years of service, which can be spent on a variety of benefits including long-term care insurance, IRAs, vision care, additional dental or medical care, child and elder dependent care, extra vacation, or cash. Employees can redesign their coverage as their circumstances change from year to year.

The Commerce Clearing House points out that organizations are implementing flex-benefits programs for a variety of reasons such as (1) containing costs, (2) providing a greater choice for employees, (3) aiding recruitment, (4) improving the organization's image, and (5) easing the pressure for additional benefits from some segments of the workforce (Commerce Clearing House, 1988). The following examples illustrate how flex-benefits programs assist both the organization and its employees.

The flexible policies of Ventura County, California, have been beneficial to women on maternity leave and mothers easing back into their jobs. Keith Turner, director of the county's planning department, was flexible and creative in keeping productivity on track when five women in his department became pregnant last year, a challenge that he says was a good learning experience.

"I see now that we can devise a maternity plan that makes sense for us. With the support of the personnel department I was able to manage a department with a job vacancy rate of 20 percent, which was further affected by overlapping maternity leaves. We brought in a temporary workforce and shifted job assignments and case loads to meet our short- and long-term needs. For those employees who needed to maintain two incomes, we allowed the mothers to continue their jobs while they were at home with their babies. We let them work at home on a part-time basis and, in some cases, work on interim projects throughout their leave. In terms of productivity and benefit to management, the women who had worked at home during their leave were back up to speed soon after they returned to the office."

Steelcase offers its employees a "cafeteria style" benefits plan that enables them to tailor benefits to meet specific needs. Employees are allotted benefits dollars and allowed to select from a menu of choices.

There are eight medical plans, three dental options, and various forms of long- and short-term disability and life insurance options.

Security Pacific Corporation provides its employees with an allotment of "benefit dollars" that are used to purchase benefits. Some of the benefits that employees can select are medical, dental, and vision coverage; life insurance; long-term disability coverage; and vacation benefits. They can also set up a personal spending account to pay for health care and dependent care expenses with pre-tax dollars.

Under Apple's FlexBenefits program, employees can design their health benefits package. The available options include various medical plans, vision care, substance abuse rehabilitation, dental coverage, life insurance, and a flexible spending account for dependent care.

Flex-benefits need not be limited to large corporations. Even small companies can maximize their use of benefits dollars and accommodate their employees.

BGS Systems, Inc., a 130-employee computer systems software development company in Waltham, Massachusetts, is one of the first small companies in the United States to introduce flex-benefits. In 1985, with the help of a consultant and insurer, the company designed and implemented the BGS Flexible Benefits Plan.

Prior to implementation of this plan, rising medical and dental costs had prompted the company to survey its employees about benefits. They found that many employees didn't need full medical coverage because they had working spouses who were insured.

The new program offers three options for medical coverage: a more expensive plan with no deductible; a less expensive plan with a substantial deductible; and, for employees covered by other insurance, a rebate of their unused benefits dollars. A pre-tax reimbursement account is set up for employees to pay for premiums, deductibles, and noncovered items as well as for dependent care.

"Offering flex-benefits is a win-win situation for BGS," says Ted Kelley, director of human resources. "Creating options for employees demonstrates good faith, eliminates waste, and helps us compete with larger computer companies in the area."

Expand Employee Services

To the traditional employee assistance programs, employee cafeterias, entertainment tickets, company merchandise, and educational assistance, many organizations are adding more health, fitness, transportation, and recreational services. One way to offer this added variety is through referral services that include special arrangements with stores,

The U.S. Forest Service, Willamette National Forest, offers an exercise program to employees that appeals to their pocketbooks and their schedules. Employees can take an hour and a half of government-paid time per week for exercise. "The conditions are that they match paid exercise time with their own time, that they go through a health risk analysis, have a medical release to participate, and write up a wellness contract with their supervisor about how they will use the program," says Keith Epstein, employee development specialist. They may also receive $25 per month to match expenditures on health club membership fees, if they include the membership fees in their wellness contract.

health clubs, and other organizations. Another way is for the company itself to provide the services.

Steelcase has an on-site medical center staffed by two full-time physicians, one part-time physician, and eighteen nurses at its headquarters in Grand Rapids, Michigan. The mini-hospital is open twenty-four hours Monday through Saturday and is equipped for minor surgery, audio and pulmonary testing, physical therapy, and injury rehabilitation. There are also four Steelcase satellite medical centers in outlying plants.

Camp Swampy, a 1,700-acre recreation area with forty-two campsites, is available to Grand Rapids employees free of charge. Employees can also join a company-owned health facility that offers a swimming pool, weight room, and aerobics classes as well as health testing and wellness programs.

Ethicon offers a comprehensive "Live for Life" wellness program to its 6,000 U.S. employees. Enrollees undergo a lifestyle assessment before being eligible to participate in the program. "The lifestyle assessment focuses on wellness, versus the traditional physical exam which focuses on disease," says Dr. George Lutz, Ethicon's medical director. "The aim of our program is disease prevention and a healthy lifestyle. The key to its success is establishing a corporate culture that values wellness."

Ethicon's Live for Life Center is located at company headquarters in Somerville, New Jersey. Open six days a week, the center houses two meeting rooms, a workout room containing the most up-to-date fitness equipment, a gymnasium, a separate aerobics studio, and shower and locker facilities. Trained professionals guide employees in a physical fitness regimen and lead educational programs on such topics as aerobics, nutrition, stress management, weight control, smoking cessation, alcohol and drug abuse, parenting, and infant and toddler health.

"More than 50 percent of our hourly and salaried employees in the United States take advantage of the program and facilities," says Lutz. Sales personnel who are not located near a plant facility receive $100 a year toward membership in a local health club.

Investing in employee wellness has paid off for Ethicon. In 1989 Johnson & Johnson reported that the program saved $378 per employee by lowering absenteeism and decreasing health care expenses.

In highly congested areas and where the geographical spread or housing prices require people to live long distances from their place of employment, a number of employers have found that organizing and supporting a vanpool program is attractive to many employees. Companies in the Los Angeles area such as Aerospace Corporation, Transamerica, and Southern California Edison have had success with these programs. This practice not only helps more employees get to work with less frustration, but also helps reduce traffic congestion.

Flexible benefits and expanded employee services are primarily policy and systems changes. They truly represent the FLEX-MANAGEMENT principle of individualizing, by allowing people to customize a wide variety of packages that they can change as their needs change over time.

15

Help Employees Take Care of Family Responsibilities

WITH RISING BIRTH RATES and an aging society, increasingly large numbers of people are responsible for regular, often long-term care for a dependent. Without company support these responsibilities may hinder productivity and create extra stress for employees.

Provide Dependent Care Assistance

While the need for child care rises, the reality lags. In their 1990 survey of a cross-section of organizations, Towers Perrin report that only 25 percent provide child care information and fewer than 10 percent provide on- or near-site day care. Even fewer provide sick child care assistance (Towers Perrin and Hudson Institute, 1990).

San Francisco was the first city in the nation to pass an ordinance on child care. This ordinance requires office and hotel complexes with more than 50,000 square feet to either provide an on-site facility for child care or pay into a city child care fund.

The mayor's Office on Child Care coordinates an advisory council that helps city union employees to negotiate child care provisions in their labor contracts. Through its Family Day Care Rehabilitation Fund, San Francisco's low-income day care providers receive construction loan grants to expand or improve their facilities.

Many organizations have set up specific programs, have created internal advisory groups, or are working with external agencies to find better ways to handle the dependent care requirements of working people.

In late 1986, Eastman Kodak Company, a leading manufacturer of photographic products, chemicals, business support systems, and health-care products, established its Child Care Task Force to explore issues related to the needs of working parents. The group was made up of employees from various departments and was in contact with a management team that reviewed its recommendations. This review of work and family requirements continues under the direction of the Kodak Work and Family Issues Team. It has resulted in company-wide policies on financial assistance for adoption, flexible work scheduling, job sharing, and family leave, which consists of seventeen weeks of unpaid leave to care for a sick spouse, sick parent or parent-in-law, sick child, or new baby—including an adopted or foster child.

Kodak has also retained Work/Family Directions, Inc., a national organization that specializes in child care resources and issues, to maintain its Child Care Resource and Referral Program. Work/Family Directions contracts with community-based child care agencies throughout the country to provide Kodak employees with detailed information and referrals to child care providers. An important feature of the program is the addition of child care in areas of short supply. During the first eighteen months, Kodak's funding resulted in the addition of 650 family day care homes in communities where Kodak facilities are located.

AT&T has set up a $5 million Family Care Development Fund to sponsor family care projects and initiatives for its union employees. These funds may be used to provide training for health care providers, start-up loans for community care centers, planning grants to service agencies, and matching funds for grants to nonprofit organizations that foster family care programs. A similar fund has been set up for management employees.

IBM, based in Purchase, New York, develops, manufactures, distributes, and services computers and office equipment. The company offers its employees a child care consultation and referral service in 250 communities throughout the United States. Since its inception in 1984, the service has been used by thousands of families. Seventy percent of the children enrolled in the program are under three years old and 40 percent are under one year old. IBM's Elder Care Referral Service, established in February 1988, lists 175 community-based organizations that provide service in local areas. IBM employees, retirees, and spouses can call an experienced geriatric counselor in the area where their elder relative lives and receive information and referrals to service care providers. Prior to embarking on the program, IBM recognized the growing elderly population in the United States. A company survey revealed that 30 percent of IBM employees had some responsibility for older relatives, many of whom lived more than 100 miles away. Since its inception, more than 9,000 people have used the program.

Steelcase employs a child care administrator whose staff evaluates day care centers and family care homes. Lists are kept of approved centers and babysitters to assist employees who are looking for child care. The company houses a library on child care issues for both employees and child care providers and offers seminars and consulting services. Survey results indicate that 94 percent of the employees who use the program feel more relaxed and productive at work.

A national community-based child care resource and referral service is available to all AT&T employees. In 1991 an elder care referral will be available to provide employees with information on elder care facilities, transportation, housing, health, and Medicare.

Many companies, both large and small, have set up pre-tax expense accounts to allow their employees to deduct child care and elder care expenses. Employees at Steelcase can choose to direct benefits dollars into a dependent care reimbursement account or can elect a percentage of their pre-tax salary to supplement the total value of this account. At AT&T, employees can place up to $5,000 per year in pre-tax wages into an account for child or elder care expenses.

Set Up On-Site Dependent Care Facilities

Some companies have opted to provide on-site child care for their employees, by either providing funding to a privately run center,

The Stride Rite Corporation is a leading marketer of high-quality footwear for children and adults. In 1987 Stride Rite's chairman of the board, Arnold Hiatt, read an article in the *Wall Street Journal* that focused on the "sandwich generation"—people who are pressed between their careers and the dual responsibilities of caring for their children and their aging parents. It described a dual-career couple, both employed outside the home, who were supporting a child and an elderly parent. The article spurred Hiatt's interest in expanding the company's on-site child care center—which was opened in 1971—to include elder dependents of both Stride Rite employees and community residents.

Today, Hiatt's notion is a reality. In February 1990 the company opened the Stride Rite Intergenerational Day Care Center, which houses fifty-five young children between the ages of fifteen months and six years and twenty-four elders sixty years of age or older.

The move from the concept to the reality began with enlisting the support of nearby Wheelock College and Somerville-Cambridge Elder Services to explore the feasibility of establishing the intergenerational program. The company considered several questions: Do adult day care centers really help? Can we provide effective adult day care? Should we integrate adult day care with child care? "We also had to consider whether the program was financially feasible and manageable for us," says Karen Leibold, director of work and family programs for Stride Rite Children's Centers.

Part of the process included determining whether Stride Rite employees needed such a facility. A survey found that 25 percent of the employees provided some sort of elder care and an additional 13 percent anticipated doing so within five years.

Once the decision was made to proceed with the facility, the existing child care program became the basic model for what Stride Rite wanted to do. The program is run as a separate nonprofit corporation. Approximately one-half of its operating budget comes from the Stride Rite Charitable Foundation and the rest from fees paid by parents and from state funds.

The intergenerational center is open to both Stride Rite employees and members of the community. Employees pay a percentage of their annual household income with minimum and maximum amounts through payroll deduction. Others pay the full fee, if they can afford it. Stride Rite contracts with the state to provide both child and elder care for low-income families.

The center has an intergenerational coordinator to plan activities that will bring elders and children together. Group activities include reading and writing stories, cooking and eating, card games, arts and crafts, and field trips.

Ongoing research and evaluation of the program is expected to provide information on the effects of intergenerational care on children, elders, the workplace, families, and the community. "Stride Rite hopes its program can become a model for other public-private partnerships as well as a resource agency in the area of intergenerational care," Leibold says.

The company also has instituted a family leave policy that allows employees to take off up to eighteen weeks every two years, without pay but with job protection, to care for a sick relative. Employee seminars on dependent care topics are also provided.

operating their own center, providing space for a center, or helping to establish child care facilities in the vicinity—sometimes in conjunction with other employers.

Genentech, a pharmaceutical company in South San Francisco, opened a child care center in January 1989. The center is open from 6:45 A.M. to 7:00 P.M. and accepts children from six weeks to six years of age. Although it was built and is maintained by Genentech, the center is operated by an independent child care group. Employees pay $490 per month per child between the ages of six weeks and two years and $390 for children between two and six years old. The company offers a 50 percent scholarship to employees who earn less than $25,000.

"Providing a near-site center makes good business sense," says Linda Fitzpatrick, director of human resources. "Not only is the center a great recruiting tool, but we've found that employees come back to work sooner after maternity leave because they know that their child is receiving quality care and is close by."

Campbell Soup Company has an on-site child care center located across the street from its corporate headquarters in Camden, New Jersey. The center is open from 7:00 A.M. to 6:00 P.M. and cares for 110 children, from six weeks to five years of age. It is operated by an outside consultant specializing in child care. The company picks up 40 percent of the weekly expense for each child. The philosophy is that on-site day care cuts absenteeism, reduces distractions for employees, and gives the company an edge in hiring.

The Hacienda Child Development Center in Pleasanton, California, serves the child care needs of many employers—AT&T, Hewlett-Packard, Computerland, and Prudential Insurance Company, to name a few—in the Hacienda Business Park. Funding for construction of the facility was made by one of the major tenants. Operating costs are funded by parents' fees and, to a lesser extent, by fees paid by the businesses. The facility accommodates 200 children, from three weeks to five years of age. The center, which also serves the community, gives a discount on monthly rates to parents who work in the park.

Employees at Merck & Company headquarters in Rahway, New Jersey, have a day care center available one mile from the office. The Employees' Center for Young Children was started in 1980 by a group of Merck employees with the help of company funding. Employees can drop their children off at 7:30 A.M. and pick them up at 6:00 P.M. At another Merck location, West Point, Pennsylvania, a child care facility was expanded with company funds to give employees' children preferential admission.

Some organizations have found other ways to assist employees with family care. Many have helped to create networks of providers or have established convenient referral services.

Be Flexible with Leave Policies

Community and family values often become more important as a population ages ("How the Next Decade Will Differ," 1989). As organizations become increasingly aware of the importance of family in the lives of their employees, they are helping them to bear or adopt children by easing the strain that is often found in the attempt to balance work and family.

With birth rates on the rise again—"the Baby Boom echo"—more couples will be concerned about combining childbearing and work and will look for options such as parental leave or alternative work arrangements on their return to work. The increasing trend toward paying more attention to the work/family balance, having a stable home life, and spending quality time together is leading companies toward more consideration of the family in their policies.

Merck recognizes that lifestyles and family patterns have changed significantly over recent years, forcing more employees to balance the demands of the family with those of the workplace. It is Merck's belief that the corporation can benefit from helping the employee develop a balance between these two arenas of life.

The company provides a leave of absence of up to eighteen months for natural or adopting parents, and a medical leave of six weeks with pay for a natural mother. Child care leave is not paid, but medical and dental benefits continue for eighteen months.

After an absence of up to six months, the employee is returned to his or her previous position or a comparable one. After longer absences, the company will try to place the employee in a position consistent with his or her qualifications.

IBM offers up to three years of personal leave to its employees. Employees who leave must be available to work part time in the second and third years and are guaranteed a job when they return. Leaves must be for serious reasons such as child care, education, or care for a sick relative.

IBM employees receive six to eight weeks' pay under the sickness and accident plan for recovery from childbirth, and more if medical complications arise.

New mothers or fathers—whether natural or adoptive—may be granted up to three years of unpaid leave, with the option of working on a part-time basis during that period. Throughout the leave, employees continue to receive full benefits. A percentage of adoption expenses is also reimbursed.

Employees of AT&T may take a one-year leave of absence over a two-year period to take care of a family member who is ill. Job reinstate-

US Sprint was founded in July 1986. Three years later, less than 1 percent of its workforce had left because of family-related concerns. However, demographic shifts prompted its farsighted management to anticipate future retention and recruitment problems, especially for qualified women.

"Organizations typically are not accustomed to thinking outside the boxes," says Deborah Holt, director of human resource policies and strategic planning. "Sprint places a high priority on attracting and retaining talent. Our FamilyCare™ program was designed to accommodate individual and departmental productivity." FamilyCare became nationally recognized and captured three awards as a leading-edge initiative and program model for workplace redesign. It was designed with the help of 150 task force members representing all levels and departments within the organization.

Introduced in August 1989, FamilyCare provides multiple support programs, which include Workplace Flexibility (flextime, compressed work weeks, part-time employment, and job sharing); child care and elder care resource and referral services; on-site personal and family counseling through the Employee Assistance Program (EAP); FamilyCare leaves of absence for up to one year with job reinstatement and continuation of benefits; working partner relocation and income assistance; and a Flex Day that allows paid time off for family emergencies. These options are complemented by a cafeteria-style benefits plan that includes adoption assistance and a dependent care reimbursement account.

Throughout the first year, response to ChildCare Solution℠, ElderCare Connection℠, the EAP, and Workplace Flexibility remained positive and exceeded expected use. Currently, more than 25 percent of the workforce enjoys some form of flexible work arrangement. Moreover, because management encourages nontraditional schedules as long as they meet business goals, use is expected to expand within the next year. As a result, the company is experiencing increased productivity and has the necessary flexibility to attract and retain its quality workforce. "We know intuitively the return on our investment in employee support programs," says Holt. "The costs of these programs are inconsequential when compared with clinging to the status quo."

Sprint also offers a FamilyCare Leave of Absence, which was designed to support family adjustments and prevent high-performing employees from leaving the company. Paul Covington, manager of network information analysis, granted a year's leave to an employee who had given birth to her third child and wanted to extend her disability leave to be home with her children.

Ultimately, Covington justified the year-long leave on the basis of the employee's high performance and dedication to the company. "I was also motivated by her peers, who adamantly supported the leave and shared my belief that we should do whatever we could do to keep her."

Now, Covington has monthly meetings with the employee by phone and she comes in once each quarter. He says, "We don't want her to feel alienated from the company during her leave. By designing a way for her to stay connected with the work environment and be updated on the changes taking place, we also maintain our relationship with her." When she returns, the temporary employee will train her for approximately a month. "My goal is that this employee will have a heightened sense of loyalty and that we will all benefit from this situation," he adds.

ment is guaranteed. Employees receive full benefits for six months; after that they must pay the premium. AT&T employees may also take a one-year leave for care of a newborn child. Adoption assistance of up to $2,000 is available to employees for expenses associated with the legal adoption of a child under eighteen years of age.

Procter & Gamble's parental leave policy allows either parent to take up to one year off when a child is born or adopted. Employees have the option of working part time during this period, depending on the company's need for their services. The company also picks up adoption expenses of up to $2,000, with a $6,000 maximum per family. In addition, employees are allowed to use a portion of their annual vacation in half-day increments for personal business such as child or elder care matters, or attendance at children's school functions.

Hewlett-Packard's Flexible Time Off program gives employees fifteen to thirty days each year, depending on their length of service, to take time off for any reason; if necessary, they may take as little as one hour at a time. Art Young, benefits manager, says that the policy answers the varying needs employees may have, from caring for sick children or relatives to scheduling vacations and personal time off.

Campbell's family care leave policy allows any full-time employee to take a three-month leave without pay to care for an immediate family member, including a newborn. Flextime and part-time options also exist for employees, at the supervisor's discretion.

Handle the Unusual Need with Understanding

Paying attention to the interface between personal life and work life can pay off for the organization and the employee. Consider how one manager from a midwestern bank used flexibility and counseling practices. "One of my employees was a recovering alcoholic; her husband was in jail, and they were in the middle of divorce proceedings. She had a son with emotional and behavioral problems, leading to destructive behavior on his part, truancy in school, stealing, and so on.

"I worked with her to ensure that she could attend AA meetings and meet any unforeseen crises in her son's life. My time was spent not only in scheduling her workload and offering personal support, but also in managing her sometimes dysfunctional behavior toward myself and her colleagues—creating resentment on their part. My time was spent on lots of coaching, confronting, and managing the effect of her needs on the whole team of nine, as well as her interaction with her customers. Today Cindy continues to work at the same bank as a lender, is happily remarried, and leads a stable life."

A manager at a high-tech company held a two-and-a-half-day retreat for four district managers who reported to him and included their spouses. The purpose of the session was to provide an opportunity for the managers and spouses to discuss how job demands affected their home and family relationships and what could be done to reduce any negative impact that demanding travel schedules and company requirements had on the managers. Although they were somewhat reluctant to attend the session and discuss these issues, at the end all of them were glad they attended and spoke positively of holding more such sessions.

This manager was driven to hold the session because of "one and one-half years of strife in my own personal relationship with my wife, which ended in a divorce. I don't want to blame the company, but traveling part of approximately forty weeks each year did put a strain on our relationship, which neither of us knew how to cope with." He knew that the deteriorating relationship negatively affected his work and, although he was used to keeping his personal life separate from his work life, he eventually had to tell his supervisors what was going on.

"After I told my supervisors and others at work, several people shared similar problems with me. Obviously I was not alone. I kept thinking about what they said. Several were ten years younger than I and it occurred to me that maybe it was appropriate and important for the company to do something."

The group worked hard over the two days. The agenda included group sessions in the morning, optional private meetings with the facilitators or free time in the afternoon, and evenings that were left open for dinner and relaxation. The couples discovered that 90 percent of their misunderstandings were due to lack of communication.

The group made several recommendations to the company. One was to include spouses at annual regional meetings, although previously employees were discouraged from bringing their spouse. Although they must pay for their travel, spouses are now included in some sessions and meal functions.

Employees who travel frequently were also encouraged to take care of their health. Company-paid physicals are done more often, if necessary, and the company is willing to pay higher prices for employees to stay in hotels that offer health club services. Previously the policy toward calling home when on the road was ill defined and managers always felt they had to cover that expense personally. Now phone calls home are permitted.

Three years after the session, the manager said that he felt especially good that all the couples that attended the session are still together, including one couple that was having difficulties.

Sometimes supporting your workforce is as simple as accommodating a pregnant employee by allowing her time to rest during work hours. Diane Anderson, associate administrator for the University of Washington Medical Center in Seattle, did just that by allowing her secretary Dianna Jourdan to take a nap in her office during the lunch hour.

"Employees must work a nine-hour day, which includes a one-hour lunch break," says Anderson. "I needed to be mindful of this work-hour policy while at the same time being aware of Dianna's special circumstance.

"Dianna scheduled me out of my office every day between 1:00 and 2:00 P.M., so that it would be available for her to rest. The hospital supplied her with a mat, pillow, and blanket.

"By allowing her to take a nap during the lunch hour, we were able to stay within organizational policy while accommodating her special need."

Taking action to help employees with family and dependent care requires policy support, new systems, and a great deal of management flexibility. The organization's goal must be to ensure that employees are not distracted at work by the demands of their home life; this will increase both their job satisfaction and productivity.

PART VI

Taking Action

"Change occurs only when there is a con-fluence of changing values and economic necessity.**"**

—John Naisbitt and
Patricia Aburdene,
Reinventing the Corporation

These insightful words from John Naisbitt and Patricia Aburdene are as timely today as when they were published in 1985. Modifications in the workplace are occurring daily and more are needed. The impact of changing needs and values in the workforce is crossing paths with increasing shortages of the human capital that is required for the United States to be globally competitive.

"Reinventing" is essential to our organizations: There must be greater alignment between the commitment organizations demand from employees in order to reach high levels of performance and the management skills and supportive environment employees must experience in order to be productive and satisfied at work.

Taking action requires two levels of attention—individual and organizational. Managing differently involves the day-to-day practices of managers and supervisors, as well as the policies and systems used by the organization. The two levels must both change and be in alignment with each other to create a flexible workplace.

In the management development arena, greater attention must be focused on communication and listening skills, training to involve and empower employees, skills in developing others, training people about diversity and its management, and individual and organizational change skills. Supervisory and management training curricula should be reviewed and redesigned with the diverse workforce in mind.

Simultaneously, organization development issues also require attention. Who is in our workforce? What are their needs and preferences? What policies and systems are in and out of alignment with these needs? How can we develop both an effective organization for the 1990s and one in which the workforce is satisfied? These and other similar issues deserve special attention in organizations.

In this part we focus on the skills for managing the diverse workforce; Chapter Sixteen includes tips for improving those skills. An approach to developing a FLEX-MANAGEMENT workplace and guidelines on how to manage the changes are presented in Chapter Seventeen.

16

How to Develop Skills for Managing Workforce 2000

WHAT IS THE MOST important factor that determines success in managing the changing workforce?

A. A thorough knowledge of all cultural groups

B. Familiarity with EEO rules and regulations

C. A commitment to tailoring approaches appropriate to the individual, based on flexibility

"C," of course, is the right answer.

As a manager of the changing workforce, you must take responsibility for developing new management skills and applying these skills sensitively to specific workforce situations. In addition, you can use your skills, awareness, and personal power responsibly to influence change in your organization and provide a link between the diverse workforce and the organization as a whole.

To provide this link, you must influence upper management and your peers and advocate for changes in organizational policies and systems; without a critical mass of managers asking for these changes, upper management will be slow to listen. With a critical mass of managers asking for changes, upper management will have to respond and organizational policies and systems will stand a better chance of being changed.

It takes credible managers who are effective in their day-to-day roles and who contribute to the organization's mission and goals to influence change. By continually developing your skills, growing in your awareness, and helping to create change, you will avoid the uncomfortable phenomenon: "We have met the enemy and it is us."

Be an Effective Manager

According to research done by the Management Research Group in Portland, Maine, six behaviors, or management practices, distinguish effective from less effective managers and are important at all management levels (1985). These six behaviors hold true across industries, the private and public sectors, organization size, and type of work performed. The research, conducted with 5,300 managers, identified the following characteristics of effective managers:[1]

- *Communication.* Highly effective managers are clear in defining their expectations for employees.

- *Management Focus.* Highly effective managers are comfortable in the management role; they gain job satisfaction from performing as a manager. They are comfortable dealing with issues of power and conflict and are at ease in assuming managerial accountability.

---

[1]Validation work on the Management Effectiveness Analysis has been based on the concept that managers are successful to the extent that they positively influence the behavior of subordinates. A primary accountability for managers therefore is to increase the probability that subordinates will be successful in performing their roles. The impact a manager has on subordinates is critical to effective managerial performance. This impact is often emotional and influences subordinates' motivation to perform. In one of several studies

- *Production.* Highly effective managers are not only clear about what they expect; they also tend to expect high levels of performance.

- *People.* Highly effective managers balance their strong concern for production and performance with empathy and authentic concern for employee growth and development.

- *Control.* Highly effective managers have systems in place that allow them to periodically and consistently review and monitor employee performance. This process takes into consideration previously established expectations and objectives and is done to assist rather than police employees in their efforts to attain good job performance.

- *Feedback.* Highly effective managers provide regular, ongoing, and spontaneous feedback concerning the positive and negative aspects of employee performance. Again, feedback is based upon previously articulated expectations.

To be an effective manager, you must develop strengths in these basic characteristics of good management, recognize how the characteristics take on new twists with a highly diverse workforce, and develop additional skills that are particularly applicable to the changing workforce.

Develop Skills for the Changing Workforce

The authors have identified five skills for working with the changing workforce that build upon basic good management. These skills provide a guide with which to create ongoing individual man-

---

conducted since 1975, a total of 5,300 managers were rated on thirteen management effectiveness criteria. Each manager was rated by his or her immediate boss, the immediate peer group, and all direct subordinates. A manager remained in the research sample if he or she received consistent ratings (as measured by intraclass correlations greater than +.40) by all raters—boss, peers, and subordinates. As a result, the validation sample was reduced to a size of 2,340 managers. A "management effectiveness index" was calculated for each manager by averaging the ratings on the thirteen criteria provided by the raters. The distribution of this index was examined, and those managers who fell above the median were placed in a "highly effective" group, while managers who fell below the median were slotted in the "less effective" group. Subsequent to the criterion collection phase of the study, the direct subordinates of each manager were asked to describe the manager on sixty-six management behaviors, using a Likert-type questionnaire. The ratings on each of these behaviors were examined to determine if highly effective managers were described differently than less effective managers. A series of *t* tests were calculated; they determined that there was significant differentiation between the two management groups.

agement development plans or to form the core of a management development program.

The most effective development plan, whether it is implemented individually or in a group setting, begins with an assessment that gives managers a clear view of their current behaviors. Assessment can be achieved through feedback, analysis of incidents, or use of diagnostic assessment tools.

With a clear view of your current practices, you can improve areas of weakness. Sometimes awareness is enough to change behavior with no further training. At other times, reading, studying, training, and practicing new behaviors may be needed before the behavior becomes part of your repertoire.

A brief summary of the five skills follows:

- *Skill One: Empower others*. As a manager, you share power and information, solicit input, and reward people; manage more as a colleague than as a boss; and encourage participation and share accountability.

- *Skill Two: Develop others*. Through coaching, modeling desired behaviors, mentoring, and providing opportunities for growth, you delegate responsibility fully to those who have the ability to do the work; question and counsel employees on their interests, preferences, and careers; and work to individualize training needs.

- *Skill Three: Value diversity*. You know your own assets, liabilities, and biases; see diversity as an asset; understand diverse cultural practices; facilitate integration among people; and help others identify their needs and options.

- *Skill Four: Work for change*. You support employees by adapting policies, systems, and practices to help meet their needs; you identify and influence organizational changes.

- *Skill Five: Communicate responsibly*. You clearly communicate expectations, ask questions to increase your understanding, listen and show empathy, develop clarity across cultures and language differences, and provide ongoing feedback with sensitivity to individual differences.

The following section describes these skills more fully and offers tips that you can use in your individual development.

Skill One: Empower Others

Power, as defined by Rosabeth Moss Kanter in *Men and Women of the Corporation* (Kanter, 1977), is the ability to mobilize resources. When you mobilize resources you depend less on your power of position, gained through your job title and credentials, and more on your personal power—your skill in influencing others to act, even without formal authority. You use your power to enable others to act with creativity and authority.

Peter Block, author of *The Empowered Manager,* emphasizes that empowerment is a state of mind—not just a result of position, policies, and practices. Managers become more powerful as they nurture the power of others (Block, 1987).

The skill of empowering others addresses the desire of the contemporary workforce to have greater personal choice and freedom, be recognized for one's competence and accomplishments, and take pride in one's work. Empowering others allows them to become more involved in the organization.

In an earlier mindset, only managers were paid to think and control, holding power closely and taking all the credit. In effective contemporary organizations, most workers are seen as being capable of making significant contributions.

As a manager who empowers others, you will act as a colleague more than as a boss, relying on influence, respect, and relationships to work with employees. Empowering managers share power. They recognize and reward people for their accomplishments, contributions, and ideas. They encourage participation, solicit input, and involve people in decisions, giving credit to those who have earned it.

You may also empower people by sharing information and accountability. Figuring out the appropriate balance of information to share is a critical skill for managers to develop. Some operate on a need-to-know basis and only share the information necessary to perform a specific task. At the other extreme, an executive might give an entire history of the accounting department when only a balance statement was requested. You must balance your preferences about sharing information with your employees' preferences. Some employees want and need the total picture, whereas others prefer to have only the specifics required to do their job.

In order to share accountability, all employees must understand how their responsibilities contribute to the bigger picture. Keeping employees well informed helps make this possible. Information about the organization's structure, policies, products, services, competition, and current technology; the industry; and the political and economic climate are all useful.

Tips for Empowering Others

- Read current management literature on power and empowerment. *The Empowered Manager* (Block, 1987), *The Quest for Staff Leadership* (Bellman, 1986), and *Men and Women of the Corporation* (Kanter, 1977) are good resources.

- Encourage spontaneity. Set up situations in which employees feel comfortable discussing issues openly.

- Allow others in the department to run meetings or to jointly manage projects.

- Work side by side with employees and use team decision-making processes frequently.

- Search for opportunities for staff persons to receive recognition. For example, allow an employee who contributed to a project to participate in presenting it to top management.

- Ask for input on issues and decisions.

- Study ways to involve others in decision making. One useful resource that offers specific techniques is *How to Make Meetings Work* by Michael Doyle and David Strauss (1976).

- When the inclination to be strongly directive is felt, stop and ask if that is the best way to proceed. If not, look for more collaborative ways to handle the problem.

- Interview each employee and your peers to find out how they like to receive information. Agree on the information-sharing process.

- Use a variety of techniques for sharing and soliciting information. Some people are best reached with written memos, whereas others respond better to personal meetings or telephone conversations.

- If there is a lot at stake in the information being solicited or provided, practice with a group of supportive observers, ask for feedback, and refine the process.

- Make sure that contributors' names are included in reports and memos.

- Use "we" when talking about the work unit.

- Clarify employees' responsibility on projects.

- Establish goals, not only for the group as a whole, but also for individual members. Share these goals with the team. Balance group and individual goals. Be careful not to lose sight of the individually oriented objectives.

- Ask individuals and the team what rewards they prefer.

- Ask all members to discuss their responsibilities with the unit; identify and resolve areas that lack clarity or that overlap.

- Discuss job concerns with employees and involve them in designing goals and objectives for their positions.

- Ask employees how the unit might be able to make a greater impact on the organization. Not only will good ideas flow, but people will feel involved and empowered.

Skill Two: Develop Others

Workers who value development will be responsive to a manager's efforts to increase their potential; others will gain new career opportunities through managerial support. Managers who develop their people reinforce their commitment to empowering others.

As a manager, your most effective role may be that of a teacher; it is also one of the most challenging. In working to develop others, you may choose to mentor, coach, delegate, train, or be a role model.

Mentoring is a one-on-one, often intense development process that usually extends over a period of time. The mentor may be the supervisor or someone else inside or outside of the organization.

Coaching consists of providing suggestions, advice, and support on the job. A coach may also hold career discussions that question and focus interests, preferences, and goals, as well as identifying organizational opportunities.

Delegating provides an opportunity to give increasingly difficult assignments in areas that are to be developed. It allows employees to use new skills or strengthen old ones. For example, if one-on-one career discussions reveal that an employee would like to move into a managerial position, provide that employee with opportunities to chair task forces and manage portions of projects.

Training consists of either direct, on-the-job instruction or internal or external training programs for employees.

Managers who are *role modeling* behave in the same way that they would like employees to behave. For example, to encourage employees to arrive on time, you also should consistently be on time.

The skill of developing others supports the FLEX-MANAGEMENT strategies of matching people and jobs and managing and rewarding performance. It acknowledges that employees want respect and dignity in the workplace, more involvement at work, pride in their work, and a chance to develop themselves.

Tips for Developing Others

- Talk regularly with employees about their preferred work assignments. Take notes and create a system that will help match tasks with the person who would benefit most.

- Study larger tasks to see if they can be divided into smaller ones that might be delegated.

- Analyze and prioritize each person's present job responsibilities. If there are gaps in people's abilities, design training that will close those gaps.

- Let employees know if promotions depend on taking more responsibility. If so, encourage them to suggest ways of being more involved and using their skills more fully.

- Give employees authority to do the job. Ask for progress reports— oral or written—at reasonable intervals.

- Encourage employees to develop skills through volunteer assignments in the community.

- Give employees opportunities to relate individual success stories at group meetings—how difficulties were overcome and how seemingly impossible goals were attained.

- Conduct developmental discussions during performance appraisals.

- Determine the major career paths available in various departments. Assess the skills and knowledge needed for each job and look for a match among employees. Experiment with planning paths for career growth.

- Quickly build on successful experiences on or off the job. During these times, the individual's courage and capabilities are expanded. Offer challenges that will take employees to the next developmental step.

- Get to know employees' competencies, motivations, and task preferences.

- When people are hired, thoroughly review their resume, and meet with them to discuss goals and expectations.

- Meet once a month with employees in the department to keep informed concerning their progress, feelings about their work, and future interests.

Skill Three: Value Diversity

"**V**aluing diversity" is a term that was first coined by Copeland Griggs Productions. "Valuing diversity," they say, "means recognizing and appreciating that individuals are different, that diversity is an advantage if it is valued and well managed, and that diversity is not to be simply tolerated but encouraged, supported and nurtured" (Copeland Griggs Productions, n.d.). In this new view, individual differences are assets, not liabilities.

If this attitude were integrated into all management functions and supported by leadership, organizations would realize enormous benefits. Higher-quality solutions are found when a team of people view problems from different perspectives, expertise, and styles, which may be based on their differences in cultural background, gender, age, education, disability, or values.

Effective managers are self-reflective. They understand their own strengths, weaknesses, and biases, and they know how their personal viewpoint affects their interaction with people who are different from themselves. In *Leaders: The Strategies for Taking Charge,* Warren Bennis and Burt Nanus say that leaders recognize strengths and compensate for weaknesses (Bennis and Nanus, 1985). The ability to reflect on your own attitudes and to assume a strategic balanced approach is essential to managing a diverse workforce.

As a contemporary manager, you make an effort to be sensitive to individual differences and cultural practices. You try to understand the diversity of values, interests, and preferences that you encounter; you also facilitate integration among people and help them to develop a quality work life.

Valuing diversity supports all four FLEX-MANAGEMENT strategies and is consistent with the contemporary workforce trend of valuing respect and dignity at work.

Tips for Valuing Diversity

- Adapt training to the learning styles of culturally diverse groups.

- Provide training in diversity for your workforce.

- Recognize individual differences and take advantage of them.

- Use cross-training to help people work together.

- Assess and explore the impact of biases and stereotypes through experiential training.

- Become aware of your own reaction to change, as well as your ability to interact with others, your adaptability to alternative solutions and unstructured situations, your mental flexibility, and your intellectual curiosity.

- Choose a colleague to meet with regularly who also wishes to manage with more sensitivity to differences. Share goals, set milestones, and report on progress.

- Learn about differences in the workforce through reading, attending workshops, fostering relationships with people who are different, and participating in diversity-related activities.

- Plan time to talk with individual employees. Listen to their opinions, and share your knowledge about ways in which the organization can meet their needs.

- Conduct team-building activities where people can get to know each other.

Skill Four: Work for Change

"**S**uccessful managers of the future will take responsibility for results and will lobby to change organizational conditions that don't respond to employee needs. Greater organizational productivity is going to rely on a flexible approach," says Lynda McDermott, management consultant and president of EquiPro International in New York City.

When you are unable to respond to an employee's request for flexibility because of rigid systems and policies, you may choose to work toward organizational change. This may involve advocacy for the individual. For example, if a valuable employee believes that her productivity would increase by working from her home, you may put together a proposal with the employee to show how the organization would actually gain by agreeing to the request. You might also work for larger-scale change by suggesting that a task force be formed to study flexible work arrangements for the entire organization.

Other ways to demonstrate managerial commitment to change might include supporting middle-aged and older workers, who may be more concerned with retirement planning, health care and wellness, and reward systems that include sabbaticals, perks, and time off than they are with a strict emphasis on financial incentives. You may also work to restructure leave policies to accommodate child care and elder care needs.

A primary way to support today's workforce is by offering a wide variety of flexible benefits and employee services, providing opportunities for a flexible time and place to work, assisting with parental responsibilities and dependent care needs, and helping employees balance family and work. Working for change responds to contemporary employees' desire for an improved quality of life—on and off the job.

Tips for Working for Change

- Work with other managers to develop consensus and priorities for change.

- Take anonymous climate surveys from time to time to discover ways in which organizational systems and policies may inhibit productivity and job satisfaction.

- Analyze and highlight any positive benefits that recent changes have produced.

- Study the literature on the management of change or attend a workshop on change. The Resources section in this book lists several firms that offer such workshops.

- Listen to employees' requests and ask them questions. Maintain a problem-solving attitude when responding to their requests.

- Read and implement the principles in Chapter Seventeen of this book.

Skill Five: Communicate Responsibly

The varied linguistic backgrounds, cultural values, and educational levels present in the contemporary workforce can be barriers to clear understanding. People often have different perspectives, ethics, work values, and nonverbal behaviors that filter messages. In order to plan and work together, communication skills are critical. Among your managerial skills, communicating expectations clearly is essential. You must also check to make sure that your requests have been understood, and you must listen carefully and sensitively to learn what motivates and satisfies your employees.

As a responsible communicator, you recognize that you are not the source of all wisdom, information, and knowledge; you demonstrate respect by staying open to new information, listening, and showing empathy. This helps to develop the basis of a strong personal relationship within the work context.

Often, managers value action and urgency over relationships. For such managers, slowing down, listening, or showing empathy seems like a waste of time. However, other employees and peers may not talk or operate at as fast a pace as the manager. Highly educated employees may want more discussion than the manager is accustomed to; other employees may not have a command of the English language or may come from a culture that gives them less experience and confidence in speaking with people in authority.

Providing feedback with sensitivity to individual differences takes on greater importance today. Although some managers may value directness and straightforwardness in giving feedback, this approach may not be effective with all members of the workforce. In some cases, a softer, more indirect style may be appropriate. Versatility and flexibility are, again, what is needed.

Traditional managers were supposed to be tough and to have the attitude that only wimps showed that they cared about employees. However, today's astute manager recognizes that productivity is achieved through people and that caring and empathizing contribute to long-term productivity.

Responsible communication is a tool that supports the FLEX-MANAGEMENT strategies of informing and involving people and managing and rewarding performance. Empathetic listening and requests for information accord respect and dignity to the individual and reinforce involvement at work.

Tips for Communicating Responsibly

- Develop skills in active listening.

- Be attentive to mood changes among employees. Acknowledge these emotional states in a supportive way.

- When employees are experiencing a difficult personal situation, such as a divorce or a death in the family, talk to them privately to find out what support may be useful and to express your concern.

- Ask for ideas to help individuals meet performance standards.

- Always make sure you are understood, whether you are communicating in writing or verbally. Have employees repeat or respond in some way to show that they understand a new perspective.

- Identify key cultural differences in the use of language and train the staff to recognize these differences.

- Create a pocket reference that lists guidelines for giving and using feedback. Add variations applicable to the various populations in your organization.

- Keep the praise-to-criticism ratio at roughly 3 to 1. Notice and acknowledge the positive things people do, and set criteria for evaluating positive achievements. Recognize even small steps along the way as valuable accomplishments.

- Ask employees about contributions that group members have made. Acknowledge these people in a meeting or write a note expressing your appreciation.

- Don't hesitate to give rewards for intelligent mistakes. Recognize thoughtful performance that rises above simple adherence to the rules.

- Establish a system to warn employees when there has been a serious breach of conduct or a marked lack of performance.

- Communicate and reinforce your expectations concerning performance or development. Show that you care.

A new breed of manager is needed—one who is competent at basic management tasks and who can develop the five special skills just described. Managing with diversity requires new initiatives. This is a time for action by both individuals and organizations. As a manager, you must use your personal power and responsibility to respond to the changing workforce and to initiate change.

When you recognize the importance of flexibility, you move beyond the limitations of using only one approach; you will have learned to pursue all options and to make the choices that will be most effective for your employees. Fortunately, it is your day-to-day behavior that creates this effectiveness—and behavior can be changed!

17

How to Manage the Change to a Flex-Management Workplace

ORGANIZATIONS THAT RESPOND by developing a FLEX-MANAGEMENT workplace will have the human resource edge that will allow them to succeed in the 1990s and beyond. Unresponsive organizations will be hard pressed to recruit or retain the highly skilled workers they need to stay competitive.

Creating a FLEX-MANAGEMENT workplace will require a transformation in the mindset and skills of managers and in the policies and systems of the workplace. It will involve fundamental shifts in the way people are managed as well as changes in the organization's culture.

Transforming the way an organization operates requires a systematic, planned approach to change. Mandates, fragmented activities, and piecemeal programs rarely generate desired outcomes. Because many FLEX-MANAGEMENT strategies are interrelated, it may be ineffective to jump into isolated solutions or to implement only a few or partial strategies. In addition, failure created by limited solutions may make the real changes that are required more difficult to implement.

Understand Barriers to Change

If the FLEX-MANAGEMENT concept is appealing, why haven't more organizations adopted it? The reason is that change is never easy and it must contend with existing barriers.

Economic considerations, the ability to pay for change, can be a constraint. In the 1980s, organizations experienced widespread cost cutting, downsizing, restructuring, and expensive mergers and acquisitions.

Years of *adversarial union/management contracting* and *government-mandated personnel law* have worked toward developing and assuring more rights, more rigid rules, and more sameness. Many of the conditions handled in labor/management contracts and in personnel law at least in part address the protection of employees from arbitrary and malicious management. Rigid, inflexible, and in some ways burdensome layers of contract understanding and work rules exist mainly to assure workers of good working conditions and equal pay, hours, treatment, and rights.

Much of personnel law seems to stem from the same roots. What organizations weren't able to do for their people, the government did. It created mandates in such areas as compensation, affirmative action, hiring and discharge practices, and work hours. Now even dependent care may go the route of being dictated by government policy.

Existing union contracts, memorandums of understanding, and personnel law work against the concept of FLEX-MANAGEMENT and the need to manage differently with the changing workforce. After decades of regulations and detailed union contracts, it will be very challenging to work *within* these realities to change them in such a way that management can operate more flexibly. Nonetheless, the implications of the changing workforce necessitate new directions for management. If labor, management, and government can recognize why the constraints of the past are in place and understand that it is time to think differently about the workplace today, it will be possible to arrive at new solutions that meet all parties' needs.

Change is also hampered by *resistance* and the difficult process of *individual transition*. Resistance is quite natural. The processes used to plan and manage change can either minimize or increase resistance.

Managers and employees may resist change for a variety of reasons:

- They may be pleased with or believe they prefer the status quo.

- They may fear personal loss.

- They may lack understanding or information about the change.

- They may feel criticized or blamed for the way things *were* being done—as though they were responsible for the need for change.

- They may resent not having had input into the change.

- They may be cautious due to a lack of trust or respect for the change initiators.

Individual transitions are also difficult and take time. Moving from previous ways of doing things to new ones involves letting go of the old, going through a transitional period, and beginning the new (Bridges, 1980, 1988). Individuals facing change typically have the following reactions:

1. If the change isn't welcomed, they begin by feeling shock or anger, followed shortly by feelings of guilt or defensiveness. They may withdraw, rebel, or become disoriented.

2. From that initial state, they move into the transition of rethinking, exploring, and analyzing themselves, the situation, and what it means. In this period, they can feel empty and alone. Confusion is paramount.

3. Finally, with hard work and support, those responding to change will typically arrive at an understanding and acceptance of the new and will work on identifying with new roles or behaviors and integrating them into their life.

When the causes of resistance are understood, processes can be designed to minimize and manage it through involving vested interests, working with the reasons for the opposition, acquiring valid information concerning the need for change, and communicating well and often.

These processes require time, focus, and help. People don't just slide through them during a weekend team-building retreat! The individual and organizational changes inherent in understanding and accepting diversity, and in creating flexibility in organizations and their managers, will require deep personal transitions for many in the workplace. Therefore, the success of change in general and the creation of a FLEX-MANAGEMENT workplace in particular are enhanced when the transition processes are planned for and well managed. While barriers to change are real, they are not insurmountable.

Plan Organizational Change

Creating a new workplace will require planned organizational change—a systematic process of diagnosis, design, and implementation. Inventing a FLEX-MANAGEMENT organization alters the culture—the underlying values in operation—and the policies, systems, and practices that manifest it. The organization's underlying values, which are internalized and are acted out through a critical mass of people (or at least by the most powerful people) in the organization, shape behavior and decisions, thus influencing "the way we do things here." The goal today is to instill, manifest, reinforce, and reward new underlying values—a new corporate mindset—a FLEX-MANAGEMENT culture!

Understanding planned change can help greatly in developing strategies and processes that will move an organization from where it is today to the desired future. Social scientists have developed reasonable consensus about some basic principles (Argyris, 1970; Margulies and Raia, 1978):

- Planned change involves a deliberate, purposeful, and explicit decision to engage in a process of improvement.

- The *processes* used for problem finding, problem solving, decision making, and implementation are critical to success.

- People who are affected by the change should be included in the process.

- Generally, a manager—one who is responsible for the operation of his or her organization—works in collaboration with a change specialist to design and implement the change.

- Planned change includes the use of valid information to examine and modify the current state.

- Planned change generally follows the sequence of entry, diagnosis, planning, implementation, and evaluation.

- Changes generally come in the form of one or more new or different ways of doing some aspect of the organization's operation (its actions).

- To be effective, actions require valid information about the present, free choice among alternatives, and internal commitment to the course of action by those affected.

These principles should be built into the change process. Important questions include what information is needed, how it surfaces, who becomes involved, how people are informed, what the selection processes will be, and what roles will be needed in taking action. "Go slow to go fast" is sound advice from Michael Doyle, a San Francisco–based change consultant. Careful preplanning, process design, diagnosis, and identification of strategy help to ensure successful implementation of complex changes.

Manage Change

The first important consideration is to decide who will guide and manage the change project. The options range from an individual to various groups coordinated by a steering committee. Many organizations use task forces, change teams, or internal or external consulting resources. Membership should include

- Groups or individuals with expertise on the changing workforce, its implications, and organizational responses

- Management and human resource professionals

- Representatives of different perspectives: the organization's diversity, departments and functions, levels, technical human resource systems, and human relations concerns

- Groups or individuals with organizational influence and credibility

Whoever is chosen to manage the project, whether it is an individual or a group, is responsible for overall design, coordination, and guidance. The individual or group will

- Coordinate information and the involvement of others

- Research other organizations, as well as obtain quantitative and qualitative information from the organization involved in the change project

- Weigh alternatives, balance needs and resources, and make choices

- Use the principles of planned change in designing both diagnostic and implementation processes

With the change management structure in place, an organization can execute a change process to move toward FLEX-MANAGEMENT by using the classic concepts of Beckhard and Harris (1987) through the following six-step plan of action:

1. Define the organization's diversity.

2. Understand the organization's workforce values and needs.

3. Describe the desired future state.

4. Analyze the present state.

5. Plan and manage transitions.

6. Evaluate results.

Step One: Define the Organization's Diversity

Since diversity suggests that no two organizations' employees will be alike, it is most important to begin with a valid picture of the current and potential workforce. While the general trends in demographics and values mark the direction of change in the labor market, a particular organization's workforce could be quite different; it is therefore important not to make assumptions about the composition of the workforce or what its members value.

Take, for example, the case at Mobil Oil Company (Trost, 1989). Mobil realized that it was having trouble keeping its investment in younger women, yet it didn't sense a problem among its older female senior managers and vice-presidents. After analyzing 2,206 questionnaires and interviewing 400 departed employees—including many with strong future potential—and 100 spouses of current employees, the company found the answer that explained the discrepancy between the younger and older women.

The senior women were atypical and different from the younger women. Many had sacrificed a family life for their careers. Over half of the female managerial and supervisory employees between thirty-five and forty-five years old were single, and 90 percent didn't have children. For them, family issues were irrelevant. However, among the promising women under thirty-five who left the organization, 44 percent left in part to start a family or devote more time to their family. They were leaving because of a lack of supportive family policies. In response to the facts generated through information gathering and analysis, Mobil has changed many of its family-related policies.

Who Is in the Workforce Now?

The first step in planning workforce-related change in an organization is to identify its members demographically. The five demographic categories discussed earlier—age, gender, ethnicity, education, and disability—along with other demographically relevant factors such as years of work experience and marital and parental status, can be used to profile your workforce.

For example, you might begin broadly by creating a matrix that captures relevant information about your workforce in percentages. Beginning with gender, suppose that women represent 35 percent of your 5,000-person workforce, or 1,750 employees. Women can be further characterized, as shown in Table 1, by age categories, educational levels, and ethnicity.

In addition, it could be quite relevant to further describe the female workforce in terms of years of work experience, marital status, and parental status (whether or not the women have children and whether those children are at home or under a certain age), as shown in Table 2.

More detail might be relevant for your workforce. For example, you may wish to factor in information about physical, mental, and medical disabilities; years of work experience; educational level; and age, which might have important implications for job matching, performance management, or ways to support the employee. Likewise, the number and ages of children and the marital status of employees could be helpful in designing policies concerning benefits, leave, and work hours.

TABLE 1

Workforce Profile for Women by Age, Education, and Ethnicity

Age	20–30	31–40	41–50	51–60	Over 60
Percent of workforce	25	10	35	20	10

Education	Less than 12 years	High school	High school +2 years	College	Advanced degree
Percent of workforce	5	28	32	25	10

Ethnicity	White	Black	Asian	Hispanic	Native American	Middle Eastern
Percent of workforce	44	19	12	20	0	5

TABLE 2
Workforce Profile for Women by Years of Work Experience,
Marital Status, and Parental Status

Years of experience	0–4	5–10	11–15	16–20	Over 20
Percent of workforce	35	20	8	12	25

Marital status	Single[a]		Married	
Percent of workforce	70		30	

Parental status	No children	Children, under 18, living at home	Children, over 18, not living at home
Percent of workforce	30	50	20

[a] Divorced, separated, widowed, or never married.

With basic information on employee demographics, various combinations can be isolated for analysis. For example, you may want to better understand which ethnic groups have particular levels of education, parental status, and marital status. Alternatively, you might wish to explore the types and levels of jobs by age, gender, or ethnicity.

An organization's study of its workforce can be as detailed or simplified as necessary to obtain a valid, clear picture of the composition of its workforce.

Who Will Be in the Future Workforce?

Looking into the future requires an examination of the organization's projected labor market. Study the trends. In what ways is the potential market changing in composition, size, or geographic dispersion? Local and regional government agencies, such as planning departments, district and county educational agencies, and the U.S. Census Bureau are good sources of data.

It is valuable to organize projected data in formats similar to those used for organizing current workforce information in order to know and respond to the current workforce as well as to study how it might change over the next five to ten years. The combination of information is important for establishing policies and systems that will be useful over time and that have enough flexibility to be adaptable to the continuing and future workforce.

Step Two: Understand the Organization's Values and Needs

Once an organization has an accurate picture of the composition of its current workforce and a forecast of its potential workforce, it is important to assess the values and needs of both workforce groups. This is a complex undertaking, because assumptions often are not true, biases may be highly inaccurate, and stereotypes are rarely representative of more than a small percentage of any group.

It is important to understand values, because they define what people want from employment and what is important in their life. Needs can be derived from life situations, such as being a single parent, or from lifestyle choices, such as where one lives or the type of leisure activities in which one participates. Different needs for regular work hours, time flexibility, transportation to and from work, or dependent care assistance can all be derived from a study of values.

Many approaches can be valuable in obtaining information about employees' values and needs. The value trends identified in Chapter Two can be used as the basis for employee surveys, interviews, or discussion groups. Needs can be identified by talking to or collecting information from employees with similar life circumstances and lifestyles.

A variety of methods can be used to collect information in this step of the process, including

- Special discussion groups representing common, larger segments of the workforce (e.g., single parents or older, white males) or that specifically mix different workforce diversities, organizational functions, or organizational levels

- Advisory groups with special expertise or perspectives

- Task forces for special studies

- Surveys of all or a sample of employees

- Individual interviews

No matter which approach is used to gather this information, it will be essential to make sure that there is accurate representation of the many portraits in the workforce. What is important at this point is to generate a descriptive—not judgmental—analysis of values and needs as they are patterned across the workforce.

Successful completion of steps 1 and 2 leads to a clearer understanding of what the organization's workforce looks like, what its members want, and what is likely to change in the future.

Step Three: Describe the Desired Future State

Having looked at who the members of the workforce are and what they want, it is now possible to use people from various segments of the population to envision the ideal future state: how the four strategies of the FLEX-MANAGEMENT model should be carried out; what policies, systems, and services will be available; how the organizational processes will work; and what management practices will be needed.

It is important to have a clear picture of what the ideal organization will be doing with its workforce. There will be plenty of opportunities to test reality, to consider economics, and to study the tradeoffs; for now, the *desired* future state should be considered.

One possibility for this step is to form a design team or teams made up of representatives from the largest demographic segments (for example, college-educated, single white males; Asian females in dual careers with children; or low-education, younger immigrants) and key value/need groupings (such as dependent care, transportation/commuting, wellness, or work schedule). The design team could be charged with developing its own consensus of how the four FLEX-MANAGEMENT strategies should occur to meet its needs. The team could also gather additional information and ideas from other organizations and from its constituent groups through interviews, questionnaires, and discussion groups.

Questions can be asked to help people be descriptive of the desired future state. In each FLEX-MANAGEMENT strategy, policies, systems, and practices should be portrayed. In addition, questions should probe how the basic tenets of FLEX-MANAGEMENT—individualizing, providing choices, seeing people as assets, valuing differences, encouraging greater self-management, and creating flexibility—might be carried out. The frame of reference for this step is for people to respond *as if they were five years in the future and the strategies have changed in the desired ways:*

- *Matching people and jobs.* How are jobs profiled and advertised? What are people looking for in job interviews? How do potential internal and external candidates find out about job opportunities? How do you assess the skills and preferences of job candidates? How do employees become oriented to the organization, the job, and how things get done? How do employees transfer, rotate, or "try out" jobs? How do managers and employees design and discuss careers? How do managers and employees ascertain "fit"? How are jobs redesigned? How are employees promoted?

- *Managing and rewarding performance.* How are role expectations and task clarity determined? How are goals and standards established? What is recorded? What is discussed? Are forms used? When are discussions held? Do performance discussions include feedback and coaching? How are training needs determined? How are performance evaluations handled? What reward possibilities exist and how are they determined?

- *Informing and involving people.* What information is shared? How and when is it shared? Who shares with whom? What mechanisms exist to communicate up, down, or horizontally? How do employees provide input? What mechanisms for delegation are in place? What opportunities exist to participate in planning, problem solving, and decision making? How is teamwork fostered?

- *Supporting lifestyle and life needs.* How are diverse needs handled? How are schedules, assignments, vacations, time off, and leaves determined? What life- and lifestyle-supporting programs are in place? Can employees tailor benefits? What social and leisure services are available? What attention is paid to career/family balance?

Once the future state has been described in a clear and detailed manner, the organization has a target, a backdrop against which decisions can be made, resource restraints can be reviewed, and tradeoffs can be more accurately considered.

Step Four: Analyze the Present State

With a potential future state in mind, the next step is to determine how the present state is operating, by examining how the four FLEX-MANAGEMENT strategies are used today and by comparing the current policies, systems, and practices to those that would operate in the future state. Suppose, for example, that in the desired, five-year-out future, people were able to "test drive" jobs—try them out for short, temporary periods. The analysis of the present state would ask whether this could happen now and how it could be done. Do current policies, structures, and systems allow it or work against it?

Looking through the four strategy "windows" allows us to fully diagnose what organizational policies or management practices may be in or out of synch with workforce needs and preferences today or in the future, and therefore what issues to pursue; in addition to this analysis, it is helpful to also review the present organizational reality through its existing policies, systems, and practices.

Policies

One approach to use with policies is to create an analysis activity based on the concept of "putting yourself in someone else's shoes" to truly understand that person's perspective. This is a great concept for "trying on" policies from the point of view of representatives of the prevalent sets of portraits, values, and needs. Working through this task will help to identify gaps, contradictions, policies with little or no flexibility or value to an organization's workforce, or simply outdated philosophies.

Policies can be reviewed through the four strategies in the FLEX-MANAGEMENT model to ascertain how well they allow for individualizing or providing options and whether or not they're really needed. Consider the following possibilities:

- *Matching people and jobs.* Policies about assessment practices may be narrow and limited or may restrict transfers and rotation. There may be no policy about job posting to provide information to employees about opportunities.

- *Managing and rewarding performance.* Policies may limit all forms of rewards or mandate the number, structure, and focus of goals. There may be no policy on individualizing development plans.

- *Informing and involving people.* There may be some outdated policies that restrict information access and dissemination or that dictate cumbersome approval and decision-making levels.

- *Supporting lifestyle and life needs.* Policies related to benefits, leaves, work hours, and "perks" are all candidates for being restrictive, demeaning, or useless to a particular segment of the workforce. For example, benefits that are liberal in retirement contributions could be inappropriate for a relatively younger workforce that is interested in more money and time off. An organization with an excellent child care program will still be perceived as unresponsive if its workforce is primarily composed of aging workers dealing with elder care issues.

Any modifications in policies must take into account existing laws, union contracts, and economics. Because of these realities, it is important to involve members of the workforce in the review and design process. They will find that some policy areas or existing agreements may be changed now or in the future; that although some needs can be met, others cannot; and that economics may require tradeoffs. Remember that ownership and commitment to solutions are developed through the involvement of those who will live with them.

Systems

It is important to analyze systems and their structure—forms, processes, and procedures—in their present state. The systems that should be analyzed are primarily human resource management systems and those that are used to run the organization, such as communication, information, planning, and decision-making systems. How these systems are designed and used can have a great impact on their effectiveness for today's workforce. Do they control or empower? Do they elicit passivity or action? Do they foster collaboration or conflict? These kinds of questions are important in order to understand the present state in new ways.

Particularly important systems—ones in which personal style, education, age, culture, disability, or values could greatly influence an organization's approach and methods—include performance planning, performance appraisal, recruiting, assessment, training, rewards, communication, and compensation. How these systems are created—and implemented—can either help or hinder the ability of managers to individualize for a diverse workforce.

Practices

How empowering are today's management practices? Are managers able to individualize their development of employees? Do managers use participation? Are they culturally aware? Are they skilled at understanding and integrating differences? Are they clear in their communication and versatile in their feedback approaches? Do managers practice flexibility in meeting employee needs? Is anyone working for organizational change? These and other similar questions focus on what managers are doing and help to analyze the existing work culture.

Potential changes in practices are numerous:

- It is likely that many managers are controlling, directing, and disempowering. Sometimes these practices are subtle and are not readily seen.

- Similarity and sameness may be prevalent in the treatment of employees. Years of working with everyone in the same ways may make individualizing rare today.

- Practices such as mentoring, coaching, and feedback may have been used less in the past and managers may be less skilled in these practices.

- Valuing diversity is new for most people. A manager's assets, liabilities, and biases may not be readily known. For many managers, it may be difficult and frightening to work with differences; they may have no experience in attempting to understand employees' needs.

- Clarity of communication often is not necessary among homogeneous groups. The importance of clarity in speaking and listening takes on new meaning in communicating with people from diverse cultures or linguistic backgrounds.

- Many managers may have been rewarded for not being flexible and not pushing for change. They may need training to improve their practices in these areas as well as new rewards for risk taking and innovation.

The ongoing, day-to-day practices of managers should also be reviewed in the present state. It can help to use the key skills outlined in Chapter Sixteen as a starting point.

Analyzing the present state, with the desired future state in mind, can help immensely toward seeing alternative solutions and preparing people to design and manage transitions to the more desired future.

Step Five: Plan and Manage Transitions

In this step of the process, managers and employees "reality test" the ideal future state, designing more specific plans, developing choices, building commitment, and implementing new ways of working and managing. Planning involves asking what tasks will be required, what methods will be used, who will now need to be involved, what communication is needed, how resistance can be overcome and commitment built, what timeline is estimated, and what planning and implementation strategies will be used.

Basically, the hard work and the *magic* in successfully planning and managing transitions lies in

- Developing a comprehensive task plan with its associated methods, people, and timelines

- Developing strategies for building commitment, managing the politics of the organization, and highlighting successes

- Managing and adapting the implementation steps, sequences, and timing

When developing a plan, it is first necessary to identify the work to be done. This will help in determining design alternatives, as well as ways to keep managers informed; deal with resistance; and put new policies, systems, and practices in place.

Some considerations for a task plan include

- Collecting additional data

- Researching what others have done

- Drafting policies or designing new systems

- Performing pilot tests on ideas

- Managing individual transitions

- Using different means of communication with different audiences

- Establishing task priorities and sequences

When considering how to move in new directions, it is again helpful to look at policies, systems, and practices.

Policies

One overall direction could be to simplify and minimize the need for large numbers of policies. They are increasingly difficult and cumbersome to work with, usually require a great deal of interpretation, set up legal constraints, and often push people toward inaction rather than action. New policies are needed whose wording provides wider latitude in the methods managers and work groups can use to meet their work and personal needs. Policies that need more managerial judgment also have greater risk, which must be balanced with anticipated gains in productivity or satisfaction.

A second direction could be to create a positive orientation. Policies could become statements of values and intention with wider latitude in how managers implement them. Policies often state what people can't do and have tended to have a negative and discipline-oriented focus.

Systems

Many systems can be made more flexible in order to bring the organization's future state "to life":

- Performance planning should vary in participation, frequency of contact, and number and types of goals; forms and discussion formats used in performance appraisal should vary in much the same way.

- Recruiting should vary in methods used to market positions; content of job profiles; length, number, and depth of interviews; use of style and "fit" tools; or use of assessment groups. What is appealing to a candidate will vary with demographics and values. Assessment methods may also need to vary with such factors as a candidate's cultural background, education, work experience, and/or disability.

- Training needs and formats should be customized for individuals and groups by using various media to accommodate different learning styles and a varied structure and pace to adapt to different educational levels, ages, maturities, cultures, and values.

- Rewards are most notably related to what people value, which in turn often varies with cultural background, education, age, lifestyle and life needs, and, possibly, disability.

- An organization must choose effective communication systems for its workforce. Considerations such as regularity, types of media (print information, public announcements, departmental meetings, and so forth), channels (number, access, restrictions, and flexibility), and content are used in the custom design of communication systems that work.

- Compensation and related classification systems may be the greatest hindrance to customizing for individual needs, differences, and merit. Fewer, broader classifications; flexible role definitions; and better design of jobs could facilitate job shifts, promotions, raises, or demotions. Optional forms of compensation should be more available. These could include team pay, skill-based pay, bonuses, stock options, dependent care accounts, educational expenses, and deferred compensation.

Practices

Managers' day-to-day behaviors with their workforce are often rooted in who they are accustomed to dealing with and what they have been doing. In identifying changes for moving to a FLEX-MANAGEMENT workplace, management practices should be assessed and management development approaches implemented.

Clarifying the management skills desired for more effectively managing the diverse workforce is an important first step. Building on the five key skills described in Chapter Sixteen, you can define the best management skill mix for your organization.

Training and other forms of learning should be developed and carried out. Development of new skills can benefit from reading, classroom instruction, new assignments, or coaching. Some skill areas, such as empowering and developing in an individualized way, communicating effectively across diversities, or appreciating differences and their integration, may be newer and therefore may require more integration.

Since change requires systematic action, the development of new practices is essential to support changes in policies and systems. Flexibility in managing employees must be in alignment with organizational flexibility in systems and policies.

All of these considerations help to identify the comprehensive set of tasks to be completed. With the list in mind, the task plan can be put in place by determining *how* the tasks should be done (methods), *who* should be involved in each task (individuals and groups), and *how long* it might take (timelines).

In designing this plan, it is also important to develop strategies for building commitment, managing organizational politics, and highlighting successes.

Some of the strategies involve the choices you make about how to be successful, *given the realities of your situation*. The number and levels of resisters, the influence of stakeholders, political alignments, and organizational culture all greatly influence outcomes and must be considered. For example, it is important to know about and plan strategies for dealing with influential stakeholders; these could include understanding resisters' points of view, building commitment among supporters, using political allies, and defending against political adversaries.

It is also helpful to understand your culture and strategize to work within it. How are decisions really made? What are the central values that must be addressed? What traditional practices can be modified? What "rules" can be bent? How can you build upon current aspects of the culture to help the change?

Strategies to highlight successes are also helpful. This often involves thinking strategically about how and when information is disseminated, who attends particular activities, how to celebrate, or how to use the informal system.

Developing strategies and blending them with tasks, methods, people, and timelines does produce a good plan, but that's not enough. Active management and adaptation are needed during implementation of the plan.

Managing implementation is critical, since most human systems are only partially predictable and most transition plans aren't perfect. *Active* monitoring, coordination, review, and adaptation are needed. Unexpected changes may arise, other events in the organization may interfere, tasks may be added or dropped, or timing may expand or contract. It is therefore important to have a good feedback system, both formal and informal, in order to learn—and learn quickly—what is working and what is not, to respond to unanticipated reactions, or to accept new perspectives. Managers of change must always be prepared, without shock or surprise, to alter or reshape their efforts.

Planning and managing transitions is complex and requires custom approaches. Given the variety of organizational realities, no two processes will be the same. Yet they all must work well in order for change to ever be successful.

Step Six: Evaluate Results

Evaluating results is always complex in organizations. However, evaluation becomes more realistic with an understanding of the desired future state. The fundamentals of the evaluation process include determining what outcomes to look for (identified when planning for the future state); what indicators (both quantitative and qualitative) would be present in the desired future state; how it can be known if they are present; and which elements can be monitored, measured, and observed.

In organizational change, it is helpful to consider two types of evaluation: "during-implementation" and "after-implementation" (Cummings and Huse, 1989). After-implementation evaluation provides feedback on whether changes have actually been implemented as intended. During-implementation evaluation takes into account that many changes require trial-and-error and incremental installation and involve modifications in behavior and procedures that may take time to achieve. Changes should be in place and working before one moves on to assessing their effects.

After-implementation evaluation focuses on reviewing outcomes or expected results and comparing them to what was outlined as the desired future state. This is possible when, earlier in the change process, the future state was translated into indicators that could be measured in some way and methods were chosen that were appropriate for evaluating these indicators.

Measures can be objective numbers or subjective perceptions of managers concerning desired outcomes. They can be obtained from organizational records, individual or group interviews, surveys, or observation. The important questions are: What should be looked at that will indicate the desired outcomes? How can such information be obtained validly? Each organization needs its own evaluation processes with specific indicators and measures.

The focus in this book is on developing a FLEX-MANAGEMENT workplace; therefore, there are a variety of possible indicators that could be considered:

- The basic tenets and values of FLEX-MANAGEMENT (outlined in Chapter Three)

- The view of the kind of organization that is desired (outlined in Chapter One)

- Turnover and retention

- The size and quality of the applicant pool being attracted

- The effectiveness of recruitment

- Morale and satisfaction

- Productivity

- The organization's reputation

- The number of grievances and other personnel actions

- Movement of the nontraditional workforce into key positions

- Salary equity

Creating change in organizations can be an exciting and complex endeavor. It is the only way to create the new workplace needed in the 1990s. Many organizations have changed and continue to change in very innovative ways. The know-how exists, but change is never painless or effortless.

Thoughtful, systematic action is called for. By using a planned approach to organizational change, organizations can develop a FLEX-MANAGEMENT workplace in which they do the right things and do things right.

PART VII

Resources for Gaining the Diversity Advantage: Where to Go for Help

"Learning to manage diversity is a change process, and the managers involved are change agents.**"**

—R. Roosevelt Thomas, Jr.,
"From Affirmative Action
to Affirming Diversity"

Gaining the diversity advantage will require some effort. You may choose to implement FLEX-MANAGEMENT using internal resources, external resources, or a combination of the two. If you choose to use external resources, you'll find this section helpful.

In the sixty-five resources listed, we've included independent consultants and consulting firms, suppliers of diversity-related materials, and nonprofit societies and associations. Resources were included because we knew of their work, they were highly recommended by persons we knew, or they were mentioned repeatedly in the literature about Workforce 2000 issues. Each organization wrote its own description, which we edited for length and consistency. It was not our intention to produce a comprehensive list of resources or to independently evaluate the quality of the work of each resource; therefore, please consider this listing only as a way to begin your search for outside assistance.

Here are some suggestions to follow in your assessment of resources:

1. Have a clear idea in mind of what assistance you need, and be open to suggestions from the resource.

2. If the resource is an independent consultant or consulting firm, ask for several references, but remember that this field is emerging, so don't expect a consultant to have performed exactly the work you need.

3. Be sure the consultant or consulting firm models the behaviors and shows evidence of having the values you desire in your managers and workforce.

4. The consultant or consulting firm should work with you to assure that any work done is in concert with an overall strategy. You want to be sure the resource will help you avoid a piecemeal approach.

5. Don't limit your reference check to the ones the consultant or firm provides. Use your network of managers and human resource professionals to learn about any experiences they've had with a person or firm.

The symbols for each listing are designed to help you quickly identify a resource for a specific need. There are eleven symbols—one for each of our six categories of diversity, the four FLEX-MANAGEMENT strategies, and "General," which indicates either that all categories and strategies are covered or that the resource's services didn't neatly fit the categories or strategies. The symbols are:

Aging

 Matching

 Women

 Managing

 Ethnicity

 Involving

 Education

 Supporting

 Disabilities

 General

 Values

We realize that this is not an exhaustive list and would welcome your referral of other resources we should include. Please contact us or the publisher with your recommendations.

Active Parenting Publishers

Contact: Carol Artigues
Director of Sales
80 Franklin Court, Suite B
Marietta, GA 30067
800/825-0060
404/429-0565
fax: 404/429-0334

Active Parenting Publishers produces video-based parental education programs. "Parents with Careers" recognizes the issues facing working parents and shows them ways to cope with their special needs. The group discussion format provides an opportunity for parents to share their concerns, such as finding good child care and time management, and even addresses the guilt and stress involved in balancing their responsibilities. Parents will also learn from the experience and collective wisdom of the other participants. "Parents with Careers" offers parents viable options that allow them to thrive in both their home and work environments.

Age Wave, Inc.

Contact: Ken Dychtwald, Ph.D.
1900 Powell Street, Suite 800
Emeryville, CA 94608
415/652-9099
fax: 415/652-8245

Age Wave, Inc., focuses on the needs and characteristics of middle-aged and older Americans. Its business includes the publication of videotapes, special reports, and newsletters; educational presentations; training to educate companies' workforces; and consulting with businesses on designing, developing, and marketing products and services. All of these products and services spring from the emerging needs of older adults and the increasing importance of the older population in the United States.

The American Association of Retired Persons (AARP)

Contact: Joan L. Kelly
Manager, Business Partnerships
Program, Worker Equity
1901 "K" Street, NW
Washington, DC 20049
202/662-4888
fax: 202/775-8373

The Business Partnership Program publishes *How to Recruit Older Workers, How to Manage Older Workers,* and *How to Train Older Workers*—a three-part series designed to assist managers in attracting and keeping older workers.

The Association maintains a free data base, the National Older Workers Information System (NOWIS), which is available to employers. NOWIS lists more than 180 programs concerning older workers. AARP has published a survey of 400 employers' perceptions of older workers called "Business and Older Workers: Current Perceptions and New Directions for the 1990s."

American Demographics, Inc. (a subsidiary of Dow Jones and Company)

Contact: Peter Francese
Publisher
P.O. Box 68
Ithaca, NY 14851
607/273-6343
fax: 607/273-3196

American Demographics is a monthly business magazine on consumer markets that reports on the demographics, lifestyles, media preferences, and buying behavior of American consumers. A special section covers the consumer information industry and the technology that is changing the way companies collect and distribute data. The magazine sponsors an annual conference on consumer trends and markets.

The Numbers News, a monthly newsletter that reports on the facts behind consumer market trends, analyzes the latest numbers from public and private sources in a quick-read format.

Marketing Tool Alert is a catalog of consumer information products available from American Demographics and other publishers.

The American Institute for Managing Diversity, Inc.

Contact: Terri Kruzan
        Associate Director
        P.O. Box 38
        830 Westview Drive, SW
        Atlanta, GA 30314
        404/524-7316
        fax: 404/524-0649

Founded in 1984 by Dr. Roosevelt Thomas, the Institute is a nonprofit applied research and educational enterprise, a pioneer in managing employee diversity in the workforce. Multicultural work environments require fundamental adjustments in managerial philosophies and practices, and within corporate culture. The Institute's programs in organizational studies, training, in-house presentations, national public seminars, management consulting, and public service support these fundamental changes.

American Productivity & Quality Center

Contact: Marie A. Jensen
        Associate Director
        Vice President, Marketing
          and Development
        123 North Post Oak Lane
        Houston, TX 77024
        713/685-4638
        fax: 713/681-8578

Since 1977, The American Productivity & Quality Center has been working with people in organizations to improve productivity, quality, and quality of work life. The Center provides educational, advisory, and information services and researches new methods of improvement. It has developed a number of improvement models that are applicable in creating flexible policies, practices, or systems to respond to the changing workforce. Write or call for a complete packet of information. Visitors' Days are the last Tuesday of each month. Call to register or for more information.

American Society for Training and Development (ASTD)

Contact: Helen Frank Bensimon
Director of Public Relations
P.O. Box 1443
1630 Duke Street
Alexandria, VA 22313
703/683-8123
fax: 703/683-8103

With more than 55,000 national and chapter members, ASTD is the pre-eminent professional organization in the field of workplace learning.

ASTD recently completed a $1.3 million research project, sponsored by the U.S. Department of Labor, which identified the best practices in training and development and how training is delivered and evaluated in the United States.

The Society launched "Train America's Workforce—Put Quality to Work," an information and action campaign on the importance of a well-trained workforce.

ASTD offers its members conferences, networking opportunities, publications including the *Training and Development Journal, Technical & Skills Training* magazine, *National Report, Info-Line,* and other professional products and information services.

American Training Systems (ATS)

Contact: Neel Advani
Ann Foudy
Managing Partners
100 Marin Center Drive, Suite 6
San Rafael, CA 94903
415/479-6631

ATS is a human resource firm specializing in applied techniques and solutions to increase productivity and profitability within organizations. It offers comprehensive systems design, organization development techniques, and tailored training programs to help managers deal effectively with current issues. Its programs focus on increased cultural diversity, changing value systems, declining literacy levels, the need for objective yet flexible performance appraisal systems, and the empowerment of the individual employee.

ATS can provide full service to an organization or can develop systems and programs for an organization's internal personnel to use on an ongoing basis.

Pat Arnold & Associates

Contact: Patricia H. Arnold, Ph.D.
3000 Hillsboro Road, Suite 105
Nashville, TN 37215
615/383-9791

Pat Arnold & Associates offers presentations, seminars, and workshops on managing diversity, building diverse teams, integrating women and minorities into the workplace, and preventing intentional and unintentional discrimination against people who are different. Pat Arnold has been working on these issues in Fortune 500 companies for fifteen years, from the executive level through hourly workers, with particular emphasis on training for first-line supervisors and middle managers. She consults with management and EEO professionals regarding strategies for using, developing, and promoting their diverse employees, particularly women.

Atlanta Resource Associates

Contact: Peggy G. Hutcheson
President
1708 Peachtree Street NW, Suite 305
Atlanta, GA 30309
404/892-2336
fax: 404/892-9599

Atlanta Resource Associates works in partnership with organizations to develop flexible human resource systems and processes that meet individual goals and needs as well as those of the company. Nationally recognized, it provides consulting and training in career systems development, personal career management, and the manager's role in employee career development. Its quarterly newsletter, *Career Impact,* supports individual responsibility for career growth and development. The company offers consulting and training on human resource issues in organizations, including career paths, plateauing, managing in transition, and self-managing work teams.

Being First, Inc.

Contact: Linda Ackerman Anderson
Dean Anderson
Principals
1130 Besito Avenue
Berkeley, CA 94705
415/549-0717
fax: 415/649-8148

Being First, Inc.™, provides training, consulting, speaking, and published materials on managing organizational and personal change. It assists clients in designing their future, identifying barriers to shaping their future, and successfully achieving their desired outcomes. Being First specializes in empowerment, management style, culture, and behavioral change on the personal side, and structures, systems, and policies on the organizational side. Flexibility and evolution are central themes in the company's approach. It teaches managers how to manage the process of change over time and develops executives toward change and the challenges of change, providing pragmatic strategies and tools that allow desired changes to come to fruition.

Blue Sky Productions, Inc.

Contact: Sandra Janoff
President
5918 Pulaski Avenue
Philadelphia, PA 19144
215/844-4444
fax: 215/844-5785

Since 1987, Blue Sky Productions, Inc., a Philadelphia-based video production company, has been serving the international business community by producing and distributing video workshops designed for the new paradigm, the team-oriented workplace. These video workshops use concepts developed by Marvin R. Weisbord in his book *Productive Workplaces,* which deals with issues of employee empowerment and whole systems improvement.

Video packages that are currently available include "Building Productive Workplaces: Change Strategies for the 21st Century," "Supervisors: The Changing Role of Supervision in the Workplace," "Managers, Workers, and Supervisors Speak Out on the Changing Workplace," and "Transforming Bureaucracies: Using Meetings People Have Anyway."

BNA Communications, Inc.

Contact: George Stillman
Vice-President, Sales and Marketing
9439 Key West Avenue
Rockville, MD 20850
800/233-6067
301/948-0540 (in Maryland)
fax: 301/948-2085

BNA Communications, Inc., a subsidiary of the Bureau of National Affairs, Inc., has produced an eight-module video-based training program designed to train managers and supervisors in new techniques to manage and motivate a diverse workforce. The video program—"Bridges: Skills to Manage a Diverse Workforce"—comes with manuals for trainers and participants. The series and manuals develop and reinforce awareness of cultural/racial/ethnic/gender differences and explore and practice skills for managing diversity. Each video runs approximately twenty-five to thirty minutes. Other video-based training programs include "Choices," "Intent vs. Impact," "A Costly Proposition," and "Fair Employment Practice." Write or call for more information.

Career Systems, Inc.

Contact: Caela Farren
Farren & Associates, Inc.
7361 McWhorter Place,
Suite 310
Annandale, VA 22003
703/256-5712
fax: 703/256-9564

Beverly Kaye
Beverly Kaye & Associates
3545 Alana Drive
Sherman Oaks, CA 94103
818/995-6454
fax: 818/995-0984

Zandy Leibowitz
Conceptual Systems, Inc.
1010 Wayne Avenue, Suite 1420
Silver Spring, MD 20910
301/589-1800
fax: 301/589-8932

Career Systems is a publishing company that specializes in training materials to support career development in organizations. These materials are used to train managers in career coaching and employees in career planning. Supporting materials are also available to train trainers in these areas. The firm's principals offer assistance in building and creating career development systems in organizations. Clients include numerous Fortune 500 companies.

Carlson Learning Company/Performax Systems (CLC)

Contact: Sandra Burk
Supervisor, Customer Service
Carlson Parkway
P.O. Box 59159
Minneapolis, MN 55459-8247
612/449-2824
fax: 612/449-2861

As a division of CLC, Performax publishes assessment instruments and packaged training programs. Many are helpful for the diverse workforce, including the Personal Profile System, a self-scored behavioral styles tool that helps people understand themselves and others and blend and capitalize on each others' styles; the Values Analysis System, which helps people understand value systems that drive behavior; and the Activity Perception System and Job Factor Analysis, which help people gain clarity on job requirements. Performax materials are available through a network of consultants. Call for the nearest representative.

Catalyst

Contact: Sabrina Schmidt Gordon
Referral Coordinator
250 Park Avenue South, 5th Floor
New York, NY 10003-1459
212/777-8900
fax: 212/477-4252

Catalyst is a national, not-for-profit organization that works with corporations to foster the career and leadership development of women. Catalyst's programs, products, and services are designed to help senior management and human resource professionals recruit, develop, and retain management women. Through qualitative research, one-on-one advisory interactions, and publications, Catalyst provides managers with knowledge and information on corporate concerns and on issues related to women in the workforce. By working continuously with corporations, Catalyst enables top management to respond effectively to these issues through the development of innovative policies and practices.

Center for Independent Living

Contact: Michael Winter
Executive Director
Marcia Ortiz
Employment Services Coordinator
2539 Telegraph Avenue
Oakland, CA 94704
415/841-4776
fax: 415/841-6168

Since 1972, the Center for Independent Living has provided assistance in entering the job market to individuals with a wide variety of disabilities. Its goal is to help clients achieve independence through self-support. The employment services department provides work-site analysis; offers technical accommodation instruction; and arranges disability awareness seminars for personnel, supervisory, and management staff and for employees. The Center advises employers on their obligations concerning fair employment, dispels stereotypes of disabled workers, and gives technical advice on what physical modifications employers can make to provide "reasonable accommodation."

Richard Chang Associates

Contact: Richard Y. Chang, Ph.D.
President
41 Corporate Park, Suite 230
Irvine, CA 92714
714/756-8096
fax: 714/756-0853

Richard Chang Associates is a nationally recognized human resources consulting firm that provides diversified, systems-oriented services and products in the areas of organization development, training, media and communications, and personnel services. Its full-service approach to the management of changing human resource demands includes specialized support in areas that include organizational diagnosis, integration of new business values and philosophy, Total Quality Management, workplace diversity, leading in a multicultural environment, implementation of major change efforts, installation of recognition systems, and job design-redesign. In addition, The Learning Advantage®, a division of Richard Chang Associates, features corporate-proven management and professional skills training programs in a public setting.

The Conference Board

Contact: Randall Poe
Director of Communications
845 Third Avenue
New York, NY 10022
212/339-0234

The Conference Board is a business network that enables executives to shape and share ideas through councils, conferences, and other meetings. This network is supported by a broad research program that identifies key areas of changing management practices and tracks economic issues in more than 3,000 companies worldwide. The Conference Board publishes *Across the Board,* a business magazine widely read by CEOs and other top management. This publication is an authoritative source of information for companies, government agencies, and world media.

Contact Center, Inc.

Contact: Su Perk Davis
Director of Clearinghouse Services
Emily Herrick
Literacy Director
P.O. Box 81826
Lincoln, NE 68501-1826
Hotline: 800/228-8813
402/464-0602
fax: 402/464-5913

The Contact Literacy Center, a division of Contact Center, Inc., serves as the clearinghouse for the Coalition for Literacy, using a toll-free telephone system to respond to requests for information and referrals. Contact maintains a data base of over 10,000 literacy resources nationwide; information on 25,000 human services agencies supplements the literacy files and can be used for requests, as deemed appropriate. The National Literacy Hotline handles approximately 15,000 calls per month and is manned by bilingual (Spanish/English) interpreters.

Copeland Griggs Productions

Contact: Lewis Griggs
Executive Producer
302 23rd Avenue
San Francisco, CA 94121
415/668-4200
fax: 415/668-6004

"Valuing Diversity" is a seven-part video series that helps managers and employees at all levels in the organization recognize that diversity is an advantage if it is valued, nurtured, and well managed. There are seven subtitles: "Managing Differences," "Diversity at Work," "Communicating Across Cultures," "You Make the Difference," "Supervising Differences," "Champions of Diversity," and "Profiles in Change."

Corporate Child Care Consultation

Contact: Louise Rush
President
2510 Bush Street
San Francisco, CA 94115
415/922-3578
fax: 415/922-3580

Serving the San Francisco Bay Area since 1981, Corporate Child Care Consultation introduces cost-effective dependent care options that address management and employee concerns. Clients receive assistance in assessing company needs as well as in program design, implementation, and evaluation. In addition to consultation, employee services include work-site seminars, work-family resource libraries, and guidebooks on selecting dependent care.

Elsie Y. Cross Associates, Inc.

Contact: Elsie Y. Cross
President
7627 Germantown Avenue
Philadelphia, PA 19118
215/248-8100
fax: 215/242-3328

Elsie Y. Cross Associates, Inc., provides consultation, training, and strategy development with organizations committed to working toward the full integration of men and women of color who are African-American, Caribbean, Hispanic, Native American, and Asian as well as of white women. The focus is on the elimination of racism, sexism, and other forms of systematic discrimination. The change process includes education and awareness, changes in policies and practices, and implementation of cultural change. Clients include major corporations, universities, and government agencies.

The Dartnell Corporation

Contact: Ann Chesney
Customer Service Representative
4660 Ravenswood Avenue
Chicago, IL 60640-4595
312/561-4000
800/621-5463
fax: 312/561-3801

The Dartnell Corporation, a publisher for business and industry since 1917, offers a variety of training materials and programs.

"One of Our Own," available in video and film, is a powerful human story that communicates vital information about AIDS in the workplace. Designed to help protect organizations and employees from legal, social, and business repercussions, it shows how one company responded to AIDS.

Drake Beam Morin, Inc. (DBM)

Contact: William J. Morin
Chairman and CEO
100 Park Avenue
New York, NY 10017
212/692-7700
fax: 212/692-7700

DBM provides career management services in 100 offices worldwide. It specializes in helping corporations to appropriately manage employee selection, performance, and transition. DBM's consulting services include outplacement for senior executives and group programs for employees at all levels. Its Corporate Revitalization Management Program assists companies in planning and implementing restructuring or other organization-wide changes. The firm also includes DBM Publishing, which offers a variety of "off-the-shelf" materials for use by managers and human resource professionals.

Drug Prevention Strategies, Inc.

Contact: B. Dana Lindstrom
Vice-President, Sales and Marketing
3150 Bristol, Suite 220
Costa Mesa, CA 92680
800/245-6336
fax: 714/641-8402

With offices in Oakland, Chicago, Atlanta, and Costa Mesa, Drug Prevention Strategies, Inc., is a national substance abuse consulting firm specializing in policy and program development, training, and education. It provides comprehensive technical assistance services that include policy and procedure development, drug crisis management, supervisor training, and employee awareness. Materials and services are designed to prevent substance abuse in the workplace and ensure compliance with federal and state laws and regulations.

Effectiveness By Design

Contact: Michele Wyman
Managing Partner
5351 W. 99th Place, Suite 4
Los Angeles, CA 90045
213/397-1680*
fax: 213/649-2560

Effectiveness By Design provides assistance in assessment-based, role-specific development. The primary emphasis is on leadership, management, and sales/service practices. Assessments can provide the basis for effective matching of people and jobs and for creating desired management practices for the diverse workforce. Effectiveness By Design's processes help to identify strengths, developmental needs, and customized strategies for change. Feedback and planning can occur in private sessions or group workshops.

* Effective November 2, 1991, this area code changes to 310.

Alan Emery, Ph.D., Consulting

Contact: Alan Emery, Ph.D.
President
360 Church Street, Suite G
San Francisco, CA 94114
415/431-7942

Alan Emery consults with organizations across the country on a variety of human resource and training issues including disability and reasonable accommodation, effective communication, the drug-free workforce, and AIDS/HIV. He focuses on developing strategies, policies, and model programs to keep pace with the challenges of the rapidly changing workforce. His articles and papers are featured in national professional journals, and he speaks and leads workshops at conferences and professional meetings throughout the United States, Canada, England, France, Australia, and Brazil. His book, *Managing AIDS in the Workplace,* was published by Addison-Wesley.

Executive Communications, Inc. (ECI)

Contact: William H. Fueller, Ph.D.
President
620 Alpha Drive
Pittsburgh, PA 15238
412/967-2736
fax: 412/963-1480

ECI produces and distributes educational video conferences and telecourses via satellite. It began in health care as the American Rehabilitation Educational Network (AREN); in 1986 the company began offering management development programs to health care and corporate leaders. Management and clinical techniques are presented through visual presentations delivered directly to the customer's workplace. Topics include "The Changing Workforce: Strategies for Future Management" by Julie O'Mara and David Jamieson, "Corporate Wellness: Impact on Productivity and Liability" by George Pfeiffer, "Emerging Technologies: Impact on the Manager of the '90s" by Mark Fox, and "Individual and Corporate Creativity" by Karl Albrecht.

Executive Diversity Services, Inc. (EDS)

Contact: Donna M. Stringer, Ph.D.
President
10311 20th, NE
Seattle, WA 98125
206/522-6267
fax: 206/522-0585

EDS provides customized management and employee training programs designed to improve productivity through understanding and valuing diversity. EDS's multicultural teams of trainers teach people how to identify and understand individuals' cultures and values; how to recognize different communication, conflict, and learning styles; and how to most effectively manage and communicate across those differences in positive and productive ways.

The Families and Work Institute

Contact: Ellen Galinsky and Dana Friedman
Co-Presidents
330 Seventh Avenue
New York, NY 10001
212/465-2004
fax: 212/465-8637

The Families and Work Institute, a nonprofit organization, serves as a national clearinghouse and center for policy research on work and family life. The Institute is currently conducting a number of policy studies, including a national study on the workforce. Its services to companies include consulting with task forces, designing needs assessments, conducting manager interviews and focus groups, synthesizing data, conducting competitive analyses and community needs assessments, and recommending strategies to solve employee problems productively. The Institute, in conjunction with Work/Family Directions in Boston, also provides management training in response to the changing workforce.

FutureScan

Contact: Roger Selbert, Ph.D.
President
2210 Wilshire Boulevard, Suite 826
Santa Monica, CA 90403
213/451-2990
fax: 213/459-1820

FutureScan is a four-page newsletter that provides a comprehensive trend report—economic, social, political, technological, demographic, lifestyle, consumer, business, management, workforce, and marketing. Dr. Roger Selbert, a corporate futurist, independent author, speaker, and consultant writes, edits, and publishes the report. Subscribers receive thirty-six issues annually of features and news analysis on the forces shaping the social and business environment of the future. Write or call for a free sample issue. Dr. Selbert is available for keynote presentations, industry- or company-specific research, and personal consultation involving strategic business foresight.

Hanamura Consulting

Contact: Steve Hanamura
9500 SW Barbur Boulevard,
Suite 115
Portland, OR 97219
503/246-2261

Hanamura Consulting frequently uses workshops, seminars, and individual consulting to help persons at all levels in an organization promote individuality, belonging, and harmony. Much of its work is focused on race, gender, and disability awareness, as well as other areas of diversity. Topics and issues addressed include cross-cultural training; managing conflict from diversity; risking—how to be different and contribute; dealing with trauma; and committing to personal empowerment.

The Hay Group

Contact: Doran Twer
Director, Marketing & Communications
229 South 18th Street
Philadelphia, PA 19103
215/875-2337
fax: 215/875-2891

The Hay Group is one of the world's largest human resource management consulting organizations, with ninety offices in twenty-seven countries. Founded in Philadelphia in 1943, Hay today consults in almost every area of human resource management, including human resource planning, organizational analysis and design, organizational effectiveness, strategic management, employee attitude surveys, corporate culture studies, market analysis and planning, total compensation planning, executive compensation, job evaluation and analysis, actuarial and employee benefit services, compensation surveys, and corporate and employee communication.

Hudson Institute

Contact: Neil Pickett
Director, Program Management
P.O. Box 26919
5395 Emerson Way
Indianapolis, IN 46226
317/545-1000
fax: 317/545-9639

Hudson Institute is the author of the landmark book *Workforce 2000: Work and Workers for the 21st Century*, which documents the changing demographic makeup of the U.S. labor force and its implications for the economy and for business. Hudson offers presentations for business groups of all kinds based on *Workforce 2000*. These presentations describe the workforce changes coming in the 1990s and propose policies businesses can use to meet the challenges of the future.

The Intercultural Communication Institute (ICI)

Contact: Milton Bennett, Ph.D.
Janet Bennett, Ph.D.
Directors
8835 SW Canyon Lane, Suite 238
Portland, OR 97225
503/297-4622
fax: 503/297-4695

ICI is a nonprofit operating foundation that sponsors educational and professional development programs in the area of intercultural relations. ICI's
Summer Institute for Intercultural Communication includes an intensive
five-day workshop on the topic "Managing Multicultural Organizations,"
as well as fourteen other workshops for trainers, educators, and administrators. Throughout the year, the ICI staff is available to make referrals
and to help locate intercultural materials. Through their consulting company, Communication Perspectives, the Bennetts develop and conduct
programs on the intercultural approach to managing and valuing diversity
for corporations and other organizations.

The International Center for the Disabled (ICD)

Contact: Elisa Lederer
Director, Placement and Employee
Rehabilitation Services
340 East 24th Street
New York, NY 10010
212/679-0100
fax: 212/889-2440

ICD, the first rehabilitation center in the United States, provides physical
rehabilitation and vocational training to people from all walks of life, conducts research, and offers professional education courses. ICD develops
model programs that are available to other agencies and rehabilitation
personnel internationally. As a rehabilitation partner of the business community, ICD offers consultation to corporations on the recruitment of
disabled employees. It also provides rehabilitation and return-to-work services for employees injured or disabled in the workplace. ICD serves
disabled persons on the sole basis of need, without regard to race, color,
religion, or ability to pay.

Jamieson Consulting Group (JCG)

Contact: David W. Jamieson, Ph.D.
President
2265 Westwood Boulevard, Suite 310
Los Angeles, CA 90064
213/397-8502*
fax: 213/397-0229*

JCG is a management and human resource consulting organization with associates nationwide. It provides expertise for managing the changing workforce through assisting organizations in the development of policies, systems, and structures for the diverse workplace, and through developing contemporary management practices.

With over twenty years' experience, JCG takes a generalist orientation to organizational issues and focuses primarily on organizational change, management and executive development, certification training in the use of FLEX-MANAGEMENT, human resource systems design, culture analysis and change, team development, and facilitation. JCG works collaboratively with organizations of varying sizes and types—including public, nonprofit, and private industries—and at all levels.

* Effective November 2, 1991, this area code changes to 310.

Job Accommodation Network (JAN)

Contact: Barbara Judy
Manager
WVU—809 Allen Hall
Morgantown, WV 26506
U.S.: 800/526-7234
Canada: 800/526-2262

JAN's human factors consultants provide accommodation information to businesses, rehabilitation professionals, or people with disabilities about employment issues. There is no cost for the service, but callers are asked to be willing to share their accommodation experiences with others. Telephones are available in voice or TDD, and print material is available in English, French, or Spanish as well as in Braille or on tape.

McLagan International, Inc.

Contact: Ron Kirsch
Vice-President
1700 West Highway 36, Suite 36
St. Paul, MN 55113
612/631-2034
fax: 612/631-1258

McLagan International helps organizations manage and develop their people. The company is known for its work in performance and flexible job design. Services include (1) consulting and workshops to assist individual and group goal setting and performance communication, (2) creating "people development" strategies and training individuals on how to manage their own development and coach others, and (3) planning the organization's human resource and succession strategies. The company's work emphasizes self-management and individualized development and communication in the context of high standards of quality, productivity, and customer focus.

Maritz Inc.

Contact: Duane Christensen
Senior Vice-President
1375 North Highway Drive
Fenton, MO 63099
314/827-4000
fax: 314/827-3708

Maritz Inc. is a world-wide company with over 5,000 employees involved in assisting clients with a variety of performance improvement systems ranging from all-employee cost reduction programs to quality and productivity improvement plans. With sales of more than $1 billion annually, Maritz has firmly established itself as the performance improvement leader, providing full-service incentive programs, multimedia business communications, research, and analysis services. Maritz programs are particularly applicable for involving employees in the organization and for rewarding improved performance.

Risa Martyn Communications, Inc.

Contact: Risa Martyn
President
52 Longview Avenue
San Anselmo, CA 94960
415/457-8344
fax: 415/457-8727

Risa Martyn Communications, Inc., provides both large corporations and small and minority-owned and women-owned business enterprises with consulting and training services that increase and develop their competitiveness and profitability.

Services include cross-cultural communications; procurement systems; troubleshooting and needs assessment; training programs and team building; development of total quality management programs for Minority/Women Business Enterprise–Small Business (M/WBE-SB); and recruitment of appropriate M/WBE-SB suppliers and assistance with their long-term business development.

MMHA The Managers' Mentors, Inc.

Contact: Margo Murray
President
2317 Mastlands Drive, Suite A
Oakland, CA 94611
415/531-9453
fax: 415/531-0944

MMHA, Inc., provides consulting services on improvement of quality and productivity, design and implementation of competency-based performance systems, and related programs and materials. Featured services are a Quality Productivity Performance System©, a Facilitated Mentoring Model©, and coaching for managers. Published programs include "Using TIME," "Communication = My Competence + Communication," "Feedback Principles and Techniques," "Planning and Conducting Meetings," "Facilitator Feedback Skills," and "The Personal Skills Map."

National Alliance of Business (NAB)

Contact: Foster C. Smith
Senior Vice-President
1201 New York Avenue, NW
Washington, DC 20005
202/289-2845
fax: 202/289-1303

NAB, a nonprofit organization, works to build business partnerships with government, labor, and education to improve the quality of the American workforce. NAB believes that to remain internationally competitive, the business community must eliminate the growing disparity between the abilities of Americans entering the workforce and the skills necessary for their jobs. NAB assists the business community in applying its strengths and capabilities toward educational change. It helps corporations develop internal company-specific plans for long-term corporate involvement with local and state schools, as well as formulating policies that promote educational reform at the local, state, and national levels.

National Center for Employee Ownership (NCEO)

Contact: Corey Rosen
Executive Director
2201 Broadway, Suite 807
Oakland, CA 94612
415/272-9461
fax: 415/272-9510

NCEO is a private, nonprofit membership and research organization formed in 1981 by Karen Young and Corey Rosen—its managing and executive directors, respectively. Since then the Center has expanded to 1,600 members internationally. Its principal activities are research; nationwide workshops; an international annual conference; and an extensive series of publications on employee ownership, Employee Stock Ownership Plans (ESOPs), and employee participation. The Center produces two serial publications, *The Journal of Employee Ownership and Finance* and an annual newsletter for members.

National Institute on Drug Abuse (NIDA)

Contact: James Lipari
    Acting Chief, Workplace Policy
      Research Branch
    Project Officer, Drug-Free
      Workplace Helpline
    5600 Fishers Lane, Room 9A-53
    Rockville, MD 20857
    301/443-0802
    Drug-Free Workplace Helpline: 800/843-4971

The Workplace Policy Research Branch develops policy and provides consultation to researchers, federal agencies, and private sector employers on workplace responses to drug abuse issues. The Branch develops and disseminates research results, scientific and technical materials, and model programs and policies for drug-free workplaces, including drug-testing and employee assistance programs.

    NIDA's Helpline, established for private sector use, is available to answer questions and provide technical assistance in developing and implementing a comprehensive drug-free workplace program. The Helpline staff can help managers, CEOs, and union representatives assess their needs and prepare their organizations to deal with current or potential problems caused by drugs in the workplace.

New England Corporate Consortium for AIDS Education

Contact: Paul A. Ross, Ed.D.
    Chair
    185 Franklin Street
    Boston, MA 02110
    508/264-1418   493-5111

Nine major Greater Boston businesses formed this consortium to promote workplace AIDS education and provide leadership and advocacy in legal and medical areas through policy statements, community relations, and corporate philanthropy. The Consortium has produced a comprehensive, affordable AIDS education package for the workplace. The kits include a twenty-two-minute videotape, "Living and Working with AIDS," narrated by Dr. Timothy Johnson; a *Corporate Program Planning Guide* on how to establish an AIDS education program; a *Supervisor's Manual* with concrete suggestions for managing AIDS-related situations; and an *Employee Brochure* that answers common questions about AIDS.

New Ways to Work (NWW)

Contact: Suzanne Smith
Co-Director
149 Ninth Street
San Francisco, CA 94103
415/552-1000
fax: 415/552-9070

New Ways to Work is a resource organization that advocates and promotes the use of alternative work schedules such as flextime, the compressed work week, job sharing, regular part time, and phased and partial retirement. NWW helps businesses nationwide as more managers recognize the need for flexibility in times of social and economic change. NWW carries out its work through research, publications, consulting, and training. Information on publications, training, and membership is available by telephone or mail. NWW members receive *Work Times,* a quarterly newsletter, and a discount on all other group publications.

ODT, Inc.

Contact: Connie Hamilton
Program Director
P.O. Box 134
Amherst, MA 01004
413/549-1293

ODT, Inc., offers products, delivers training, and creates customized train-the-trainer programs on topics of employee empowerment and valuing a culturally diverse workforce. The group's expertise includes upward influence (how to manage your boss, upward appraisal, and personal power) and self-directed work teams, as well as skill-building programs on how to receive a performance appraisal and a delegated assignment. ODT's diversity awareness programs include "How to Avoid Stereotyping," "Dealing with Subtle Discrimination," and "Managing a Culturally Diverse Workforce." The free product catalog lists seventy-two items ranging from single audiocassettes to programmed-instruction learning modules.

O'Mara and Associates

Contact: Julie O'Mara
President
5979 Greenridge Road
Castro Valley, CA 94552
415/582-7744*
fax: 415/582-4826*

O'Mara and Associates, a full-service human resource development firm since 1972, works with organizations to develop policies, systems, and management practices that link the strategic direction of the business with the skills, needs, wants, and values of its people.

The firm works collaboratively with managers and human resource and organization development professionals to determine the most effective ways to manage the diverse workforce. Its services include executive briefings; certification training on the use of FLEX-MANAGEMENT; general consultation on strategies to address issues of the changing workforce; needs assessment; management, leadership, and sales effectiveness; program implementation; training; and speeches and workshops of varying lengths.

* Effective September 2, 1991, this area code changes to 510.

Phoenix Associates, Inc.

Contact: Ed Kur
President
1204 East Steamboat
Tempe, AZ 85283
602/831-1911
fax: 602/253-4611

Phoenix Associates, Inc., conducts workshops that help people to lead and work in organizations characterized by diverse workforces and changing values. These workshops include (1) "Developing High Performance Organizations," in which people at all levels develop principles for changing their own organizations into high-performing systems; (2) The Leadership Institute, which teaches leadership skills appropriate with diverse workforces; (3) "Developing Shared Vision," a program in which members of an organization draw on their common and unique values to develop a shared sense of purpose; and (4) team development retreats that help members of work groups draw on individual differences to build effective teamwork.

Pope & Associates

Contact: Patricia C. Pope
Vice-President
1313 East Kemper Road, Suite 350
Cincinnati, OH 45246
513/671-1277
fax: 513/671-1815

Pope & Associates are personnel consultants specializing in workforce diversity and multicultural management training. Established in 1973, the firm helps diverse organizations improve work relationships, boost performance, and increase productivity. Its strategic affirmative action seminars include "Leading a Diverse Workforce" for executives, "Managing Personnel Diversity" for managers/supervisors, and "Enhancing Work Relationships" for co-workers. Two public seminars are "Increasing Self-Development: Minorities" for minority managers and professionals and "Managing Personnel Diversity" for managers/supervisors.

Bob Powers & Associates, Inc.

Contact: Bob Powers
The Mill
Three Bridges, NJ 08887-0177
201/369-8402
fax: 201/369-6027

Bob Powers & Associates, Inc., exists to help organizations and individuals achieve desired business results and enhance life in the workplace. The firm, founded in 1982, focuses on matching people to jobs; defining jobs and job expectations; ensuring that employees have the tools, training, and other support mechanisms to perform; providing feedback that reinforces and develops good performance; and providing reward systems that are valued by employees and managers. The firm operates on the belief that people will perform if these components are effectively aligned and implemented; its goal is to help organizations move toward such a system.

P.S. Consultants, Inc.

Contact: Joan H. Linder, Ed.D.
President
3104 Sheldon Road, Suite 150
Middletown, OH 45042
513/424-0775
fax: 513/424-0775

P.S. Consultants, Inc., offers services in organizational consultation; needs assessment; and the design, delivery, and evaluation of training. The firm concentrates on team building, leadership development, customer service, management and supervisory development, interviewing, communication, and train-the-trainer programs. Based on her research, Dr. Linder facilitates custom-designed workshops that focus on helping couples and individuals balance and integrate their work and personal lives. She is also available for keynote presentations on a variety of topics, including "Balancing and Integrating Work and Family."

Resources for Child Care Management (RCCM)

Contact: Robert Lurie
President
261 Springfield Avenue, Suite 201
Berkeley Heights, NJ 07922
201/665-9070
fax: 201/665-9231

RCCM works with leading corporations and developers to create innovative child care solutions. Projects include the design and development of (1) the John Hancock Child Care Center, Boston; (2) the Johnson & Johnson Child Development Center, New Brunswick, N.J., which RCCM will manage; and (3) Wegmans Child Care Center, Rochester, N.Y., serving both employees and customers, the latter through an innovative drop-in program. RCCM has been planning a work/family policy for Sandoz Pharmaceuticals, reviewing options for Metropolitan Life Insurance Company's four regional claims operations centers, and designing an enrichment center at a major office park developed by the Rockefeller Group.

John Thomas Group, Inc.

Contact: C. T. Dortch
Chairman
P.O. Box 2144
Lake Arrowhead, CA 92352
714/337-6049
fax: 714/337-9421

The John Thomas Group, Inc., has developed two processes that assist managers or human resource professionals to assess people, jobs, and the work environment. The Job•Person•Match™ (JPM) process uses two copyrighted inventories—the Personal Preference Inventory (PPI) and the Job Perception Inventory (JPI)—to gather information regarding ten key motivational/behavioral characteristics of individuals, using these characteristics to determine expected or required behaviors for specific jobs.

The Job•Person•Environment™ process adds an environmental measure to the PPI and JPI to generate information about the support the organizational climate provides in achieving top productivity and quality.

Towers Perrin

Contact: Margaret Regan
Principal
245 Park Avenue
New York, NY 10167
212/309-3593
fax: 212/309-3760

Towers Perrin specializes in helping management evaluate, develop, finance, and communicate human resource programs of all types. The firm designs and administers retirement, health, and flexible benefits programs, compensation plans for both executives and their employees, and individual and group incentive pay programs. Towers Perrin consultants help organizations communicate effectively with employees, develop a focus on quality, create alternative working arrangements to support increased productivity, and promote change in the human resource environment. In tandem with these activities, Towers Perrin works with management in the areas of strategy and organizational effectiveness to help achieve a sustainable competitive advantage and improved performance.

Training & Culture Newsletter

Contact: Barbara Deane
Editor
13751 Lake City Way NE, Suite 10
Seattle, WA 98125-3615
206/362-0336
fax: 206/368-6850

The *Training & Culture Newsletter* is a bimonthly publication for professionals who manage, train, and conduct business amid diversity. The newsletter monitors trends in multicultural and international human resource management and provides new ideas and tips for gaining intercultural competence.

The *Training & Culture Bulletin*—a calendar for multicultural/international conferences, seminars, and other events—is published every month except August. Call or write for a free copy of the newsletter. Subscription rates are $59 for organizations and $39 for individuals. (Add $5 for Canada and Mexico, and 8.1 percent sales tax for Washington state.) Other international subscriptions are $69. Group rates are available.

TriNet Employer Group, Inc.

Contact: Martin Babinec
President
525 Estudillo Avenue, Suite E
San Leandro, CA 94577
415/352-5000
fax: 415/352-6480

The TriNet Group provides contract staffing services to companies that want to maximize flexibility with longer-term contingency employees. These include project staff, reemployed retirees, and others who work for extended periods but who will not be hired as regular employees. The client firm selects the employees and determines their compensation. Contract employees are placed on TriNet's payroll and receive health and other benefits as well as human resource support through the TriNet office. Even with the cost of health benefits included, the total markup for this service can be up to one-half the fees charged by temporary agencies or payrolling services.

University Associates, Inc. (UA)

Contact: Richard L. Roe
Vice-President, Publications
8517 Production Avenue
San Diego, CA 92121
619/578-5900
fax: 619/578-2042

University Associates is internationally known for publishing, training, and consulting in the field of human resource development. UA is a source of practical, experientially based materials, books, workbooks, instruments, and tape-assisted learning programs, as well as workshops that are customized to meet specific client needs.

UA's practical, applied, theory-based approach is evident in its training and consulting activities in both the public and private sectors, where it conducts programs to train trainers and consults with organizations and communities to solve human and organizational problems. UA provides workshops on fundamental and current topics in human resource development and organization development.

The U.S. Learning Corporation

Contact: Paul Roelofs
President
1150 Foothill Boulevard, Suite F
La Canada, CA 91011
800/869-1310
fax: 818/790-4910

The U.S. Learning Corporation's one-day program, "Managing Workforce Diversity," creates awareness of subtle cultural and value differences and provides managers with the critical skills needed to effectively manage diversity. It helps managers to understand their own biases and the negative assumptions they may make about the behavior of their diverse workers. Managers learn how to build on individual differences to enhance jobs and unlock the potential of each member of the work group. Participants learn a reliable process for identifying barriers to productivity and overcoming them through the application of key communication skills. The result is an improved working relationship with their diverse workers.

Vanguard Consulting Group

Contact: Stephanie Jackson
Senior Partner
100 Larkspur Landing Circle, Suite 104
Larkspur, CA 94939
415/461-6126
fax: 415/461-8930

Vanguard works with organizations that are undergoing complex or difficult change. Its services include helping organizations to clarify and communicate values and to translate strategies and values into day-to-day behavior, examining the effects of key organizational influences on behavior, implementing training and development programs, conducting management work sessions, and helping organizations build their capacity to successfully initiate or adapt to continuing change.

Vanguard specializes in helping organizations build effective linkages through working partnerships among organizational units and between organizations, and through effective communication and consistency of direction across organizational levels.

Work/Family Directions, Inc.

Contact: Johanna Schulman
Director, Corporate Relations
930 Commonwealth Avenue, South
Boston, MA 02215-1212
617/566-1800
fax: 617/566-2806

Since 1983, Work/Family Directions has offered American corporations the services, products, and skills they need to meet the challenges of the changing workforce. Work/Family Directions has established a national reputation through (1) high-quality child care and elder care programs for employees and retirees, (2) innovative labor force strategies for corporate flexibility and career mobility, (3) unique management training programs on work and family issues, and (4) formulation of new human resource responses to the changing work and family arena.

World Future Society

Contact: Edward S. Cornish
President
4916 St. Elmo Avenue
Bethesda, MD 20814
301/656-8274
fax: 301/951-0394

The World Future Society is an association of over 30,000 people interested in how social and technological developments are shaping the future. The Society's bimonthly journal, *The Futurist,* frequently covers demographic and workplace issues, and more than 30 *Futurist* articles are collected in *Careers Tomorrow: The Outlook for Work in a Changing World.* Recent Society reports of special interest to managers of the changing workforce include "Nine Forces Reshaping America" and "Into the 21st Century: Long-Term Trends Affecting the United States." A variety of books on work, business, and social issues are available from the Society's Futurist Bookstore.

Milt Wright & Associates, Inc.

Contact: Milt Wright
President
19151 Parthenia Street, Suite D
Northridge, CA 91324
818/349-0858
fax: 818/349-0987

Milt Wright & Associates, Inc., specializes in training to eliminate attitudinal barriers regarding people with disabilities. The firm assists the employer community in recruiting, hiring, training, and supervising persons with special needs. For further information regarding seminars, in-house training of trainers, technical assistance, material development, keynote speeches, or conference presentations, contact Milt Wright. A catalog describing the firm's services and products is available at no cost.

Afterword

We believe this book is a start—a start at better understanding the reality of workforce diversity now and in the future, and a start at taking a management and organization perspective on the issues of a changing American workforce.

We are pleased that organizations in America are responding, innovating, experimenting, and responsibly struggling with the growing workforce diversity. Much still needs to be done and much could be at stake.

FLEX-MANAGEMENT is our way of organizing the thinking and action that are needed for managing in the 1990s and beyond, as viewed through the diverse workforce lens. We hope that we have captured what you are doing or have stimulated you to think about new approaches.

During the years in which we have been developing our concepts and learning about what's happening in organizations, we have had the pleasure of hearing good stories that captured examples of managers and organizations "doing the right things" with their diverse and changing workforce. Unique policies, customized practices, and flexible systems have surfaced throughout the country, in small and large organizations, and in the public and private sectors. We salute the pioneers and innovators.

While the percentage of organizations that are responding to the changing workforce seems to be growing, the percentage that is systematically initiating change at the individual and organizational levels is woefully small. We hope that this situation is changing and will continue to change.

As we wrote this book, shortly after each draft was completed new ideas would emerge and new examples would surface. We finally had to stop adding information in August 1990. Therefore, we are very aware that we could not possibly have covered all the changes that are taking place throughout organizations, but we are anxious to know about them!

We would like to hear from you about what you and your organizations are doing

- In the FLEX-MANAGEMENT strategies

- Within diversity categories

- In addition to either of the above

Respond to: David Jamieson, 2265 Westwood Boulevard, Suite 310, Los Angeles, CA 90064, 213/397-8502*; or Julie O'Mara, 5979 Greenridge Road, Castro Valley, CA 94552, 415/582-7744*.

* Effective November 2, 1991, the current 213 area code changes to 310. Effective September 2, 1991, the current 415 area code changes to 510.

References

"A Look at Alternative Work Schedules." *Training: The Magazine of Human Resource Development,* March 1988, p. 74.

American Productivity Center. *Reward Systems and Productivity: A Final Report for The White House Conference on Productivity.* Houston: American Productivity Center, 1983.

Argyris, C. *Intervention Theory and Method: A Behavioral Science View.* Reading, Mass.: Addison-Wesley, 1970.

Beckhard, R., and Harris, R. *Organizational Transitions: Managing Complex Changes.* (2nd ed.) Reading, Mass.: Addison-Wesley, 1987.

Bellman, G. *The Quest for Staff Leadership.* Glenview, Ill.: Scott, Foresman, 1986.

Bennis, W., and Nanus, B. *Leaders: The Strategies for Taking Charge.* New York: Harper & Row, 1985.

Berkman, L. "Working 7 to 5—Four Days a Week." *Los Angeles Times,* November 30, 1989, pp. D1–D8.

Block, P. *The Empowered Manager: Positive Political Skills at Work.* San Francisco: Jossey-Bass, 1987.

Braham, J. "No, You Don't Manage Everyone the Same." *Industry Week,* February 6, 1989, pp. 28–35.

Bridges, W. *Transitions.* Menlo Park, Calif.: Addison-Wesley, 1980.

Bridges, W. *Surviving Corporate Transitions.* New York: Doubleday, 1988.

Chisman, F. P., and Associates. *Leadership for Literacy: The Agenda for the 1990s.* San Francisco: Jossey-Bass, 1990.

Commerce Clearing House Editorial Staff. *Flexible Benefits: Will They Work For You?* Chicago: Commerce Clearing House, 1988.

Copeland Griggs Productions. "What is Valuing Diversity? Definition and Short History." San Francisco: Copeland Griggs Productions, n.d. (in-house document).

Cummings, T., and Huse, E. *Organization Development and Change.* (4th ed.) St. Paul, Minn.: West Publishing, 1989.

Deutsch, R. E. "Tomorrow's Work Force: New Values in the Workplace." In E. Cornish (ed.), *Careers Tomorrow: The Outlook for Work in a Changing World.* Bethesda, Md.: World Future Society, 1988, pp. 17–19.

Dortch, C. T. "Job•Person•Match," *Personnel Journal,* June 1989, pp. 49–57.

Doyle, M., and Strauss, D. *How to Make Meetings Work.* New York: Berkley Publishing Group, 1976.

Emery, A., and Puckett, S. *Managing AIDS in the Workplace.* Menlo Park, Calif.: Addison-Wesley, 1988.

Employee Benefits Research Institute. *Business, Work, and Benefits: Adjusting to Change.* Washington, D.C.: Employee Benefits Research Institute, 1989.

Gardner, R., Robey, B., and Smith, P. "Asian Americans: Growth, Change, and Diversity." *Population Bulletin,* Oct. 1985, *40*(4).

"How the Next Decade Will Differ." *Business Week,* September 25, 1989, pp. 142–156.

"Human Capital: The Decline of America's Workforce." *Business Week,* September 19, 1988, pp. 100–141.

International Center for the Disabled. *The ICD Survey II: Employing Disabled Americans.* New York: International Center for the Disabled, 1987.

Johnston, W. B., and Packer, A. E. *Workforce 2000: Work and Workers for the 21st Century.* Indianapolis, Ind.: The Hudson Institute, 1987.

Kanter, R. M. *Men and Women of the Corporation.* New York: Basic Books, 1977.

Kur, C. E. "New Applications for Self-Managing Work Teams." *High Performance Practices,* November 1989, pp. 1–2 (newsletter).

Kutscher, R. "Projections Summary and Emerging Issues." *Monthly Labor Review,* 1989, *112* (11), 66–74.

Lawler III, E. E. *High-Involvement Management: Participative Strategies for Improving Organizational Performance.* San Francisco: Jossey-Bass, 1986.

Lawler, E., Renwick, P., and Bullock, R. "Employee Influence on Decisions: An Analysis." *Journal of Occupational Behavior,* 1981, *2,* 115–123.

Leibowitz, Z., Farren, C., and Kaye, B. *Designing Career Development Systems.* San Francisco: Jossey-Bass, 1986.

Linder, J. "Dual-Career Couples Change the Rules." *Cincinnati Enquirer,* February 29, 1988, p. D-2.

McAdams, J. "Performance-Based Reward Systems." *Canadian Business Review,* Spring 1988, pp. 17–19.

McLagan, P. "Flexible Job Models: A Productivity Strategy for the Information Age." In J. P. Campbell, R. J. Campbell, and Associates, *Productivity in Organizations: New Perspectives from Industrial and Organizational Psychology.* San Francisco: Jossey-Bass, 1988.

McLagan, P. *Models for HRD Practice: The Models.* Alexandria, Va.: American Society for Training and Development, 1989.

Management Research Group. *Management Effectiveness Analysis Technical Considerations.* Portland, Maine: Management Research Group, 1985.

"Managing Now for the 1990s." *Fortune,* September 26, 1989, p. 46.

Margulies, N., and Raia, A. *Conceptual Foundations of Organizational Development.* New York: McGraw-Hill, 1978.

Morhman, A. M., Resnick-West, S., and Lawler, E. *Designing Performance Appraisal Systems: Aligning Appraisals and Organizational Realities.* San Francisco: Jossey-Bass, 1989.

Naisbitt, J., and Aburdene, P. *Reinventing the Corporation.* New York: Warner Books, 1985.

O'Dell, C., and McAdams, J. "The Revolution in Employee Rewards." *Management Review,* March 1987, pp. 30–33.

Salisbury, D. (ed.). *America in Transition: Implications for Employee Benefits.* Washington, D.C.: Employee Benefits Research Institute, 1982.

Schwartz, F. "Management Women and the New Facts of Life." *Harvard Business Review,* January–February 1989, pp. 65–76.

Selbert, R. "Women at Work." *Future Scan,* no. 554, November 16, 1987, pp. 1–3 (newsletter).

Selbert, R. "Benefits Growth." *Future Scan,* no. 599, September 26, 1988, p. 1 (newsletter).

Shaw, J. "Peter Drucker Looks at Future, Sees New Firms." *San Francisco Business Times,* September 25, 1989, p. 17.

Thomas, R. R., Jr. "From Affirmative Action to Affirming Diversity." *Harvard Business Review,* March–April 1990, p. 116.

Towers Perrin and Hudson Institute. *Workforce 2000: Competing in a Seller's Market.* Valhalla, N.Y.: Towers Perrin, 1990.

Trost, C. "New Approach Forced by Shifts in Population." *Wall Street Journal,* November 22, 1989, pp. B1–B4.

Valdivieso, R., and Davis, C. *U.S. Hispanics: Challenging Issues for the 1990s.* Population Trends and Public Policy Series, no. 17. Washington, D.C.: Population Reference Bureau, 1988.

Index